The Legal Protection of Personality Rights

Chinese and Comparative Law Series

VOLUME 5

The titles published in this series are listed at *brill.com/ccls*

The Legal Protection of Personality Rights

Chinese and European Perspectives

Edited by

Ken Oliphant
Zhang Pinghua
Chen Lei

BRILL
NIJHOFF

LEIDEN | BOSTON

Library of Congress Cataloging-in-Publication Data

Names: Oliphant, Ken, editor. | Zhang, Pinghua, 1974- editor. | Chen, Lei
  (Lawyer), editor.
Title: The legal protection of personality rights : Chinese and European
  perspectives / edited by Ken Oliphant, Pinghua Zhang, Lei Chen.
Description: Leiden ; Boston : Brill/Nijhoff, 2018. | Series: Chinese and
  comparative law series; 5 | Includes index.
Identifiers: LCCN 2017048717 (print) | LCCN 2017049186 (ebook) |
  ISBN 9789004351714 (E-book) | ISBN 9789004276291 (hardback : alk. paper)
Subjects: LCSH: Personality (Law)--Comparative studies. | Personality
  (Law)--China. | Personality (Law)--Europe.
Classification: LCC K627 (ebook) | LCC K627 .L44 2017 (print) |
  DDC 346.01/2--dc23
LC record available at https://lccn.loc.gov/2017048717

Typeface for the Latin, Greek, and Cyrillic scripts: "Brill". See and download: brill.com/brill-typeface.

ISSN 2213-4875
ISBN 978-90-04-27629-1 (hardback)
ISBN 978-90-04-35171-4 (e-book)

This book is printed on acid-free paper and produced in a sustainable manner.

Printed by Printforce, the Netherlands

Contents

PART 3
Special Topics Relating to the Protection of Personality Rights by Private Law

Preface

This publication collects together papers delivered at the first Sino-European Private Law Forum, held at Yantai University, China, in September 2013, organized jointly by the Sino-European Tort Law Institute of Yantai University, the Institute for European Tort Law of the Austrian Academy of Sciences and the University of Graz (ETL, Vienna) and the European Centre of Tort and Insurance Law (ECTIL, Vienna) in the context of their collaboration agreement. Alongside the revised versions of the presentations delivered there, additional contributions by Chen Lei, Wang Jia and Ernst Karner have been included in order to further the aim of the research, namely to examine the aims of, and divergences in, the protection of personality rights in tort law within the Chinese and European legal traditions. Given the substantial period between the conference and the date of publication, an opportunity to revise the reports was offered to contributors in the first half of 2016 and (for minor updates only) when making proof corrections.

With this research, the editors hope to have contributed to a mutual understanding of the different modes of thought of Chinese and European legal scholars. This has been attempted on the example of a topically important subject intensively debated in the context of the coming Chinese Civil Code. This codification discussion is particularly clearly reflected in the contributions on Chinese law, but similar themes equally arise in the discussion of a potential unification of European tort law by the European authors. We hope that this investigation of the legal protection of personality rights in Europe and China will both inform the Chinese debate and introduce non-Chinese readers to the arguments made and their legal context.

At this point we would like to thank all of the contributors for their enthusiastic cooperation and commitment in participating. Additionally, we would like to express our special thanks to the Executive Director of the Sino-European Tort Law Institute of Yantai University, Associate Professor Zhang Yudong, for his valuable and active support in the organisation of the conference, as well as to the staff in Vienna, in particular Donna Stockenhuber, Kathrin Karner-Strobach, Andrew Bell, Simona Buss, Thomas Thiede, Eva Ondreasova, David Messner and Lisa Zeiler, for their engagement throughout the project.

Ken Oliphant, Zhang Pinghua and Chen Lei

List of Authors

Asian Scholars

CHEN Lei　　　　　　　　　陳磊
Hong Kong City University　　　香港城市大学
School of Law　　　　　　　　法律学院
Centre for Chinese and Comparative　中国与比较法研究中心
Law
83 Tat Chee Avenue　　　　　　达之路83号
Kowloon　　　　　　　　　　九龙
Hong Kong SAR　　　　　　　香港特别行政区

DING Chunyan　　　　　　　丁春艳
City University of Hong Kong　　香港城市大学
School of Law　　　　　　　　法律学院
Centre for Chinese and Comparative　中国与比较法研究中心
Law
83 Tat Chee Avenue　　　　　　达之路83号
Kowloon　　　　　　　　　　九龙
Hong Kong SAR　　　　　　　香港特别行政区

FAN Liying　　　　　　　　范李瑛
Yantai University　　　　　　烟台大学
Law School　　　　　　　　法学院
30 Qingquan Road, Laishan　　山东省烟台市莱山区清泉路
Yantai　　　　　　　　　　30号
Shandong 264005　　　　　邮编：264005
P.R. China　　　　　　　　中国

WANG Jia　　　　　　　　王佳
Guangdong University of Foreign　广东外语外贸大学
Studies
School of Law　　　　　　　法学院
South China Institute For International　华南国际知识产权研究院 &涉外
Intellectual Property　　　　法律研究服务中心
Centre for Foreign-related Legal
Research with Going Abroad Strategy
Guangzhou, 510006
P.R. China

The Hong Kong Polytechnic University,   广东省广州市番禺区广州大学
Faculty of Business   城（南校区）
Hong Kong SAR   邮编：510006

                                         中国

                                         香港理工大学工商管理学院
                                         香港特别行政区

ZHANG Pinghua   张平华
Yantai University   烟台大学
Law School   法学院
30 Qingquan Road, Laishan   山东省烟台市莱山区清泉路
Yantai   30号
Shandong 264005   邮编：264005
P.R. China   中国

European Scholars

Monika HINTEREGGER
University of Graz
Institute for Civil Law, Foreign and Private International Law
Universitätsstrasse 15/D4
8010 Graz
Austria

Ernst KARNER
Institute for European Tort Law
Reichsratsstrasse 17/2
1010 Vienna
Austria

Ken OLIPHANT
University of Bristol Law School
Queens Road
Bristol BS8 1RJ
United Kingdom

Eva ONDREASOVA
Institute for European Tort Law
Reichsratsstrasse 17/2
1010 Vienna
Austria

Barbara STEININGER
Institute for European Tort Law
Reichsratsstrasse 17/2
1010 Vienna
Austria

Thomas THIEDE
Institute for European Tort Law
Reichsratsstrasse 17/2
1010 Vienna
Austria

Laura WEISSEL
Institute for European Tort Law
Reichsratsstrasse 17/2
1010 Vienna
Austria

Introduction

Ken Oliphant, Zhang Pinghua and Chen Lei

I   Starting Points

1 Three recent decisions provide informative case studies of how Chinese courts
have had to grapple with the complexities of liability for interference with personality rights in the years since the turn of the century:

> Without obtaining permission, Life Style newspaper used a picture of Liu
> Xiang, superstar of Chinese track and field athletics who won the gold
> medal in the 110 metre hurdles at the 2004 Beijing Olympics, to advertise
> the opening of a new department store. Liu claimed RMB 1.25 million
> in damages, but was ultimately awarded only RMB 20,000, this amount
> being compensation for his mental anguish rather than disgorgement of
> Life Style's unjust enrichment; the court also ordered Life Style to make
> a public apology.[1]

> A group of medical students doing internships at the defendant hospital
> observed a woman's abortion surgery without her knowledge and con-
> sent. As the operation was under anaesthetic, the patient was unaware
> of this at the time, but she felt deeply offended when she learned of it
> afterwards. She sued the hospital for invasion of her right to privacy and
> was awarded RMB 10,000 as compensation for mental suffering.[2]

> The plaintiff conducted searches on Baidu, the largest Chinese search
> engine service provider, using the terms 'weight loss,' 'breast enhance-
> ment' and 'abortion.' When she subsequently accessed other websites,
> advertisements relating to the search terms popped up in her browser.
> She claimed that Baidu had used cookies to collect her personal infor-
> mation and disclosed that information to third parties for commercial
> advertisement. She requested an injunction and damages for mental dis-
> tress. However, the court found that the information was not personal

---

1 *Liu Xiang v Life Style Newspaper* [2005] Beijing No 1 Immediate Court, Civil Appeal case no
   8144. See *Chen Lei*, Codifying Personality Rights in China: Legislative Innovation or Scare-
   mongering?, this volume, no 30.
2 *Liang v Qingdao People's Hospital* (unreported, 2003), cited by *Ding Chunyan*, Protection of
   Patient Personality Rights in China, this volume, no 22.

to her as cookies identify only the browser being used and not the user. Further, Baidu had placed a notice on its search page to inform users that they could opt out of the use of cookies and so, by proceeding to use the search engine without opting out, the plaintiff had impliedly agreed to accept cookies. Her claim therefore failed.[3]

2 In fact, the recognition and protection of personality rights in China is not a creation of the 21st century but goes back at least as far as the General Principles of Civil Law (GPCL) of 1986, in which the following are specified as 'personal rights' (art 98 ff): life and health; personal name; portrait; reputation; honour and marriage by choice.[4] The Tort Liability Law (TLL) of 2009 expressly adds to this (non-exhaustive) list the right of privacy (art 2).[5] These legislative texts are reinforced by authoritative interpretations and guidance issued by the Supreme People's Court.[6] Yet the legal protection of personality rights remains a much discussed and controversial issue in China and this debate has been given renewed impetus in recent years by repeated calls to introduce new legislation. Indeed, Chen Lei states at the outset of his chapter in this collection that how to legislate personality rights has been 'the most controversial issue in Chinese civil law' in the last few years – in particular, whether there should be a separate book on personality rights in the future Chinese Civil Code.[7]

3 Against that backdrop, we hope that this investigation of the legal protection of personality rights in Europe and China will both inform the Chinese debate and introduce non-Chinese readers to the arguments made and their legal context.

II   The Structure of this Book

4 This book is divided into three parts, providing general overviews of the legal protection of personality rights in Europe (Part 1) and in China (Part 2),

---

3 *Beijing Baidu Technology Ltd v Zhu Ye* (2014) Ning Min Zhong Zi no 5028, cited by *Wang Jia*, The Right to Privacy in the Internet Age: The Chinese Perspective, this volume, no 39 ff.

4 English translation available at http://www.npc.gov.cn/englishnpc/Law/2007-12/12/content_1383941.htm. As to the statutory framework, see further Chen (fn 1) no 5 ff.

5 English translation available at http://www.npc.gov.cn/englishnpc/Law/2011-02/16/content_1620761.htm.

6 Chen (fn 1) no 8.

7 Ibid no 1.

before addressing a number of specific contexts in which protecting personality rights raises important and distinctive issues (Part 3).

A   *The Legal Protection of Personality Rights in Europe*

5 In her helpful remarks in Chapter 1, *Barbara Steininger* sets out the basic questions that should be answered in investigating the protection accorded by law to interests in personality.[8] The three questions she highlights are the following: (1) What interests in personality does the law protect and what is the scope of such protection?; (2) Which legal mechanisms are employed to provide this protection?; and (3) How are the general rules applied to specific areas such as the mass media and the internet? The ways in which European legal systems answer the first and second of these questions are then pursued in further detail in the contributions to this volume of *Eva Ondreasova*[9] and *Monika Hinteregger*.[10]

6 Looking at the interests protected, *Ondreasova* first provides an overview of the historical evolution of different approaches from the time of Roman law onwards, then highlights for systematic analysis the issue of whether the law should recognise a single, all-encompassing personality right or a 'bundle' of specific rights. In her view, each approach has its competing advantages and disadvantages. The adoption of a single personality right of general scope gives the courts freedom to develop the law in response to social change, allowing new aspects of personality to be granted recognition and protection as the need becomes apparent. Conversely, the task of filling in the content of the general right is left to the courts, who may be ill-suited to resolving difficult questions of balance as between the opposing interests involved. It is not clear that courts are better placed than legislators to identify and reflect social values and attitudes. Specifying a long list of protected aspects of personality, on the other hand, has the merit of making explicit what elsewhere has to be drawn out by interpretation, but it may leave gaps as well as (one might add) tending to 'fossilise' the law in an area that is peculiarly subject to changing social attitudes. Further, in the absence of any explicit hierarchy of interests, it may be understood as placing all aspects of personality on the same level, thereby obscuring some important differences between the different aspects of personality that are legally protected.

---

8   *Barbara C Steininger*, The Protection of Personality Rights in Comparative Perspective: Basic Questions, this volume.

9   *Eva Ondreasova*, Personality Rights in Different European Legal Systems: Privacy, Dignity, Honour and Reputation, this volume.

10   *Monika Hinteregger*, The Protection of Personality Rights in Private Law: Remedies, this volume.

7 In fact, whichever approach is adopted, it is important to bear in mind that personality rights (narrowly so-called) are a subset of interests in the person that differ from the absolute rights to life, health and bodily security by virtue of the qualified protection they receive. The rights to honour, reputation and privacy are qualified rather than absolute rights – in the sense that they must be weighed against opposing interests such as freedom of expression and the freedom of the press. This balancing process is of the essence in determining whether a violation of personality rights has occurred, irrespective of whether the 'single right' or 'bundle of rights' approach is taken.

8 The final section of *Ondreasova's* paper examines the scope of protection given by different European legal systems to particular interests in personality: dignity, honour and reputation; privacy; image and likeness (with separate analysis of the topic of commercial appropriation); personal identity; and self-determination. She submits persuasively that privacy is the overarching category into which all legally protected interests in personality other than dignity, honour and reputation can be fitted.

9 Addressing the legal mechanisms that protect the various interests in personality, *Hinteregger* identifies four distinct aims: (1) compensation; (2) prevention; (3) restoration of the pre-existing state of affairs (*status quo ante*); and (4) restoration of unjustly acquired gains. The law of tort is crucial to the first of these aims, and arguably to the second and third too – assuming one views injunctions as remedies in tort. Tort compensates for the losses consequential on the interference, and the threat of liability in damages provides an incentive that deters future interference. Injunctions constitute a more direct mechanism to prevent the repetition or continuation of behaviour that violates personality rights (prohibitory injunctions) and to require the defendant to take positive steps to restore the plaintiff's pre-tort position (mandatory injunctions). It may be added that, in modern legal systems, such orders are often supplemented by specific provisions relating to (for example) the removal of offensive content from websites or the printing of apologies or corrections in respect of defamatory newspaper stories.[11]

10 In principle, a rational legal system would make the remedy proportionate to the circumstances that allow it to be invoked. Greater fault, for example, warrants a remedial response of greater severity, all other things being equal. Along these lines, *Barbara Steininger* suggests in her chapter that injunctions, typically involving less serious consequences for the defendant, should be available in a wider range of cases than the remedy of compensatory damages – for example, where there is an immediate risk of harm but no fault (even in circumstances where fault would be needed to establish a liability in damages).[12] No doubt

---

11   As explored in some of the contributions in Part 3 of this volume.
12   *Steininger* (fn 8).

the proposed principle of proportionality embodies good legal sense, but it is not clear that all would accept that injunctions generally involve less serious consequences for the defendant than compensatory damages. Common law systems, in particular, have traditionally been reluctant to grant injunctions or other forms of what is known as 'specific relief,' precisely because the interference with the defendant's liberty of action thereby entailed is viewed as typically more serious than the imposition of an obligation to pay damages – which may be viewed as licensing or at least tolerating the defendant's interference with the plaintiff's rights. Thus, it is a general principle that no injunction should be granted where damages would be an adequate remedy – and this applies not only for past infringements but also for possible infringements in the future, which may be 'licensed' in advance.[13]

11 The three chapters mentioned so far in relation to Part 1 of this book were conceived as and form a coherent set. The fourth – by *Ernst Karner* – was not written as part of the same set, but it nevertheless usefully ties together some of the themes elaborated in the other contributions, while exploring in more detail the influence in this area of human rights law.[14] He emphasises the manifold and diverse character of interests in personality and the consequent need to identify different categories attracting different degrees of protection. He also underlines that personality rights are interdependent with constitutional rights, the latter not being directly enforceable in ordinary private law but having indirect effect. As an example he cites the 1975 decision of the Austrian Supreme Court to award damages for non-pecuniary loss consequent upon false imprisonment by the Austrian State – notwithstanding earlier decisions going the other way – having regard to the right to liberty and security recognised in art 5 of the European Convention on Human Rights (ECHR).[15] *Karner* then shows how the European Court of Human Rights (ECtHR) has acted as a driving force behind legal harmonisation in Europe, especially in resolving the conflict between the competing rights of privacy (art 8 ECHR) and freedom of expression (art 10 ECHR). The same may also be said in respect of the final area that *Karner* touches upon – the legal consequences of a violation of personality rights – as the ECtHR's jurisprudence has been influential in several legal

---

13   See generally *K Oliphant*, Injunctions and Other Remedies, in: *id* (ed), The Law of Tort (3rd edn, 2015).

14   *Ernst Karner*, Human Rights and the Protection of Personality Rights in Europe: Comparative Reflections, this volume.

15   OGH in SZ 48/69 = JBl 1975, 645, cited in *Karner* (fn 14) no 22.

systems in encouraging awards of non-pecuniary damages for violations of personality rights even where there is no express basis for this in national law.[16]

B   *The Legal Protection of Personality Rights in China*

12 Opening Part 2 of this book, *Chen Lei* examines the extent to which personality rights are currently protected in China, highlighting the plethora of legal provisions that perform this function and the fragmented and unsystematic approach that results.[17] As noted at the start of this Introduction, the GPCL and TLL both identify in non-exhaustive terms a variety of interests in personality that are protected by law, the latter in more detail than the former. Article 2 TLL expressly protects the right to life, the right to health, the right to name, the right to reputation, the right to honour, the right to self-image, the right of privacy and the right of marital autonomy. The extent of this protection is clarified by authoritative interpretations and guidance promulgated by the Supreme People's Court. Additionally, a number of other legal sources – including not only the Constitution but also the laws of civil and criminal procedure, substantive criminal law, administrative law and consumer law – address personality rights in ways that augment or overlap with the protection provided by the TLL. A table on p 105 f provides a helpful overview of the personality rights protected by Chinese law, the source of that protection, and the remedies available on their violation (see especially art 15 TLL, which refers amongst other things to cessation of infringements, removal of obstacles, rehabilitation and elimination of ill effects, in addition to compensation for damage). In a very useful annex to his chapter *Chen* provides English translations of legislative texts relating to the protection of specific personality rights.

13 Mirroring the discussion in Part 1 of the book, *Chen* then discusses the interplay between the rival approaches based respectively on one general personality right and on a set of specific personality rights. In his view, the concept of a general personality right is too abstract to be practically useful as it is still necessary to concretise specific rights of personality on the varied facts of individual cases. He doubts whether Chinese courts, given their limited resources, can be entrusted with the task of identifying new instances of such rights in responsible fashion, in view of social changes. Hence, he proposes that it would be practical for China to develop a legislative model which combines a 'stick'

---

16   *K Oliphant*, Comparative Remarks, in: H Koziol/BC Steininger (eds), European Tort Law 2007 (2008) no 5 f.

17   *Chen* (fn 1).

of specific rights entailing the various remedial measures with the recognition of general rights located in the general part of a future Chinese Civil Code.[18]

14 *Chen* then provides an overview of the debate currently raging as to the desirability of codifying personality rights as an independent book in a future Chinese Civil Code. He concludes that the form that personality rights protection takes is less important than its substance. For him, in so far as there is a declarative provision recognizing protection of personality rights in the general part of a future Chinese Civil Code, coupled with concrete remedial provisions in the TLL or in a separate book on personality rights and restitution for unjust enrichment, that would not cause many concerns.

15 The issue of the introduction of a statutory right of personality is also taken up, at a rather more abstract level, by the other contribution in Part 2 of the book, written by *Zhang Pinghua*.[19] Stressing the multi-dimensional structure of the interest in personality, Zhang distinguishes between its inherent and derivative aspects. Only the former is essential to what makes humans human. The influence of European, particularly German, legal theory here is especially evident in *Zhang's* appeal to the socially typical and manifest nature (in German: *sozialtypische Offenkundigkeit*) of this inherent interest in personality. By contrast, the derivative interests in personality have not received the same degree of social acceptance and are not protected to the same extent. *Zhang* argues that introducing a statutory right of personality would enable clarification of its boundaries and a distinction to be drawn between specific rights in personality as such, which cannot be sold or otherwise transferred, and rights which are more akin to rights in property, such as the right to the commercial value of one's image.

C   *Specific Aspects of the Legal Protection of Personality*

16 As *Barbara Steininger* explains in the first chapter of this collection,[20] one of the basic questions relating to the legal protection of personality is how the general rules specifying the interests protected, the scope of that protection and the legal mechanisms employed to provide it are applied in specific contexts. This, the subject matter of Part 3 of the book, provides particularly

---

18   In the civil rights section of the General Provisions of Civil Law, which was passed on 15 March 2017, art 113 provides for a list of personality rights which fall within the scope of the Law's protection.

19   *Zhang Pinghua*, The Structure of the Interest in Personality and the Introduction of a Statutory Right of Personality, this volume.

20   *Steininger* (fn 8).

illuminating evidence of the qualified rather than absolute character of personality rights and the consequent need to weigh them against opposing interests such as freedom of expression. The papers collected here demonstrate that cultural and social context plays a large role both in the identification of relevant rights and countervailing interests, and in the balance to be struck between them.

17 The first two papers encountered here look at the particular threats to personality interests posed by the internet and the specific responses to them in Europe and China respectively. Modern social media make it easy to post, tweet or otherwise comment on others in derogatory, offensive or intrusive fashion, thoughtlessly, and under the cloak of anonymity. Being unconstrained by physical form, such communications can often be read by anyone anywhere in the world. At the same time, 'big data' technologies instantaneously and almost costlessly accumulate massively large, diverse and complex datasets whose subjects are increasingly vulnerable to damaging breaches of privacy in cyberspace.

18 In her paper on personality rights and the internet in Europe, *Laura Emilia Weissel* inquires specifically into the potential subjects of tortious liability (the internet user, the internet service provider (ISP) or even the search engine) and identifies the cardinal question regarding the liability of host providers in particular as the extent of their obligation to monitor stored information.[21] The same actors face liability under boadly equivalent provisions of Chinese law, which are identified and critically analysed in the paper contributed to this volume by *Wang Jia*.[22] Both *Weissel* and *Wang* highlight recent litigation regarding the particular position of search engines: in China, the *Baidu* case mentioned above; in Europe, a set of cases in different countries addressing Google's liability for 'auto complete' suggestions and 'snippets,' and litigation around 'the right to be forgotten' in the EU Court of Justice.[23] The global reach of the internet means that the same issues will arise for resolution around the world, but *how* they are resolved will inevitably reflect both the applicable legal rules and wider social and cultural factors.

19 Regarding China, *Wang* highlights how privacy was not included amongst the personality rights specified in the General Principles of Civil Law of 1986 and, despite the inclusion of a right to privacy among the 'civil rights and interests' whose infringement is subject to tortious liability (art 2 TLL), its recognition is limited to the area of tort law and thus remains incomplete – hence the calls for

---

21   *Laura Emilia Weissel*, Personality rights and the Internet in Europe, this volume.
22   *Wang Jia*, The Right to Privacy in the Internet Age: The Chinese Perspective, this volume.
23   *Weissel* (fn 21) no 22 ff.

an independent law of personality rights. In *Wang's* view, this would facilitate the application of remedies not available under the TLL, notably the disgorgement of profits obtained through the unauthorised commercial exploitation of personal information. She stresses, however, that privacy is only one of several goals that warrant legal protection and have to be balanced against each other in modern Chinese society; these also include security, self-development, freedom of speech, accountability and social productivity.

20 The balance between personality rights and freedom of expression is further pursued in the context of the mass media in the next chapter of the book, authored by *Thomas Thiede*.[24] Like *Karner* in his paper in Part 1, summarised above, Thiede underscores the role of the European Convention on Human Rights in driving developments in national law, particularly in the balance to be struck between the right to private life (art 8 ECHR) and freedom of expression (art 10 ECHR). He offers a survey of leading decisions by the European Court of Human Rights, in which he identifies a change of emphasis over time: press freedom is no longer accorded the same priority it once had, at least when if comes to statements of fact rather than opinion, and the constraints on its exercise when it impinges on countervailing interests – including the personality rights of others – have become notably more significant over the years. *Thiede* broadly approves of this trend and in particular applauds the willingness of the ECtHR to limit freedom of expression in respect of intrusions by mass media into the private lives of individuals where this does not contribute to a relevant public debate but satisfies only the prurient interests of the consumer.

21 The final two papers in this collection take us to other, perhaps less obvious areas of Chinese law. First, *Ding Chunyan* looks at the protection of personality rights in the medical context, especially through the ideas of patient autonomy (reflected in the right to informed consent specified in art 55 f TLL) and privacy, the latter embracing both freedom from intrusion and rights over private information.[25] She finds that current Chinese law is too ready to restrict the protection given to patients' personality rights for reasons of medical paternalism, social morality and the public interest in security, justice and public health. It thereby creates a risk of undermining the inherent value of human dignity and the scope for personal development.

22 Lastly, *Fan Liying* considers personality rights in the context of the laws of marriage in China, with reference to the freedom to choose one's family name on

---

24   *Thomas Thiede*, Personality Rights, the Mass Media and the European Convention on Human Rights, this volume.

25   *Ding Chunyan*, Protection of Patient Personality Rights in China, this volume.

marriage, and the right to return to one's original name on divorce, bereavement or even during the marriage, each spouse's right of cohabitation, and how it is reconciled with their right of sexual freedom, and their right to reproductive autonomy.[26] Her account reveals a set of complex interactions between personality rights and both the countervailing rights of others and the public interest, in an area where the legal principles are strongly shaped by cultural values and liability rules have to find their rightful place amongst a range of other legal responses (eg divorce).

---

26   *Fan Liying*, On the Independence of Personalities and Restrictions on the Status of Spouses, this volume.

PART 1

On the Legal Protection of Personality Rights in General: Europe

∴

The Protection of Personality Rights in Comparative Perspective: Basic Questions

Barbara C Steininger

I   Introduction

1 The aim of the present book is an examination of the various questions arising in the context of personality rights – both from a European and from a Chinese perspective. I was asked to discuss the basic questions from a European point of view. My task is therefore considerably easier than that of my colleagues, as I will only have to identify the basic questions, while they are expected to provide the answers.

2 The legal problems related to personality rights are diverse. It is therefore particularly useful to narrow down what questions we are actually focusing on. While personality rights are sometimes defined very broadly to include interests such as life, freedom and bodily integrity,[1] the term is often understood in a narrower sense as the less obvious rights connected to the person such as honour, dignity, privacy and the like.[2] Without intending to thereby make a choice between these positions, we will focus our presentations on personality rights in the narrower sense with honour, dignity and privacy as the core elements.

3 When looking at the basic questions in relation to these personality rights I will first examine the interests protected, then look at the ways in which such protection may be enforced and, finally, I will briefly deal with specific challenges, namely those related to mass media and the internet. But let me start with the question of which interests are protected and how such protection

---

*   The manuscript for this text was finalised in late 2014. Only minor changes have been incorporated since that time.

1   See eg *H Koziol/A Warzilek*, Austria, in: H Koziol/A Warzilek (eds), The Protection of Personality Rights against Mass Media (2005) 3 no 4 ff; *H Koziol*, Österreichisches Haftpflichtrecht I (3rd edn 1997) no 4/24; *E Karner*, Human Rights and the Protection of Personality Rights in Europe: Comparative Reflections, in this volume; *J Neethling*, Personality Rights, in: JM Smits (ed), Elgar Encyclopedia of Comparative Law (2nd edn 2012) 662.

2   See *G Brüggemeier*, Protection of personality rights in the law of delict/torts in Europe: mapping out paradigms, in: G Brüggemeier/A Colombi Ciacchi/P O'Callaghan, Personality Rights in European Tort Law (2010) 6. Brüggemeier defines personality rights as the non-bodily aspects of the persona.

© KONINKLIJKE BRILL NV, LEIDEN, 2018 | DOI 10.1163/9789004351714_003

is implemented, a topic which will later be examined in more detail by *Eva Ondreasova*.

II   Interests Protected

4 When looking at personality rights from a theoretical point of view, one can, to start with, distinguish different approaches.[3] A first model would be that of a general personality right covering all personality interests.[4] While this has the advantage of covering all potential personality interests and remaining open for adaptation to future developments, the diversity of personality interests – ranging from the protection of one's image to that of one's reputation – makes it impossible to have uniform rules for all the personality interests covered. This means that, notwithstanding the starting point of one single personality right, one will have to narrow down certain specific areas of protection.[5] Secondly, one could instead focus on individual (narrower) personality rights, which are then defined in more detail, such as the right to privacy or one's image.[6] While this allows for greater accuracy concerning the individual rights, it might lead to gaps in protection. A third, completely different starting point, is not to look at the interests themselves but rather, as the English do, at the conduct endangering a certain interest.[7] Thereby it is the respective tort and the proscribed conduct encapsulated by such tort that is focused on and not the underlying personality interest. While this again allows very specific solutions, it can – even more than the approach focusing on individual rights – entail a danger of

---

3   For further details see *E Ondreasova*, Personality Rights in Different European Legal Systems: Privacy, Dignity, Honour and Reputation, in this volume no 41 ff.

4   This approach is eg followed in Germany: *G Wagner*, Germany, in: H Koziol/A Warzilek (eds), The Protection of Personality Rights against Mass Media (2005) 137 no 7 f; *T Thiede*, Internationale Persönlichkeitsrechtsverletzungen (2010) no 2/1 ff. See also *C-W Canaris*, Grundprobleme des privatrechtlichen Persönlichkeitsschutzes, Juristische Blätter (JBl) 1991, 205 ff.

5   For an overview from a comparative point of view including a discussion of advantages and disadvantages of the different approaches see *A Warzilek*, Comparative Report, in: H Koziol/A Warzilek (eds), The Protection of Personality Rights against Mass Media (2005) 613 no 6 ff. Cf also Neethling (fn 1) 662 f.

6   Cf eg the situation under French law: *K Anterion/O Moréteau*, France, in: H Koziol/A Warzilek (eds), The Protection of Personality Rights against Mass Media (2005) 117 no 1 ff.

7   See on this *WVH Rogers*, England, in: H Koziol/A Warzilek (eds), The Protection of Personality Rights against Mass Media (2005) 59 no 1 ff.

gaps in protection which has to be taken into account.[8] Consequently, it clearly makes a difference which systematic starting point a system chooses. While it therefore makes sense to take the starting point chosen by a certain system into account in a comparative analysis, one should not forget that a starting point will not necessarily be decisive for the result. The latter will instead be highly dependent on the way the system in question deals with the advantages and disadvantages connected with the respective starting point.

5   Irrespective of this more theoretical question of the choice of a systematic approach, the more practical problem to be solved by the various jurisdictions is to what extent they want personality interests to enjoy protection. Results in the various jurisdictions are even more diverse than the personality interests involved.[9] A decisive factor for the existence of these huge differences is the fact that the personality interests we are discussing in the framework of this publication are, on the one hand, not clearly defined or obvious[10] and that they are, on the other hand, usually not the only interests involved. Quite often other opposing rights such as the freedom of expression or the freedom of the press will come into play. When carving out the shape and determining the extent of protection of personality interests, one will therefore regularly also have to decide about the extent of protection of these 'opposing' rights. The jurisdiction in question therefore has to strike a balance between the opposing interests involved.[11] Only on the basis of such a weighing of interests can it be determined against which conduct the respective personality interest will be protected. When looking at personality interests from a comparative perspective, one of the most interesting questions therefore is how such balance is struck for the different personality interests in the various jurisdictions. Thereby it has to be taken into account that different techniques may be applied for such weighing of interests for specific personality interests in a certain system. One option would be, for instance, to limit the concept of what constitutes a violation of a personality interest to situations where the balance struck by the system was disregarded; alternatively, the weighing of interests could for instance also be effectuated by providing for defences. Irrespective of the

---

8   In the context of privacy *M Lunney* and *K Oliphant*, Tort Law: Text & Materials (5th edn 2013) 771 speak of a 'scatter-gun approach.'

9   For a brief comparative overview see *G Brüggemeier/A Colombi Ciacchi/P O'Callaghan*, A common core of personality protection, in: G Brüggemeier/A Colombi Ciacchi/P O'Callaghan, Personality Rights in European Tort Law (2010) 568 ff.

10   Cf *E Karner*, Human Rights and the Protection of Personality Rights in Europe: Comparative Reflections, in this volume no 13 ff.

11   The importance of a weighing of interests is also stressed by *Warzilek* (fn 5) 53 ff.

question of which technique for implementing such a weighing of interests is chosen, the necessity of weighing the different interests involved will naturally lead to great diversity in the results, not only between the different personality interests in question but also between the respective jurisdictions.

6   Notwithstanding this potential for great diversity in detail, it can be stated that the rough lines tend to coincide: If, on the one hand, the other interests involved weigh very high, the personality interest may enjoy no or only very limited protection; it may, for instance, only be protected against certain very specifically defined manners of conduct. On the other hand, protection will be the more extensive the closer one comes to the core area of certain personality interests, where other interests will be of less importance.[12]

7   Let me exemplify this on the basis of a violation of honour. Against true statements a person's honour will enjoy only very limited protection throughout Europe.[13] Here freedom of expression is a strongly weighing counterpart to the interest in one's honour. Only if such (true) statements are made in a particularly degrading form will protection of the person's honour prevail in some jurisdictions.[14] The situation is quite different if the allegations made are untrue, as the interest in disseminating untrue information is not valued very highly and therefore has limited capacity to outweigh a person's interest in protection of his or her honour.[15] A similar line can be drawn when the protection of privacy is concerned. While core areas like a person's intimate life will normally enjoy extensive protection, so that other interests which could justify disclosure – for instance the public's interest in being provided with information – will only exceptionally prevail over the personality interest, the result is quite different when acts in a public sphere are concerned. These will normally only enjoy limited protection and will therefore regularly rank lower than other interests involved such as freedom of the press or freedom of expression.[16]

8   As we have seen, we are faced with different systematic starting points and an extreme diversity concerning the extent of protection of personality interests. Although we are focusing on personality rights and their protection in private law, we will, in our attempt to look at personality rights from a comparative

---

12   See *Karner* (fn 10) in this volume no 13 f.

13   Cf *Thiede* (fn 4) no 2/13 for Germany; Rogers (fn 7) no 15 ff for England where 'truth' is an absolute defence; *Anterion/Moréteau* (fn 6) no 13 for France.

14   Cf *Warzilek* (fn 5) 29. For German law see *Thiede* (fn 4) no 2/13.

15   The situation might, however, be different in media cases where freedom of the press comes into play. See on this *W Berka*, Persönlichkeitsschutz und Massenmedien im Lichte der Grundfreiheiten, in: H Koziol/A Warzilek (eds), The Protection of Personality Rights against Mass Media (2005) 493 no 92 ff.

16   In this sense also *Thiede* (fn 4) no 7/30.

perspective, moreover, have to take into account that protection of personality rights can be situated in various areas of the law. In particular, constitutionally granted rights play an important role here. Their interpretation will normally have direct consequences for the interpretation on the corresponding civil personality right. The same is true for the European Convention on Human Rights, irrespective of the question of whether the jurisdiction in question grants this Convention constitutional status or not.[17] Apart from constitutional law and the ECHR, rules for the protection of personality interests can regularly also be found in the area of criminal law. Although the rationale underlying criminal law rules for the protection of personality rights will differ from those of private law rules, the design of such criminal law rules may nevertheless influence private law protection.[18] In some jurisdictions granting protection under private law will even depend on the existence of a violation of criminal rules in this respect.[19]

9   This leads us directly to the next set of basic questions – namely how the protection, if granted, can be enforced, a topic that will be dealt with in more detail by *Monika Hinteregger*.[20]

III   Enforcement of Protection

10   Regardless of the extent of protection granted to a personality right, protection will only ever be as good as the remedies available. Naturally, the best possible protection is to avoid any infringement. Without regard to possible deterrent effects of other remedies,[21] the potential victim of a personality right violation is therefore best served by a *preventive injunction* prohibiting certain conduct imminently endangering a specific personality interest,[22] as for instance the publication or republication of articles or photos in a newspaper.

11   Such claims for preventive injunctions are, on the one hand, less far reaching than compensation claims and may therefore be granted more easily than for

---

17   On the protection of personality rights through the Charter of Fundamental Rights of the European Union see *Berka* (fn 15) 55 ff (though that text was drafted before the Charter became binding).

18   Cf for instance French law, where reference to criminal law provisions is a common approach in personality rights cases. See on this *Anterion/Moréteau* (fn 6) no 18 ff.

19   This is the case in the Nordic countries. See on this *Brüggemeier* (fn 2) 28 ff.

20   The Protection of Personality Rights in Private Law: Remedies, in this volume.

21   On the topic of the preventive function of tort law see *H Koziol*, Basic Questions of Tort Law (2010) no 3/4 ff.

22   See in this sense *Lunney/Oliphant* (fn 8) 759 f.

instance damages claims.[23] The decisive prerequisite for awarding an injunction is the imminent danger for the personality right in question.[24] However, to be able to avert an infringement of the personality right endangered, such injunctions will usually require speedy action on the part of the court to be successful. Consequently, jurisdictions provide for so-called interim injunctions granting protection only provisionally. The speed required for such protection entails a serious disadvantage of these remedies as the court will have to make its decision without having enough time for a full consideration of all the aspects of the case.[25] When taking into account that the interim injunction will not only protect the respective plaintiff's personality interest but will at the same time also interfere with rights of the defendant as for instance freedom of expression or freedom of the press, it is understandable that courts tend to be reluctant to grant such interim protection unless confronted with rather clear cases: the willingness to award protection will largely depend on the clarity of the balance of interests concerned.[26] Obviously, once the case has been fully tried, (permanent) preventive injunctions will be granted more easily. However, then the personality right in question will usually already have been infringed and the injunction will therefore usually only aim at preventing repetition of such infringement.

12 Once a violation of personality rights has taken place, victims of such violations will, in particular, aim at an elimination of such violation. One way of reaching such elimination is *reparative injunctions*, that is to say injunctions aiming at the removal of the source of the violation, for instance in the form of a retraction or correction of an incorrect statement about a person, an apology or the destruction of material used for the violation such as photos violating a person's privacy.[27] Under certain circumstances, the victim of a personality right infringement, in particular in cases of defamation, may also claim a right

---

23   In particular, preventive injunctions will regularly be granted irrespective of any culpability on the part of the defendant. *Koziol* (fn 21) no 2/7.

24   *Koziol* (fn 21) no 2/7.

25   Cf the discussion of this problem in the 19th century English case of *Bonnard v Perryman* [1891] 2 Law Reports, Chancery Division (3rd Series) Ch 269.

26   In England, it depends on the respective tort under which conditions interim injunctions are available, whereby English law is particularly reluctant to grant interim injunctions in defamation cases, cf *Rogers* (fn 7) nos 47 ff, 76, 82 ff. For German law see *Thiede* (fn 4) no 2/54 ff. On the more generous approach in this respect in French law see *Anterion/ Moréteau* (fn 6) no 34 f.

27   See *Warzilek* (fn 5) no 170 f.

to reply[28] or the publication of the judgment finding against the defendant or a summary thereof. Another possibility to achieve the elimination of the violation are claims for *restitution in kind* which may take the same form of retraction, correction, apology and the like.[29] While both reparative injunctions and claims for restitution in kind can therefore aim at the same result, the conditions for these remedies may differ.[30]

13   Generally, it can be stated that holding the person who infringed another's personality right liable in tort is one of the main remedies available to a person who suffered such infringement. In the first place, one can think of *compensatory damages*. When looking at these, a distinction can be drawn between compensation for pecuniary and non-pecuniary loss. Violations of personality interests can clearly cause persons to suffer pecuniary loss, as for instance someone who suffers income losses due to defamatory statements.[31] However, the more important category in personality rights' violation cases certainly is non-pecuniary loss suffered as a consequence of such violation. Compensation in non-pecuniary loss cases is generally more difficult than in cases in which pecuniary loss is at stake. As indicated earlier, corrections, retractions, apologies, judgment publications or the like may serve as a form of restitution in kind in particular when a non-pecuniary interest was violated.[32] If, however, such restitution in kind is impossible or seems insufficient to compensate the victim, compensation will have to be monetary. In non-pecuniary loss cases this leads to the difficult question of how to assess the non-pecuniary interest in monetary terms, a question which is, however, not a peculiarity of the area of personality interests but arises in all cases of non-pecuniary loss.[33] In this context it must be kept in mind that some jurisdictions are generally more reluctant than others to award monetary compensation for non-pecuniary loss.[34] In accordance with the general position taken towards the compensability of

---

28   Although such a right to reply may be less efficient compared to other remedies due to the way it is usually implemented by the media. See on this *H Koziol*, Sachgerechte Haftung der Massenmedien, in: H Koziol/J Seethaler/T Thiede (eds), Medienpolitik und Recht (2010) 1119 no 10 f.

29   For an overview of such claims see *Warzilek* (fn 5) nos 123, 170.

30   On the relation between reparative injunctions and compensation in kind concerning personality interests see *Warzilek* (fn 5) nos 123 ff, 170 ff. More generally *Koziol* (fn 21) no 2/15 ff.

31   Cf *Warzilek* (fn 5) no 134 with further references to national jurisdictions.

32   *Warzilek* (fn 5) no 123 ff. See also *Neethling* (fn 1) 664 f.

33   *Koziol* (fn 21) no 5/10 ff.

34   *WVH Rogers*, Comparative Report, in: WVH Rogers (ed), Damages for Non-Pecuniary Loss in a Comparative Perspective (2001) 245 no 5 ff; *R Zimmermann*, Comparative Report, in:

non-pecuniary loss, the French legal system is, for instance, rather open when compensation of non-pecuniary loss suffered as a consequence of a violation of a personality interest is concerned,[35] while German courts provide an example for reluctance to grant such awards as they require the existence of a grave violation of the personality right in question to justify monetary compensation for non-pecuniary loss.[36]

14 A noticeable feature arising in the context of damages for personality rights' violations is the regular reference to punitive aspects of damages awards, particularly in situations of structural inequality between tortfeasor and victim such as to be found for instance between mass media and individuals whose honour or privacy was infringed. The main question in this context is whether, and, if so, in which way such punitive aspects are taken into account. At one end of the spectrum, jurisdictions can reject punitive elements as factors relevant for the award of damages.[37] At the other end of the spectrum, one would situate jurisdictions foreseeing punitive, that is to say, non-compensatory damages in case of personality rights' violations.[38] In between these systems, one would find systems using the idea of deterrent and punitive aspects to increase compensatory damages, a development that will not necessarily be openly admitted. Here one could also think of systems using the profit made by the tortfeasor to assess the damages. Such an approach can, for instance, be found in Germany[39] and France.[40] The same result of depriving the tortfeasor of any profit made due to the violation of another's personality interest is reached in other systems (in a methodologically more convincing manner) via the law of unjust enrichment.[41]

15 A successful lawsuit against the tortfeasor will, however, not necessarily end with a conviction to pay damages or to repay unjust enrichment. In some jurisdictions there may instead be the possibility of a declaration by the court that

---

B Winiger/H Koziol/B Koch/R Zimmermann, Digest of European Tort Law II: Essential Cases on Damage (2011) 13/30 no 1 ff.

35 *S Galand-Carval*, Non-pecuniary loss under French law, in: WVH Rogers (ed), Damages for Non-Pecuniary Loss in a Comparative Perspective (2001) 87 nos 1 ff, 64 ff, 69.

36 *Thiede* (fn 4) no 2/49 ff.

37 This is for instance the case in Austria, although the degree of the tortfeasor's fault will be taken into account for the extent of compensation. See on this *Koziol* (fn 21) no 3/13.

38 In Europe this is the case for the Common law jurisdictions. For England see *Rogers* (fn 7) no 51 ff; *Lunney/Oliphant* (fn 8) 851, 855.

39 See on this *Wagner* (fn 4) 104 ff; *J von Gerlach*, Die Sicht des Höchstrichters, in: H Koziol/A Warzilek (eds), The Protection of Personality Rights against Mass Media (2005) 451 no 70.

40 See *Anterion/Moréteau* (fn 6) no 38 f.

41 See *Koziol* (fn 21) no 2/37.

a violation has indeed taken place, an option foreseen e.g. in the ECHR[42] and Switzerland.[43] A similar result can be reached by symbolic damages awards.[44] Moreover, Swiss law in art 49 para 2 Obligationenrecht (Law of Obligations, OR) foresees the possibility of awarding the victim a different kind of satisfaction by for instance ordering the tortfeasor to make a donation to a charitable society.[45]

16 Finally, another question of interest for a comparative analysis of personality rights and their protection from a comparative angle is what the prerequisites for the various possible consequences of imminent or already occurred violations of personality interests are. These might range from situations where only a heightened degree of fault will lead to liability[46] to strict liability scenarios.[47] Again this will depend both on the personality interest in question and the respective jurisdiction.

IV   Specific Challenges

17 In the last part of my paper I will have a brief glance at specific challenges in the area of personality rights.

A   *Mass Media*

18 The most prominent one certainly is the area of infringements of personality rights by mass media, a topic that will, with a focus on the practice of the ECHR, be analysed in more detail by *Thomas Thiede*. The reason why mass media

---

42   See on this *M Jozon*, Satisfaction by finding a violation, in: A Fenyves/E Karner/H Koziol/ E Steiner (eds), Tort Law in the Jurisprudence of the European Court of Human Rights (2011) 741; *F Bydlinski*, Methodological Approaches to the Tort Law of the ECHR, in: A Fenyves/E Karner/H Koziol/E Steiner (eds), Tort Law in the Jurisprudence of the European Court of Human Rights (2011) 29 no 2/245 ff.

43   *H Hausheer/R Aebi-Müller*, Switzerland, in: H Koziol/A Warzilek (eds), The Protection of Personality Rights against Mass Media (2005) 341 no 95.

44   See eg for France *Anterion/Moréteau* (fn 6) nos 1, 37; cf also *Warzilek* (fn 5) no 134. On symbolic awards under the ECHR see *Bydlinski* (fn 42) ibid; see also *V Wilcox*, Punitive and Nominal Damages, in: A Fenyves/E Karner/H Koziol/E Steiner (eds), Tort Law in the Jurisprudence of the European Court of Human Rights (2011) 725 no 12/19 with further comparative references in no 12/31.

45   *Hausheer/Aebi-Müller* (fn 43) 341 no 90; *Warzilek* (fn 5) no 145.

46   Eg in case of the tort of malicious falsehood. Often liability will be limited in this sense by admitting wide defences.

47   See *Warzilek* (fn 5) no 160 ff.

cases represent such a prominent challenge when protection of personality rights is concerned lies in the fact that in mass media cases the weighing of the different interests involved is of particular difficulty. On the one hand, due to the considerable impact of mass media, potential negative effects on personality interests are substantial.[48] On the other hand, the media are considered to fulfil an important control function in modern society.[49] Consequently, the interests in freedom of the press and freedom of expression carry considerable weight in mass media cases. When looking at this process of weighing of interests, three main categories can be distinguished: first, value judgements; secondly, statements of facts; and, thirdly, privacy issues.

19   When *value judgements* are concerned, we find ourselves in the core area of the freedom of expression. The interests of the person reported on will therefore have to be weighed against the freedom of expression. The question therefore is how far freedom of expression should reach, and under which circumstances it will prevail over the individual's interests in protection of his or her personality.[50] Against the background of the above-mentioned control function of the media, a system will thereby have to decide in particular the extent to which not only the importance of the topic covered but also the position the individual in question has in society is a factor relevant in the course of this balancing process.[51]

20   Concerning *statements of fact* the situation is different. Here it is freedom of the press which is the core interest to be taken into account in opposition to the protection of the personality of the individual in question. While personality rights will only exceptionally enjoy protection in case of true statements,[52] the decisive question in this area is how the law reacts to untrue statements of fact. Here a system will in particular have to decide which standards of care it imposes on the media.[53]

21   Finally, as far as protection of privacy is concerned, we will again have to weigh the public's interest in information against the personality interests of the individual involved. One of the core questions thereby being whether, and if so,

---

48   See on this *Berka* (fn 15) 493 no 13 ff.

49   See *T Thiede*, Personality Rights, the Mass Media and the European Convention on Human Rights, in this volume.

50   See *Berka* (fn 15) no 79 ff.

51   On the situation of politicians according to the practice of the ECtHR see *Thiede* (fn 49) in this volume no 3 f.

52   The most important of these exceptions being an invasion of privacy.

53   *Berka* (fn 15) no 92 ff.

the extent to which the fact of the individual in question being a public figure influences the result.[54] In contrast one could also argue that it should not be the person in question but rather the facts reported on that should be decisive for such balancing of interests.[55]

B   *Internet*

22 As a last point I would also like to refer to what could be called a contemporary or modern challenge to personality rights' protection, namely cases of personality rights infringements and the internet. *Laura Weissel* will deal with these questions in further detail in her paper.[56] I would only like to highlight some peculiarities of this relatively new area. First of all one will have to take into account that we are faced with enormous amounts of content infringing personality interests, which reaches an extremely broad audience within a minimum of time, with only limited possibilities of taking the respective content off the net again.[57] In combination with a low inhibition threshold for disseminating infringing content on the one hand and a certain lack of awareness of the sensitivity of placing content on the other hand, the internet offers a vast field of personality infringements and related litigation. The core questions will thereby be who can be held liable and what conditions apply for such liability.[58] These conditions will, amongst others, depend on the question of how close a potential defendant is related to the infringement – for instance whether he or she posted the incriminating information him- or herself, spread information posted by someone else, acted as one of the various service providers or provided information via a search engine. Although we are therefore confronted with a broad range of new cases, the basic necessity of a balancing of the opposing interests involved will equally apply in cases of personality infringements on the internet.

23 To conclude, let me summarize the core sets of questions concerning the protection of personality rights: first, which interests are protected and what is the scope of such protection; secondly, what are the means of enforcing such protection; and, finally, how can the general rules be applied to specific scenarios.

---

54   On this question see *Warzilek* (fn 5) no 78 ff.

55   See the decision of the ECtHR, *Caroline von Hannover v Germany*, 24.6.2004, no 59320/00.

56   See on this particular aspect also the 2014 special issue of the Journal of European Tort Law on Cybertorts, 5 Journal of European Tort Law (JETL) 2014, 133 ff.

57   *LE Weissel*, Personality Rights and the Internet in Europe, in this volume no 1 f.

58   See *Weissel* (fn 57) in this volume no 4 ff.

CHAPTER 2

Personality Rights in Different European Legal Systems: Privacy, Dignity, Honour and Reputation

Eva Ondreasova

I **Introduction**

1 The topic of personality rights covers a wide range of protected interests and has a long history in Europe.[1] These protected interests are, generally speaking, the interests of a person to be acknowledged as such and not to be injured in particular in a wrongful way; in other words: to have their personality protected.[2] They exist 'automatically' and do not need to be acquired, which is one of the main differences to property rights.[3] The rights to life, health and liberty are regarded as the core of personality interests. This is largely due to the fact that these rights connected to persons safeguarding against harm were developed very early and then expanded to include other personality interests such as honour and later dignity, privacy and autonomy.[4] So in a way the rights to

---

1   *C von Bar*, Gemeineuropäisches Deliktsrecht II (1999) § 1 no 81 ff. The overview given in this chapter is largely based on the works *G Brüggemeier*, Protection of personality rights in the law of delict/torts in Europe: mapping out paradigms, in: G Brüggemeier/A Colombi Ciacchi/P O'Callaghan (eds), Personality Rights in European Tort Law (2010) 5 ff; *G Brüggemeier/A Colombi Ciacchi/P O'Callaghan*, A common core of personality protection, in: G Brüggemeier/A Colombi Ciacchi/P O'Callaghan (eds), Personality Rights in European Tort Law (2010) 565 ff and the national reports contained in the book.

2   *E Adler*, Die Persönlichkeitsrechte im allgemeinen bürgerlichen Gesetzbuch, FS zur Jahrhundertfeier des ABGB II (1911) 170; *K Larenz/M Wolf*, Allgemeiner Teil des bürgerlichen Rechts (9th edn 2004) 126 ff; *H Koziol*, Österreichisches Haftpflichtrecht II (2nd edn 1984) 5; *von Bar* (fn 1) § 1 no 46.

3   *J Mauczka*, Die Anwendung der Theorie der Interessenkollisionen auf die ‚angeborenen Rechte', FS zur Jahrhundertfeier des ABGB II (1911) 284 f. Although *Mauczka* (fn 3) 285 disagrees as to when personality rights start existing. He claims some of the interests only come into existence once they can be properly exercised by the person, not with birth.

4   *Brüggemeier* (fn 1) 6; *B-R Kern*, Historische Entwicklung des Persönlichkeitsrechts in Deutschland und Kontinentaleuropa, in: A Beater/S Habermeier (eds), Verletzungen von Persönlichkeitsrechten durch die Medien (2005) 82 f, 85. See for Germany *H Coing*, Zur Entwicklung des zivilrechtlichen Persönlichkeitsschutzes (1958) Juristenzeitung (JZ) 558. For Austria *H Koziol*, Österreichisches Haftpflichtrecht I (3rd edn 1997) no 4/24 ff. A violation of the right to life,

life, health and liberty are the starting point for rights connected to the person.[5] In most jurisdictions these core rights of the personality enjoy a stronger protection,[6] as any infringement is in most cases seen as wrongful. With other personality interests one sometimes needs to first examine if said interest is even protected against violations.[7]

2 Currently there is an array of personality interests that can fall under the heading of this paper, which have been developed at specific times in different social contexts in Europe. The legal bases for their protection differ vastly from country to country. In some countries it is the constitution, in some it is their civil code or statutes, in some it is case law or codes of conduct or a combination of the above that offers protection; additionally multinational and EU legal frameworks exist which also have an impact on the legal protection of personality rights.[8] Despite all these differences, it will become apparent that certain common ground in the protection of privacy, dignity, honour and reputation exists in Europe.[9] This report will first show an analysis of the historical roots and different approaches to protecting personality interests in Austria, Germany, France, England and Sweden,[10] followed by a chapter focusing on

---

health and liberty is presumed to be wrongful, while other personality rights only enjoy protection against specific acts. Cf also Roman law and therefore also for some time German *ius commune*, which protected *corpus*, *dignitas* and *fama* through the same legal institute, the starting point having been *corpus, R Zimmermann*, The Law of Obligations: Roman Foundations of the Civilian Tradition (1996) 1052 ff, 1062 ff.

5   *Koziol*, Haftpflichtrecht I (fn 4) no 4/24 ff; *Kern* (fn 4) 83 ff.

6   Some scholars argue that all personality rights are absolute and in each case the involved interests need to be balanced against each other; however, acts against the core of personality rights will be seen as violations more often cf *Koziol*, Haftpflichtrecht II (fn 2) 6.

7   As the title suggests, this paper will solely focus on these rights and not life, health and liberty, see also *BC Steininger*, The Protection of Personality Rights in Comparative Perspective: Basic Questions, in this volume no 2. Cf for a discussion in what cases the violation should indicate wrongfulness and how the balance of interests should be struck *J Aicher* in: P Rummel, Kommentar zum ABGB (3rd edn 2000) § 16 no 14, 27 ff; *C-W Canaris*, Grundprobleme des privatrechtlichen Persönlichkeitsschutzes (1991) Juristische Blätter (JBl) 205 ff, the latter successfully arguing that the balancing act itself is the same both in cases of violations of all personality rights. Additionally compare below the balance which has to be struck between the right to privacy and the freedom of speech.

8   *Brüggemeier/Colombi Ciacchi/O'Callaghan* (fn 1) 567.

9   Cf also *Brüggemeier/Colombi Ciacchi/O'Callaghan* (fn 1) 567 ff; *von Bar* (fn 1) § 1 no 81.

10   This paper will not deal with the remedies available for violations of personality rights, cf *M Hinteregger*, The Protection of Personality Rights in Private Law: Remedies, in this volume, and *A Warzilek*, Comparative Report, in: H Koziol/A Warzilek (eds),

how European systems are currently developing some common ground which is still being expanded, and how this still leaves enough differences in the details so that formulating norms which would correspond with all the European legal systems is currently difficult. In the last chapter of this paper an overview of the systematic approaches to personality rights protection and the current extent of said protection will be given.

II   Historical Development

3 The historical progress in the legal protection of personality rights in Europe shows very interesting and different approaches to treating violations of personality interests. The different developments can be summed up in three different groups. Things started with Roman law and its protection of dignity, honour and reputation as well as its later reception into *ius commune* in most European countries. Then the development took different turns in Europe, especially with the start of the codification process: Natural law and *neminem laedere* jurisdictions on the one hand and the German school of Pandects and Scandinavian law on the other hand at first took very different routes. England had a different development altogether from both groups.

A   *Roman Law,* ius commune, *Middle Ages and Early Modern Europe*

4 Classical Roman law, in particular from the later Roman Republic onwards, alongside the bodily integrity of the free Roman citizen also safeguarded his/her 'personality'– *dignitas* and *fama* – against the most varied forms of intentional acts through tort law.[11] The protection covered dignity and reputation against acts which cause humiliation, in particular insults, and examples passed on by scholars are rife with defamation cases.[12] There was a general edict of the *praetores* against *iniuria* and three special delicts, namely *convicium, adtemptata*

Persönlichkeitsschutz gegenüber Massenmedien (2005) 642 for an overview of remedies in Europe. For Austria cf *Canaris* (1991) JBl 205, 211 ff.

11   Roman law and therefore also for some time German *ius commune*, protected *corpus, dignitas* and *fama* through the same legal institute, the starting point having been *corpus, Zimmermann* (fn 4) 1052 ff; 1062 ff with further references. Cf also *Brüggemeier* (fn 1) 18 with further references; *Brüggemeier/Colombi Ciacchi/O'Callaghan* (fn 1) 568 with further references; *Kern* (fn 4) 83 ff.

12   *Zimmermann* (fn 4) 1050 ff with further references; *Brüggemeier* (fn 1) 18 with further references. Of note are the particular similarities between modern defamation law and Roman law under the edict *convicium*.

pudicitia and *infamatio* in particular which were used in these cases. There were two different actions available to an injured party, which could be seen as covering personality interests. First, the *actio infamia* and second, the *actio iniuriarum*.[13] The civil suit of *actio iniuriarum* in particular was aimed at the satisfaction of persons unlawfully brought into public disrespect through equitable monetary compensation.[14]

5 In most European countries the *actio iniuriarum* was still part of the *ius commune* until the eighteenth and nineteenth centuries and it only protected honour and reputation and not privacy as such.[15] In the Middle Ages society in most of Europe was based on the spirit of the feudal codes of chivalry and assigned great importance to honour.[16] Unfortunately, in particular during early modern European times, honour and revenge were tied up closely with each other and in particular duelling as a form of dispute settlement was widely spread.[17] However, in a developed community it is of importance that self-help is not tolerated and disputes are settled in a peaceful manner; the *actio iniuriarum* was therefore very useful at this time in most European countries.[18] German *ius commune* for example, despite society's deep entrenchment in duelling as a form of dispute settlement,[19] attempted to provide protection against interference with man's interest in his dignity and honour through the *actio iniuriarum*, which, for a certain period of time in Germany's history, was

---

13 Or *actio iniuriarum aestimatoria*. Cf *Zimmermann* (fn 4) 1050 ff; *Kaser/Knütel*, Römisches Privatrecht (17th edn 2003) § 51, III, no 22, 323; *Brüggemeier* (fn 1) 6; *Kern* (fn 4) 84.

14 *Zimmermann* (fn 4) 1050 ff with further references; *Brüggemeier* (fn 1) 18 with further references. Of note are the particular similarities between modern defamation law and Roman law under the edict *convicium*.

15 *Brüggemeier* (fn 1) 18; for Germany *Zimmermann* (fn 4) 1062 f, 1070 f and for the modern application of the *actio iniuriarium* in South Africa 1078 ff. The protection of honour lived on in the Austrian Code, while the *actio iniuriarum* itself was according to *Mauczka* (fn 3) 257 ff abolished in Austria. The *actio* was also abolished in Germany, cf II.B (no 8 below).

16 *Zimmermann* (fn 4) 1062 f.

17 Despite the enactment of anti-duelling laws as early as in the 16th century, duelling was dominant in German society until the first World War, cf in detail *Zimmermann* (fn 4) 1062 ff, 1085 f; for the duelling laws cf also *E Kaufmann*, Die Fehde des Sichar (1961) Juristische Schulung (JuS) 85 ff. For England and a similar development cf *W Ellet*, The Death of Dueling (2004) 13 Historia 59 ff. For a general overview in Europe see *VG Kiernan*, The Duel in European History (1988) 31 ff, 165 ff, 185 ff.

18 *Zimmermann* (fn 4) 1063.

19 Despite the enactment of anti-duelling laws as early as in the 16th century, duelling was dominant in German society until the first World War, cf in detail *Zimmermann* (fn 4) 1062 ff, 1085 f; for the duelling laws cf also *Kaufmann* (1961) JuS 85 ff.

successful, in particular during the period of Natural law theory.[20] Reparation was made by a payment of money if the injured party wished but also by a formal declaration by the offender that he had made his allegation in heat and without any intention to defame, retraction of the defamatory words as being untrue, which repaired the injured person's honour, or an acknowledgement by the offender that he had done wrong coupled with a prayer that he might be forgiven (*amende honourable*).[21] A similar approach could be seen in other countries following the Natural law theory, like Austria, where not just the protection of dignity and honour was the starting point, mostly through the reception of Roman law, but also a right to personality as such was already starting to be developed.[22]

6   Germany, however, in contrast to other continental European states following the Natural law theory, had a very peculiar further development. With the fall of the Natural law theory and the rise of the school of Pandects, legal opinion started to turn against both the *actio iniuriarum* itself as well as the idea that the law of delict should protect honour and reputation in general.[23] A reason for this was that scholars argued that the remedies described above did not serve a useful restitutionary purpose. Criminal law was seen as providing sufficient remedies and therefore a separate action in private law was considered unnecessary, especially as pecuniary damages were already included in the criminal law regime.[24] In as far as damage which was non-monetary or even non-material was concerned, according to legal opinion, there was no way to assess how much money would have to be paid as compensation. In these

---

20   The Natural law scholars saw the *actio iniuriarum* as an integral part of the general law of delict and developed the idea of natural rights, innate to man and based on his natural freedom, including the right to develop one's own personality freely. Cf *Zimmermann* (fn 4) 1063 ff, 1085 ff; cf also the situation in Austria above.

21   The *actio iniuriarum* tied in well with the traditions of German *ius commune*, but its inherent flexibility rendered it superior to the system of fixed penalties dominant in the latter. Some of the mentioned possible reparations go back to German *ius commune* itself and some to Christian traditions. Cf *Zimmermann* (fn 4) 1063 ff, 1085 ff.

22   *Adler* (fn 2) 175 and below no 9 ff.

23   One of the reasons was that the *actio iniuriarum* included a penal element which was seen as not fitting for a law of delict increasingly directed towards the compensation of loss sustained. *Zimmermann* (fn 4) 1085 ff, 1088 ff with further references. For the legal opinion against the *actio iniuriarum* cf *P Gotthardt*, Persönlichkeitsrechte und Rechtssystem, in: A Beater/S Habermeier (eds), Verletzungen von Persönlichkeitsrechten durch die Medien (2005) 2 f; *N Jansen*, Die Struktur des Haftungsrechts (2003) 459; *Kern* (fn 4) 84 f, 87. Of course dissenting opinions existed cf no 18 and fn 77 below.

24   *Zimmermann* (fn 4) 1090 with further references.

cases one would have to express the value of the injured feelings in financial terms, which repelled the contemporary sense of decency; honour and good reputation were seen as being of an inestimable value.[25] Accepting monetary compensation was seen as scurrilous and some scholars suspected claimants of trying to enrich themselves.[26] Tort law was regarded as focused typically on the market and interests which have a market value and it was thought that personality rights could not be compensated in money as there was no clear loss sustained; other interests had to be protected either by societal means or criminal law.[27] For example one of the first cases concerning personality interests regarding the late Imperial Chancellor and illegally obtained images of him (the *Bismarck* photograph case of 1899[28]) had to be resolved by referring to the law of trespass.[29] Due to this change in legal opinion, the *actio iniuriarum* was formally repealed in the nineteenth century in an increasing number of German states until the German Empire followed suit.[30]

7 England had a very different development, both in defamation and in privacy law. In general English tort law recognizes individual torts, which can also protect various personality interests; it does not nominally recognise a general tort of intrusion of privacy.[31] The most prominent in the protection of personality rights is the law of defamation, which has a long history in English law. Rooted in different traditions, there are two distinct torts: written or 'permanent' defamation (libel) and oral or 'transient' defamation (slander).[32] A distinction has

---

25   *Zimmermann* (fn 4) 1090 f with further references; *K Larenz/CW Canaris*, Lehrbuch des Schuldrechts II/2 (13th edn 1994) 494.

26   *B Mugdan*, Die gesamten Materialien zum Bürgerlichen Gesetzbuch, Band II: Recht der Schuldverhältnisse (1899) 12; *Jansen* (fn 23) 459; *Brüggemeier* (fn 1) 7, 18 ff; *Zimmermann* (fn 4) 1089 ff with further references.

27   *Jansen* (fn 23) 459; *Zimmermann* (fn 4) 1085 ff; *Kern* (fn 4) 85; *Brüggemeier* (fn 1) 7, 19 f further references.

28   Reichsgericht (RG) Entscheidungen des Reichsgerichts in Zivilsachen (RGZ) 45, 170. The RG denied the personality rights of children and conventionally referred to the *ius commune actio ob iniustam causam*. Cf *Larenz/Canaris* (fn 25) 491 ff: *Brüggemeier* (fn 1) 21 with further references; *T Thiede*, Internationale Persönlichkeitsrechtsverletzungen (2010) 18 f.

29   RG RGZ 45, 170. Cf *Brüggemeier* (fn 1) 21 with further references; *Thiede* (fn 28) 18 f; *E Karner*, Menschenrechte und Schutz der Persönlichkeit im Zivilrecht (2013) Österreichische Juristenzeitung (ÖJZ) 906, 907.

30   *FC von Savigny*, System des heutigen Römischen Rechts II (1840) 1 ff; *Zimmermann* (fn 4) 1085 ff; cf *Brüggemeier* (fn 1) 8, 19 f.

31   Cf *S Deakin/A Johnston/B Markesinis*, Makesinis and Deakin's Tort Law (7th edn 2012) 706 ff, 713 ff; *M Lunney/K Oliphant*, Tort Law: Text & Materials (5th edn 2013) 783 ff.

32   Cf for the details of how to differentiate between 'libel' and 'slander' *Deakin/Johnston/ Markesinis* (fn 31) 636 ff; *Lunney/Oliphant* (fn 31) 687 ff; *Thiede* (fn 28) 60 ff; *C von Bar*,

always been made between the two and they have always been treated differently from one another and this tradition is continued today.[33]

B   *European Development after the Codifications*

8 At first in the European development there were no constitutional rights
which would have influenced the protection of personality rights. For example
in France the *Déclaration des droits de l'homme et du citoyen* of 26 August 1789
only obliged any politic body to protect the 'natural rights' of human beings.[34]
The 1919 *Weimar Constitution*[35] in Germany only included substantive constitutional civil and economic rights which were not judicially enforceable.[36]
Only after World War II did the constitutional framework start to play a more
significant role.[37]

9 The development after early modern Europe was therefore at first in most jurisdictions free of influence from public law. In some countries, however, other
parts of the civil law played a role. In France for example scholars argue that
the development of the protection of personality rights was largely aided by
the discussion regarding intellectual property rights in the nineteenth century.[38] The same does, however, not hold true for Germany.[39]

10 The civil law systems present in Europe could be again clustered into three
groups according to their views on tort law and the protection of personality
rights already described above.

11 On one side of the spectrum were jurisdictions which followed the Natural
law theory even after early modern European times or had a *neminem laedere*
clause in their codes, which recognised personality rights in one form or other
at least in most cases somewhat consistently from *ius commune* on. For Austria

---

Gemeineuropäisches Deliktsrecht I (1996) § 3 no 271 ff; for an overview of the historical
development from an outsider's perspective *Zimmermann* (fn 4) 1074 ff. He shows that the
protection was geared towards the reputation of the individual, not his honour.

33 *Deakin/Johnston/Markesinis* (fn 31) 636 ff; *Lunney/Oliphant* (fn 31) 687 ff; *Brüggemeier*
(fn 1) 25; *Thiede* (fn 28) 58 ff.

34 Article 2 of the *Déclaration*. Cf *Brüggemeier* (fn 1) 10 f and *Thiede* (fn 28) 89 with further
references. Cf *K Anterion/O Moréteau*, France, in: H Koziol/A Warzilek (eds), Persönlichkeitsschutz gegenüber Massenmedien (2005) 117 ff for the changes in the application of
the *Déclaration* over time.

35 Verfassung des Deutschen Reiches of 11.8.1919, Reichsgesetzblatt 1919, 1383 ff.

36 They were merely seen as programmatic political goals to be implemented by the legislator. *Larenz/Canaris* (fn 25) 492; *Brüggemeier* (fn 1) 21.

37 Cf below.

38 *Brüggemeier* (fn 1) 13 with further references.

39 *Brüggemeier* (fn 1) 21.

this was the broad and unique provision of § 16 of the Code from 1811 (Austrian Civil Code, *Allgemeines Bürgerliches Gesetzbuch*, ABGB)[40] coupled with the broad provisions for the law of delict (§ 1293 ff ABGB) and for France it was the extensive and general formulation of arts 1382 and 1383 *Code Civil*, which will be described in more detail below.[41] Both aided the development of personality rights, however, in slightly different ways. Parallels in the development of these two jurisdictions existed mainly during the first phase of French legal history after Early Modern Europe.

12 On the one hand in Austria the Civil Code from 1811 was strongly influenced by Natural law theory going back to *Kant*,[42] and included in § 16 ABGB a specific provision stating in its original and until today in its unchanged version that every human being has certain inborn rights, apparent from reason, and is therefore to be regarded as a person. The Austrian system therefore acknowledges in § 16 the rational freedom of a person to make decisions about their life, which is inherent to every human being, and the inborn rights needed to protect this freedom.[43] The provision is seen as a central provision of Austrian private law[44] as well as the civil law basis for human dignity[45] and the protection of the right to personality of human beings.[46] This protection includes the protection of life, liberty and health as well as privacy and dignity.[47] However, this interpretation of § 16 ABGB has not always been prevalent in Austrian doctrine.[48] Even leading scholars of the later 19th century thought

---

40 Cf for the legal protection of personality rights, in particular honour and reputation before the Code, *Mauczka* (fn 3) 257 ff.

41 *Brüggemeier* (fn 1) 11, 13; *Thiede* (fn 28) 89 with further references.

42 *Mauczka* (fn 3) 234 ff; *Adler* (fn 2) 176 ff; *O Edlbacher*, Der Stand der Persönlichkeitsrechte in Österreich (1983) ÖJZ 423, 424; Rummel/*Aicher* (fn 7) § 16 no 1.

43 *M Schauer* in: A Kletečka/M Schauer (eds), ABGB-ON (1.01 edn 2013) § 16 no 1.

44 RIS-Justiz RS0114307, RS0008993 and OGH 3 Ob 197/13m; 7 Ob 130/15s; Kletečka/Schauer/*Schauer* (fn 43) § 16 no 4 and no 11 ff; *BA Koch*, Von Sklaven und Kabarettisten. § 16 ABGB im Wandel der Zeit, in: H Barta/C Lehne/M Niedermayr/M Schennach (eds), Kontinuität im Wandel. 200 Jahre ABGB (1811–2011) (2012) 223; *W Posch* in: M Schwimann/G Kodek, Kommentar zum ABGB (4th edn 2011) § 16 no 3 with further references.

45 Rummel/*Aicher* (fn 7) § 16 no 3; Schwimann/Kodek/*Posch* (fn 44) § 16 no 3; Kletečka/Schauer/*Schauer* (fn 43) § 16 no 1; *Canaris* (1991) JBl 205, 213. Some even see it as the central norm of the entire Austrian legal system *Edlbacher* (1983) ÖJZ, 423, 428.

46 Rummel/*Aicher* (fn 7) § 16 no 3; Schwimann/Kodek/*Posch* (fn 44) § 16 no 3; Kletečka/Schauer/*Schauer* (fn 43) § 16 no 1; *BA Koch* in: H Koziol/P Bydlinski/R Bollenberger, Kommentar zum ABGB (4th edn 2014) § 16 ABGB no 3.

47 *Koziol* (fn 2) 7 f; Schwimann/Kodek/*Posch* (fn 44) § 16 no 20 ff; Rummel/*Aicher* (fn 7) § 16 no 17; *Adler* (fn 2) 189 ff.

48 Schwimann/Kodek/*Posch* (fn 44) § 16 no 1.

§ 16 had little application in practice and was only to be regarded as a mani-festo of the underlying principles of the Code; however, some of them still accepted personality rights based on other provisions in the Code.[49] Only at the beginning of the 20th century did the opinion regarding the role of § 16 ABGB begin to change.[50] An increasing number of scholars saw the open-ness of the provision as an opportunity to base and develop personality rights upon it.[51] Most prominent were *Wellspacher* and *Mauczka*,[52] who already in 1911 regarded § 16 ABGB as a potential basis for the recognition of personal-ity rights under Austrian law. *Mauczka* was even able to show that his and the current interpretation of § 16 is in line with the interpretation of the provi-sion by its drafters and the scholars from the early 19th century;[53] therefore it was an application of § 16 as envisaged by the drafters. An indication of this is that the decision as to which interests are protected by § 16 ABGB is in part judged based on the provision's predecessor – § 29[54] from the primary draft

---

49   *J Unger*, System des österreichischen allgemeinen Privatrechts I (1856) 71, fn 16; cf further *M Wellspacher*, Das Naturrecht und das ABGB, in FS zur Jahrhundertfeier des ABGB I (1911) 187; *Edlbacher* (1983) ÖJZ 423, 424; Schwimann/Kodek/*Posch* (fn 44) § 16 no 1; Kletečka/ Schauer/*Schauer* (fn 43) § 16 no 4; *Karner* (2013) ÖJZ 906 (907). Cf for a further list of these scholars *Wellspacher* (fn 49) 189; *Edlbacher* (1983) ÖJZ 423, 424.

50   Only a few scholars of the late 19th century denied § 16 its application when it came to personality rights, cf *Mauczka* (fn 3) 236 f. Some denied § 16 had any role at all, cf *Unger* (fn 49) 71, fn 16; *Adler* (fn 2) 187 f. Some of those scholars, however, considered personality rights to be protected under Austrian law without basing this protection on § 16 ABGB; cf for a list of these scholars *Wellspacher* (fn 49) 189; *Edlbacher* (1983) ÖJZ 423, 424. Dissent-ing against personality rights for a long time *K Wolff* in: H Klang (ed), Kommentar zum Allgemeinen bürgerlichen Gesetzbuch I/1 (2nd edn 1964) 130. Unclear to me is *Adler* (fn 2) 176 ff who argues that 'inborn rights' does not mean personality rights and therefore § 16 does not protect personality rights – instead it covers 'inborn' rights; but he then lists most accepted personality rights as 'inborn' rights. In my view he mostly means that § 16 itself cannot be seen as the basis of protection if other provisions do not exist, which also protect the discussed interest. Cf also *Koziol* (fn 2) 5.

51   Kletečka/Schauer/*Schauer* (fn 43) § 16 no 4. *Wellspacher* (fn 49) 187 f. Cf also *Adler* (fn 2) 165 ff who argued that the ABGB from 1811 protects personality rights even in its original version, however, he disagreed that § 16 ABGB is the basis of this protection.

52   *Wellspacher* (fn 49) 187 f; *Mauczka* (fn 3) 231 ff; dissenting against § 16 as the basis of these rights, *Adler* (fn 2) 187 f. Cf for the discussion *Edlbacher* (1983) ÖJZ 423, 424. It took a few years before this interpretation of § 16 was widely accepted by scholars, cf *Koch* (fn 44) 221 ff.

53   Cf the numerous references and citations in *Mauczka* (fn 3) 233 ff.

54   § 29 of the *Martini* draft included a demonstrative enumeration of 'inborn rights' as un-derstood by the Natural law theory: the right to preserve one's life and to acquire the nec-essary things for this purpose; the right to develop one's mental and physical prowess; the

prepared by *Martini*,[55] which was in force initially in western Galicia from 1797.[56] *Zeiller*, one of the drafters of the Code, also saw the content of § 16 ABGB as protecting the right to personality, meaning a right to the dignity of a free and reasonable human being.[57] The courts, however, have only in the last quarter of the last century begun to use § 16 ABGB as a basis for personality protection.[58] Additionally certain rights were individually protected in the Code, for example a violation of honour had to be compensated under tort law according to § 1330 ABGB already from 1812 onwards.[59]

---

right to defence; the right to argue a good repute and the right to do with one's property as one pleases. Due to political and legislative reasons, the Code later only had a general clause describing the primordial right to personality. *Mauczka* (fn 3) 232 ff; *Adler* (fn 2) 185; Schwimann/Kodek/*Posch* (fn 44) § 16 no 2.

55 Cf Rummel/*Aicher* (fn 7) § 16 no 1; *Koch* (fn 44) 217. Cf for Martini's views on 'inborn rights' *Mauczka* (fn 3) 235 and the other drafts of the Austrian Code regarding the protection of one's honour 257 ff; also *Adler* (fn 2) 176 ff, who, however, disagrees with the notion that § 16 protects what is currently seen as personality rights and underlines that the interpretation of 'inborn' rights can only be done according to Natural law theory and not current views on personality rights (187 f). In his list of what 'inborn' rights are, however, he more or less covers all the accepted personality rights (189 f).

56 *Mauczka* (fn 3) 232 ff; *Adler* (fn 2) 185; Schwimann/Kodek/*Posch* (fn 44) § 16 no 2; *Koch* (fn 44) 218. Cf on the influence of Natural law on the draft, *Wellspacher* (fn 49) 179 f.

57 *F Zeiller*, Das natürliche Privatrecht (3rd edn 1819) 64 ff; cf, however, his more reluctant interpretation of § 16 in *F Zeiller*, Commentar über das allgmeine bürgerliche Gesetzbuch für die gesammten Deutschen Erbländer der Oesterreichischen Monarchie, Band I (1811) 102 ff. Cf on detail regarding the state of the scholarly opinion at the time *Mauczka* (fn 3) 232 ff; *Adler* (fn 2) 176 ff; *Koch* (fn 44) 219 f.

58 One of the starting points was the judgment of the Supreme Court from 1978 in which a right to privacy was acknowledged as being one of the inborn rights mentioned in § 16 ABGB. 4 Ob 91/78 SZ 51/146 = Zeitschrift für Arbeitsrecht und Sozialrecht (ZAS) 1979, 176 (*Marhold*) = Das Recht der Arbeit (drdA) 1979, 394 (*Raschauer*); cf *Edlbacher* (1983) ÖJZ 423, 428. OGH 10 ObS 40/90 SZ 63/32 was one of the first decisions to use § 16 itself as the basis of a right; cf also RIS-Justiz rs0114307, RS0008993 and OGH 3 Ob 197/13m; 7 Ob 130/15s. Cf Schwimann/Kodek/*Posch* (fn 44) § 16 no 1, 3; Kletečka/Schauer/*Schauer* (fn 43) § 16 no 4, 11 ff; *Koch* (fn 44) 223; Rummel/*Aicher* (fn 7) § 16 no 3; *I Griss*, Das ABGB und die Praxis – eine wechselvolle Beziehung, in: C Fischer-Czermak/G Hopf/G Kathrein/M Schauer (eds), ABGB 2011 (2008) 46. Before the protection had been based on other individual provisions of the code and only as far as the violated interest was covered by them, cf *Koch* (fn 44) 223.

59 Cf also § 43 ABGB protecting the name of a person. *Koch* (fn 44) 223. Cf for the current view on both provisions *E Wagner* in: A Kletečka/M Schauer (eds), ABGB-ON (1.02 edn 2015) § 43 no 1 ff; *S Kissich* in: A Kletečka/M Schauer (eds), ABGB-ON (1.02 edn 2014) § 1330 no 1 ff; *H Koziol*, Basic Questions of Tort Law from a Germanic Perspective (2012) 114 f.

13 On the other hand in France the protection in the Code in contrast to the Austrian system developed in a more insular way. Not a general right to personality
as enacted in § 16 ABGB was accepted, but instead, depending on the cases before the court, individual personality rights were acknowledged and their protection insured. The judgment of 16 June 1858 on the *Rachel* case was the starting point of this development.[60] It concerned a famous actress who had been
photographed on her deathbed and unauthorised sketches were then made
of the photograph. In the judgment it was held that the reproduction of a person's likeness was seen as a sort of exclusive right to the individual.[61] Following
this decision, French law regarded a person's image, name[62] and likeness as
exclusive rights in various other judgments.[63] By the end of the nineteenth
century various personality interests were protected in France.

14 The main restriction on the protection of personality rights existed in cases
where the harmful conduct involved the media. Private life and honour were
protected against invasions by the media in the Press Act 1881,[64] which chose
to strongly protect the freedom of the press and restrict the damages available
to victims.[65]

15 In the 1950s, what is regarded as the second phase in the history of French law
on the protection of personality interests in particular regarding the right to
privacy began.[66] In the famous *Marlene Dietrich* case, a magazine published
parts of Ms Dietrich's alleged memoirs in the form of an invented interview.
It was held that facts and stories 'concerning the private life are part of the
person's moral property; ...no one may publish them ... without the express
and unequivocal authorization of the person whose life is recounted.'[67] This
was not an isolated case and, due to this flourishing case law development,
the legislature decided to reform the *Code Civil* through the Act of 17 July 1970

---

60   Tribunal civil de la Seine (Trib civ Seine), Recueil Dalloz (D) 1858, 3, 62. The overview of
      the French law development is based on the paper by *Brüggemeier* (fn 1) 11.

61   *Brüggemeier* (fn 1) 11.

62   Trib civ Seine, D 1884, 2, 22 note *Labbé*. *Brüggemeier* (fn 1) 11.

63   Damages were awarded under arts 1382 and 1383 Code Civil. The only subject of conten-
      tion was the question of the legal nature of this right and the conflict with an artist's right
      to his/her work; cf *Brüggemeier* (fn 1) 11 f.

64   The protection before the Act had been based on tort law and criminal law, cf *Anterion/
      Moréteau* (fn 34) 117.

65   *Brüggemeier* (fn 1) 13 and *Thiede* (fn 28) 89, 95 ff with further references.

66   The distinction into phases is based on the work of *Brüggemeier* (fn 1) 14.

67   Paris, *M Dietrich*, Recueil Dalloz-Sirey: Jurisprudence (DS Jur) 1955, 295. Cf for the trans-
      lation *Brüggemeier* (fn 1) 14. See also Cour de cassation, Chambre civile (Cass civ) 2,
      G Philipe, DS Jur 1967, 181.

and introduced art 9 discussed below, thereby strengthening the protection of personality rights and in particular privacy.[68]

16 What is seen as the third phase in the legal protection of personality rights in France arose due to the changed view of constitutional rights and their influence on private law. A new branch of law was created: constitutional jurisprudence (*droit constitutionnel jurisprudentiel*). This jurisprudence allows ordinary courts in France to directly refer to constitutional principles when deciding cases. This development constituted a break from established previous French legal tradition and opened up the protection of personality rights to the influence of human rights and also the European Convention on Human Rights (ECHR), which came into force in 1974 in France. The effect, as will be described in more detail below, can be seen in particular regarding the right to privacy, in particular because the Press Act 1881 has *de facto* lost its influence.[69]

17 In contrast to the legal systems following Natural law theory, the development in Germany had taken a different turn already under the *ius commune*, especially with the rise of the German school of Pandects[70] as described above. A similar approach to personality rights was also prelevalent in Sweden. The protection of honour and reputation was left to criminal law; they were not included in Germany in § 823 BGB[71] or in Sweden in § 1 of the Swedish Tort Liability Act as rights whose violation can lead to compensation.[72] The protection of honour was only permitted as far as criminal protection existed.[73] In Sweden, for example, an infringement of personality interests as a 'civil injury' only triggers liability if the infringement is punishable as a criminal act as is regulated

---

68   Loi No 70-643, Journal Officiel (JO) 19 July 1970, 6751; cf *Brüggemeier* (fn 1) 14 with further references.

69   *Brüggemeier* (fn 1) 15 ff with further references. The new interpretation of the *Déclaration des Droits de l'Homme et du Citoyen,* coupled with the influence of the ECHR, played a significant role; cf *Anterion/Moréteau* (fn 34) 123 ff.

70   Cf instead of all *A Heise*, Grundriß eines Systems des gemeinen Zivilrechts (1807).

71   See § 823 para 2 BGB and § 826 BGB. *Coing* (1958) JZ 558; *Zimmermann* (fn 4) 1085 ff; *Larenz/Canaris* (fn 25) 491 f; *Kern* (fn 4) 84; *Brüggemeier* (fn 1) 18 ff with further references.

72   The reasoning was that in contrast to the right to life, liberty and health and the right to one's name, other personality rights lack obviousness and publicity to the public and it was assumed that a constant overlap between the personality rights of multiple persons would exist, which in most cases is not typical of the above mentioned acknowledged rights; the other personality rights were therefore not included in the protection by § 823 BGB. Cf *Larenz/Canaris* (fn 25) 491; *Brüggemeier* (fn 1) 8, 19 f; *FC von Savigny*, System des heutigen Römischen Rechts, Band 1 (1840) 335 f; *idem* (fn 30) 1 ff; *Zimmermann* (fn 4) 1085 ff.

73   Through a combination of § 823 BGB and the Criminal Code, *Larenz/Canaris* (fn 25) 491; *Zimmermann* (fn 4) 1092.

in § 3 of Chapter 2 of the Swedish Tort Liability Act.[74] § 3 states that liability shall arise if anyone seriously violates the rights of others if a crime involving an assault on their person, freedom, peace or honour was committed.

18 In Germany the protection of personality rights was only allowed in specific cases, in particular the right to one's name under § 12 BGB[75] and in contrast to other private law systems – England, Austria and France – not in defamation cases without it also being a crime.[76] Dissent was formulated already before the BGB came into force, most importantly by *Otto von Gierke*, who was one of the first scholars to formulate a thesis of a general personality right.[77] However, leading scholars disagreed and therefore the field of these personality rights remained underdeveloped.[78]

19 In Germany it soon became apparent that an increasing number of important interests were left outside the protection of tort law with no real protection in other parts of law or in society. This void had to be filled.[79] Therefore, in the aftermath of the *Bismarck* case, the right to one's image was introduced

---

74   1972:207. Cf *H Andersson*, Sweden in: K Oliphant/BC Steininger (eds), European Tort Law: Basic Texts (2011) 255. Cf *E Lindell-Frantz*, Personality Rights and the Media: National Report for Sweden, in: A Beater/S Habermeier (eds), Invasions of Personality Rights by the Media (2005) 51 f; *Brüggemeier* (fn 1) 28 f; and in this direction *A Lauer/A Colombi Ciacchi*, Sweden, in: G Brüggemeier et al (eds), Fundamental Rights and Private Law in the European Union I (2010) 690 f.

75   The protection of these rights includes non-pecuniary loss, even though the argument from above against the personality rights discussed in this paper – their inestimatable value – should apply here as well. However, other personality rights were seen as having enough obviousness and publicity to others that they should be an exception. Cf §§ 847 and 823 BGB; *Zimmermann* (fn 4) 1092; *Larenz/Canaris* (fn 25) 491. Other non-pecuniary damages could not be awarded due to § 253 BGB.

76   *Larenz/Canaris* (fn 25) 491; *Brüggemeier* (fn 1) 20; *Zimmermann* (fn 4) 1091 f with further references.

77   *O Gierke*, Deutsches Privatrecht (1895) 260, 702 ff. Cf *Kern* (fn 4) 87. One of the first to discuss personality rights was *Gierke's* teacher, *Beseler*. See *G Beseler*, System des gemeinen deutschen Privatrechts III (1855) 336. One of the first to introduce the case of an unauthorised publishing of letters was *J Kohler*, Das Autorrecht, in: Jahrbücher für die Dogmatik des heutigen römischen und deutschen Privatrechts 18 (1889) 129 ff, 271 ff.

78   With a few notable exceptions, cf *Brüggemeier* (fn 1) 20 with further references; *Thiede* (fn 28) 5.

79   *Brüggemeier* (fn 1) 8. The courts were reluctant to do this at first and saw personality rights as foreign to the regime of the BGB; *Kern* (fn 4) 89 f; RGZ 69, 401, 404; further references in BGHZ 13, 334, 337. Only particular single personality rights were protected through § 826 BGB at first, a general personality right, however, denied. Cf *Larenz/Canaris* (fn 25) 491 f.

into the Artists' Copyright Act (*Kunsturhebergesetz*, KUG) of 1907.[80] Despite the introduction of a right to one's image in 1907, in 1908 the Imperial Court (*Reichsgericht*, RG) stated that a general personality right was alien to German civil law.[81] The protection remained thus isolated to images; other personality interests remained unprotected. Scholars argued that in Germanic society and therefore also in the German legal system, personality interests were protected by other means than by the law of delict.[82]

20 Similarly to France, the increased influence of constitutional rights after World War II led to a further change in the law.[83] The *Bonn Constitution* (*Grundgesetz*, GG) came into force in 1949 in the Federal Republic of (West) Germany.[84] It contained a catalogue of mandatory fundamental rights, explicitly binding all public powers (art 1 para 3 GG).[85] This led to a need for interpretation of the pre-constitutional nineteenth century civil law of the BGB that was compatible with the new GG.[86] The highest German courts – the Federal Constitutional Court (*Bundesverfassungsgericht*, BVerfG) and the Federal Court of Justice (*Bundesgerichtshof*, BGH) – played a key role. In a couple of landmark judgments they eventually developed a general personality right protecting various personality interests.[87]

21 In particular the *Schacht-Leserbrief* judgment of the BGH in 1954 led to a change in the law of personality rights.[88] The facts of the case were as follows: Dr Hjalmar Schacht was temporarily the Minister of the Economy under *Hitler* and also the president of the *Reichsbank* until 1938 during the National Socialist

---

80   The KUG was repealed by the Copyrights Act (Urheberrechtsgesetz) in 1965, however, the provision concerning the right to one's image remained in force, cf *Brüggemeier* (fn 1) 21; *Thiede* (fn 28) 18 ff. Cf on the ECtHR's case law below.

81   RG RGZ 69, 401, 403 – *Nietzsche letters. Larenz/Canaris* (fn 25) 491; *Brüggemeier* (fn 1) 18.

82   *Zimmermann* (fn 4) 1085 ff.

83   *Brüggemeier* (fn 1) 22 with further references.

84   Grundgesetz für die Bundesrepublik Deutschland of 23.5.1949, Bundesgesetzblatt 1949, 1 ff. Cf *Larenz/Canaris* (fn 25) 492; *Brüggemeier* (fn 1) 22.

85   *Larenz/Canaris* (fn 25) 492; *Zimmermann* (fn 4) 1092 ff; *Brüggemeier* (fn 1) 22.

86   *Coing* (1958) JZ 558, 559 f; *Zimmermann* (fn 4) 1092 ff; *Jansen* (fn 23) 487; *Kern* (fn 4) 90 ff; *Larenz/Canaris* (fn 25) 492 ff, 494 f; *Brüggemeier* (fn 1) 22 with further references; also *Thiede* (fn 28) 5 f, 49 f; BGHZ 13, 334, 334–340; 26, 349–359; 35, 363; 128, 1, 15; 143, 214, 218 f.

87   *Coing* (1958) JZ 558, 559 f; *Zimmermann* (fn 4) 1085 ff; *Larenz/Canaris* (fn 25) 492 ff; *Brüggemeier* (fn 1) 22. The development in Germany influenced other European jurisdictions like Italy and Portugal; cf *E Karner*, Menschenrechte und Persönlichkeitsschutz in Österreich und Europa, in: Vienna Law Inauguration Lectures III (2014) 25 f.

88   BGH BGHZ 13, 334 = Neue Juristische Wochenschrift (NJW) 1954, 1404 = JZ 1954, 695 (*Coing*). Cf *Brüggemeier* (fn 1) 22 f; *Thiede* (fn 28) 8 ff.

era. In 1952, a journal investigated his new economic activities. The claimant, the legal counsel for Dr Schacht, filed a formal brief for his client, in which he demanded the rectification of the article. The magazine printed the brief next to opinions of readers under the column 'Letters to the Editor.' Therefore, the claimant was cast in a false light as being a sympathizer of both Dr Schacht and National Socialism. The BGH for the first time developed a right of personality as constitutionally guaranteed by art 1 para 1 (respect of human dignity) and art 2 para 2 GG (right to free development of the persona).[89] Based on these provisions, the BGH stated that a person has to be protected against the altered and unauthorised publication of his/her written expression. Due to the Constitution, the general right of personality must be accepted as a constitutionally guaranteed fundamental right, which is not only directed against the State and its public bodies, but also against private parties.[90] In 1957, the general personality right was explicitly recognised as an 'other right' within the meaning of § 823 para 1 BGB.[91]

22 Despite starting out similarly, the development in Sweden, in contrast to Germany, has not yet led to such a drastic change in the law. This is mainly due to the fact that prevailing legal theory was, for some time in the past, influenced by prominent scholars who were 'Realists' and sceptical towards Natural law theory as well as the specific political framework of Sweden as a 'welfare' democracy; this backdrop has made Swedish legal theory reluctant to accept fundamental rights which could influence private law as they did in Germany.[92] Defamation, for example, still only leads to compensation under tort law if it is considered a crime.[93] In particular Scandinavian doctrines on the horizontal effect of human rights have only just and timidly begun to be developed.[94]

---

89   Together with § 847 BGB. *Jansen* (fn 23) 487; *Kern* (fn 4) 90 ff; *Larenz/Canaris* (fn 25) 491 ff, 494 f; *Thiede* (fn 28) 49 f; BGHZ 13, 334, 334–340; 26, 349–359; 35, 363; 128, 1, 15; 143, 214, 218 f.

90   Cf *Brüggemeier* (fn 1) 22 f and *Koch* (fn 44) 228 ff with further references regarding the doctrine of *Drittwirkung* (third party effect).

91   BGH BGHZ 24, 72 = NJW 1957, 1146. Cf *Larenz/Canaris* (fn 25) 491 ff; *Thiede* (fn 28) 6 ff; *H Sprau* in: Palandt, BGB (75th edn 2016) § 823 no 84. Not all scholars were in agreement with this right, cf *Brüggemeier* (fn 1) 23 with further references. Efforts to codify this new protection of the personality have not been successful.

92   *M Schultz*, Rights through Torts: The Rise of a Rights Discourse in Swedish Tort Law (2009) 6 European Review of Private Law (ERPL) 305 ff, 313 ff.

93   Cf below.

94   *Lindell-Frantz* (fn 74) 66 ff; *Lauer/Colombi Ciacchi* (fn 74) 667 ff; *Brüggemeier* (fn 1) 29. Cf also for a reason for the Swedish approach, in particular a reluctance to accept Natural law theory thinking, *Schultz* (2009) 6 ERPL 305 ff.

It was not until recently that the Swedish Supreme Court acknowledged a right to compensation directly based on the violation of an ECHR right, but so far not between private parties – only when the State commits the violation.[95] This claim, based directly on the ECHR, is seen as part of the Swedish legal system, completing the tort law protection already in existence.[96]

23 In England the development of the protection of personality rights apart from defamation cases which were protected for a long time already depended on the applicability of a pre-existing tort or the development of a new tort which would cover the violation in question. The development was slightly more selective than in other jurisdictions. On the one hand, English law was one of the first where a court recognised a right to one's own picture. In 1848, the English courts passed judgment on a case concerning the publication of drawings made by the husband of Queen Victoria, Prince Albert, of the members of the Royal Family.[97] The court granted an injunction against the publication on the basis of breach of confidence.[98] Breach of confidence, which is rooted in equity – the second strand of unwritten law next to the common law – had for a long time been the most important legal basis for the protection of privacy. It covers the misuse of private information which was confidentially given in writing or orally, and includes photographs of persons.[99] The criteria were

---

95   Nytt Juridiskt Arkiv (NJA) 2007, 584 concerns art 8 ECHR and the protection of privacy, however against the State. The other cases mostly concern violations of art 6 ECHR also by the State; NJA 2012, 211; NJA 2009, 463; NJA 2007, 295; NJA 2005, 462; NJA 2005, 726; cf *H Andersson*, Sweden, in: *K Oliphant/bc Steininger* (eds), ETL 2012 (2013) no 22 ff; *Andersson*, Sweden, in: *H Koziol/BC Steininger* (eds), ETL 2009 (2010) no 28 ff; *Andersson*, Sweden, in: *H Koziol/BC Steininger* (eds), ETL 2007 (2008) no 3 ff; *Andersson*, Sweden, in: *H Koziol/BC Steininger* (eds), ETL 2005 (2006) no 3 ff, 25 ff; *Brüggemeier* (fn 1) 29 f with further references. The ECHR has been incorporated into domestic law since January 1995 and it is an ordinary law but, in the case of a conflict with another law, the Convention should prevail: *Lauer/Colombi Ciacchi* (fn 74) 664 ff. See, however, NJA 2007, 747, which states that there is no horizontal effect and there is no claim directly based on the ECHR between private parties. Cf *Andersson*, ETL 2007 (2008) no 24 ff. A detailed overview of the change in law was published by *Schultz* (2009) 6 ERPL 318 ff.

96   NJA 2012, 211; cf *Andersson*, ETL 2012 (2013) no 22 ff.

97   *Prince Albert v Strange* (1849) 1 Macnaghten & Gordon's Chancery Reports (Mac & G) 25, 64 English Reports (ER) 293; cf also *Pollard v Photographic Company* [1889] 40 Law Reports, Chancery Division (2nd Series) (Ch D) 345. Cf *Brüggemeier* (fn 1) 25 f who regards this as an isolated case.

98   *Prince Albert v Strange* (1849) 1 Mac & G 25, 64 ER 293; cf *Lunney/Oliphant* (fn 31) 774; *Brüggemeier* (fn 1) 25 f.

99   *Pollard v Photographic Company* [1889] 40 Ch D 345. Cf *M Warby QC/A Speker/D Hirst*, Breach of Confidence, in: M Warby QC/N Moreham/I Christie (eds), The Law of Privacy

summarised in *Coco v AN Clark (Engineers) Ltd*: 'First, the information itself ... must have the necessary quality of confidence about it. Secondly, that information must have been imparted in circumstances importing an obligation of confidence. Thirdly, there must be an unauthorized use of that information to the detriment of the party communicating it.'[100] In *Campbell v MGN Ltd*[101] the court went even further and saw the breach of confidence as covering personal instead of confidential information.[102] This is seen as the starting point of a new tort, developed from breach of confidence, which provides a remedy against unauthorised disclosure of personal information and therefore covers a wide array of issues previously left unprotected. The tort protects against certain unlawful intrusions into one's private life.[103]

24 On the other hand, no other comprehensive protection of privacy exists, despite the fact that English law is one of the examples of the influence of the ECHR and human rights as enacted in the Human Rights Act (HRA) on the protection of personality interests.[104] The HRA, which was passed in 1998 and came into effect in 2000, implemented the ECHR into English law.[105] English courts are now committed to the protection of privacy according to art 8 para 1 ECHR. Even this has, however, not led to the development of a general tort of privacy so far,[106] mostly because the courts see the remedies enacted in the HRA together with the possible tort claims as sufficient protection.[107] Privacy

---

and the Media (2nd edn 2011) no 4.01 ff; *Lunney/Oliphant* (fn 31) 791 ff; *Brüggemeier* (fn 1) 26 f; *Thiede* (fn 28) 68 ff.

100   *Coco v AN Clark (Engineers) Ltd* [1969] Reports of Patent, Design and Trade Mark Cases (RPC) 41, 47.

101   [2004] 2 Appeal Cases (AC) 457. Cf *Lunney/Oliphant* (fn 31) 783 ff; *Thiede* (fn 28) 69 f.

102   *Lunney/Oliphant* (fn 31) 792; *Thiede* (fn 28) 69 f.

103   *Lunney/Oliphant* (fn 31) 791 ff.

104   *Campbell v MGN Ltd* [2004] 2 AC 457 no 16 ff per Lord *Nicholls*.

105   *Deakin/Johnston/Markesinis* (fn 31) 738 ff; *I Christie/A Wolanski*, Context and Background, in: *M Warby QC/N Moreham/I Christie* (eds), The Law of Privacy and the Media (2nd edn 2011) no 1.91 ff; *Lunney/Oliphant* (fn 31) 771.

106   Cf *Deakin/Johnston/Markesinis* (fn 31) 706 ff, 713 ff; *Lunney/Oliphant* (fn 31) 783 ff; *Thiede* (fn 28) 58 ff, cf for potential reasons why this has not happened 87 f. Unlike the common law in the United States. Cf the criticism by *von Bar*, Deliktsrecht I (fn 32) § 3 no 272 f and *idem*, Deliktsrecht II (fn 1) § 1 no 92, 94, 104 (missing is in his view for example a protection of personality rights *post-mortem*); *Zimmermann* (fn 4) 1074 ff (critical of defamation law in particular); *Karner* (2013) ÖJZ 906, 907 f.

107   *Wainwright v Home Office* [2003] 4 All England Law Reports (All ER) 969; *Lunney/Oliphant* (fn 31) 778 ff.

is seen as a value underlying the law but not a principle susceptible of direct application to individual claims.[108]

25 Recent cases make it doubtful that such a general tort will ever be developed.[109] In *Douglas v Hello! Ltd*[110] a paparazzo had taken secret pictures of the wedding between filmstars *Michael Douglas* and *Catherine Zeta-Jones* despite a ban on photographs and sold these pictures to one of OK!'s competitors – OK had the exclusive right to photographs from the wedding. The High Court judge (Chancery Division) held that, with regard to the HRA and ECHR, it would be inconsequential if the case constituted a violation of privacy, because it constituted a breach of confidence and the claimant's rights were therefore sufficiently protected. The House of Lords agreed with this view.[111]

C   *European Development after the Enactment of the ECHR*

26 When discussing the law in European countries, one also must take into account the developments in Europe as a whole as already seen in the chapter above, be it through international treaties like the European Convention for the Protection of Human Rights and Fundamental Freedoms (ECHR) or the European Union and its legal framework, in particular the Charter of Fundamental Rights of the European Union (CFR).

27 The ECHR was passed in 1950 by the Committee of Ministers of the Council of Europe and came into force in 1953. The ECHR is an international multilateral treaty, which after ratification becomes part of the legal systems of the currently forty seven Contracting States of the Council of Europe.[112] As with any legal statute, the rank of the norm in question in the domestic hierarchy as a source of law plays a role in its interpretation and application. In this regard, the Contracting States have not followed a uniform approach; in fact the rank of the ECHR differs from country to country. Thus in some countries the ECHR

---

108   *Wainwright v Home Office* [2003] 4 ALL ER 969; *Deakin/Johnston/Markesinis* (fn 31) 706 ff; *Lunney/Oliphant* (fn 31) 778 ff.

109   Cf *Brüggemeier* (fn 1) 27 f. The House of Lords (now Supreme Court) seems to prefer to leave the issue to the legislature. Cf also *Wainwright v Home Office* [2003] 4 ALL ER 969; *Campbell v MGN Ltd* [2004] 2 AC 457. The latter case was also based on breach of confidence although the requirement of a confidential relationship was missing.

110   *Douglas v Hello! Ltd* [2003] England & Wales High Court (EWHC) 786 (Ch).

111   *Douglas v Hello! Ltd* [2007] United Kingdom House of Lords (UKHL) 21. Cf also *Prince of Wales v Associated Newspapers Ltd* [2006] EWHC 522 and *Thiede* (fn 28) 72 for the balancing act necessary to decide whether information is covered by sufficient public interest. The fact alone that the person is a public figure is not sufficient.

112   *Brüggemeier* (fn 1) 31 with further references; *Thiede* (fn 28) 164 ff with further references.

is ranked above the domestic constitution, as for example in the Netherlands. In other countries it has the standing of constitutional law, as in Austria and Switzerland. In other systems it is ranked between the national constitution and statutory law, as in France, Spain or Portugal. Finally, in other jurisdictions it is ranked or was enacted in the rank of regular statutory law, like in Germany, Finland, Italy, Sweden and the UK,[113] although in the UK judges may recommend the repeal of certain statutes based on the HRA, which might elevate the standing of the Act above regular statutory law.[114]

28 The application of the ECHR is observed by the European Court on Human Rights (ECtHR), whose jurisprudence has largely influenced private law in Europe, in particular after World War II, aided in some jurisdictions by the national constitutions, also with regard to the protection of personality rights.[115] However, the ECtHR is not the only court which was the driving force behind the development in Europe: the Court of Justice of the EU (CJEU) incorporated the substance of the ECHR under the 'general principles of law' into EU law.[116] The CJEU case law has occasionally been referred to by the EU legislator.[117] Additionally, the EU passed the CFR[118] which also protects personality

---

113   Detailed overview in *C Grabenwarter/K Pabel*, Europäische Menschenrechtskonvention (5th edn 2012) 15 ff; *Brüggemeier* (fn 1) 31 f with further references. For Germany cf *Thiede* (fn 28) 56 ff.

114   *Grabenwarter/Pabel* (fn 113) 18, fn 28.

115   *N Moreham/A Coppola/I Christie*, Privacy in Europe and the Common Law, in: M Warby QC/N Moreham/I Christie (eds), The Law of Privacy and the Media (2nd edn 2011), no 3.27 ff. Cf also the examples mentioned above and below. *Brüggemeier* (fn 1) 9 f with further references calls it the process of 'Europeanisation' or 'constitutionalisation' of private law. This process has not yet reached its end, cf *Thiede* (fn 28) 188 f.

116   General principles of law are part of law in the sense of art 220 EC, now art 19 (1) TEU. Cf *Brüggemeier* (fn 1) 32 with further references. Cf for example ECJ 29/69 *Stauder v City of Ulm* [1969] European Court Reports (ECR) 419; [1970] Common Market Law Reports (CMLR) 112; ECJ 4/73 *Nold v Ruhrkohle AG* [1974] ECR 491; [1974] 2 CMLR 338; ECJ 44/79 *Hauer v Rheinland-Pfalz* [1979] ECR 3727; cf in particular ECJ 11/70 *Internationale Handelsgesellschaft v Einfuhr- und Vorratsstelle für Getreide und Futtermittel* [1970] ECR 1125.

117   In the Single European Act; Treaty on the European Union. Art 6 para 2 TEU now even obliges the EU to respect the fundamental rights enshrined in the ECHR. Cf *Brüggemeier* (fn 1) 32.

118   [2012] Official Journal (OJ) C326/391. The CFR was solemnly proclaimed on 7 December 2000 by the European Commission, European Parliament and Council of Ministers and approved by the Member States. It attained full legal effect with the entry into force of the Lisbon Treaty on 1 December 2009. See *C Paul/DB Gráinne*, EU Law: Text, Cases, and Materials (5th edn 2011) 394. Cf *Hinteregger* (fn 10) in this volume.

rights. It is due to this entire development that the diverse private law traditions and different national legal systems of Europe have found some common ground in the protection of personality rights to the extent which will be described in detail below.[119]

29 Due to the mentioned historical differences,[120] the influence of the ECHR and human rights in general has been universal across Europe but felt differently and has raised different issues in individual countries. One of the most notable influences of the ECHR can be seen, for example, on English law or Swedish law as shown above. For the former, the values expressed in art 8 of the ECHR are now seen as values that are inherent to common law and therefore courts have started awarding damages for invasion of privacy even in cases where in the past no other tort was applicable, for example by creating unauthorised disclosure of private information or analogously applying defamation or breach of confidence.[121] The latter started allowing claims based directly on the ECHR if the tortfeasor is the State or a public body.[122] In France the influence of human rights on private law was the most significant as regards personality rights via the media. The restrictive Press Act 1881 lost, *de facto*, any influence.[123] In Austria the Convention is part of the constitution. It has the greatest influence through the interpretation of general clauses, like § 16 ABGB.[124] The right to one's image, for example, enjoys additional protection in Austria through § 16 ABGB together with art 8 ECHR next to §§ 78, 87 para 2 *Urheberrechtsgesetz* (Copyright Law).[125] Lastly, in Norway courts have started following the ECtHR jurisprudence regarding art 8 ECHR in cases concerning privacy,[126] with art 10 ECHR covering the freedom of speech working as a constant border.[127]

---

119   *Brüggemeier* (fn 1) 9 f; *Thiede* (fn 28) 188 f. For the historical differences cf 11 (no 3 above).

120   For details cf above.

121   *Mosley v News Group Newspapers* [2008] EWHC 1777 (Queen's Bench, QB). *Deakin/Johnston/Markesinis* (fn 31) 701 ff; *Lunney/Oliphant* (fn 31) 791 ff; *Moreham/Coppola/Christie* (fn 115) no 3.27 ff, 3.50 ff. For art 8 ECHR cf *Thiede* (fn 28) 176 ff with further references.

122   Cf no 22 above and in particular fn 95.

123   *Brüggemeier* (fn 1) 16 with further references. Although in most cases through the new interpretation of the *Déclaration des Droits de l'Homme et du Citoyen* coupled with the influence of the ECHR, cf *Anterion/Moréteau* (fn 34) 123 ff.

124   OGH 4 Ob 91/78 SZ 51/146 = RdA 1979/24 (*Reischauer*) = ZAS 1979/24 (*Marhold*); Rummel/*Aicher* (fn 7) § 16 no 30 ff; Kletečka/Schauer/*Schauer* (fn 43) § 16 no 15; *Karner* (2013) ÖJZ 906, 907.

125   OGH 6 Ob 256/12h; Rummel/*Aicher* (fn 7) § 16 no 19; *Karner* (2013) ÖJZ 906, 910; cf for other personality interests Kletečka/Schauer/*Schauer* (fn 43) § 16 no 17 ff.

126   Cf above.

127   *Thiede* (fn 28) 167 ff.

In particular, persons fulfilling official functions have to accept criticism in a more extensive form than private persons.[128]

30 In Germany, however, the guarantee of personality rights by the national Constitution was the starting point of the change in law. Next to the national Constitution, the ECHR, which was incorporated into German law as ordinary statutory law, remained until recently mostly without much influence.[129]

31 Overall, through the influence of the ECHR, thanks to the jurisprudence of the ECtHR, some of the differences in the protection of personality interests in the European countries have disappeared. This development will surely continue in the future.

32 The harmonisation of law has been additionally aided by scholars who developed common rules of tort law out of the individual systems found in Europe: on the one hand, the Principles of European Tort Law (PETL) and, on the other hand, the Draft Common Frame of Reference (DCFR).

D   *European Development through the Eyes of the PETL*

33 In the Principles of European Tort Law, art 2:102 (2) states that human dignity and liberty are protected interests under the PETL and they enjoy the most extensive protection. To that extent, the PETL protect personality interests under the general tort law regime. The PETL also clearly follow a broad conception of the right of persons.[130] In the Commentary to the Principles, it is admitted that the rights of personality do not have such clear contours as the fundamental rights to life, bodily or mental integrity and liberty. The right to privacy is seen as being a broad grey zone.[131] Therefore, the interests of all others as regards freedom of action have to be considered. As a result, the right to honour or reputation is protected against true statements or expressions

---

128   ECtHR *Lingens v Austria*, 8.7.1986, no 9815/82, Series A 103 (1986) 11, 26 = Europäische Grundrechte-Zeitschrift (Eugrz) 1986, 424; ECtHR *Oberschlick v Austria (no 2)* 1.7.1997, no 20834/92; cf *H Koziol*, Der Schutz der Persönlichkeitsrechte gegenüber Massenmedien: Zusammenfassung und Ausblick, in: H Koziol/A Warzilek (eds), Persönlichkeitsschutz gegenüber Massenmedien (2005) 666 f; *H Koziol/A Warzilek*, Der Schutz der Persönlichkeitsrechte gegenüber Massenmedien in Österreich, in: H Koziol/A Warzilek (eds), Persönlichkeitsschutz gegenüber Massenmedien (2005) 9 ff; *Karner* (2013) ÖJZ 906, 911. Some scholars criticise this position.

129   *Larenz/Canaris* (fn 25) 491 ff; *Brüggemeier* (fn 1) 24 with further references.

130   *H Koziol*, General Conditions of Liability, in: European Group on Tort Law (ed), Principles of European Tort Law (2008) 40 ff; also *Brüggemeier* (fn 1) 30 f.

131   *Koziol* (fn 130) 43.

of opinion only to a small extent. Even if the comment cannot be shown to be true, the right of others to the free statement of opinion and the interest in full information have to be considered.[132]

E   *European Development through the Eyes of the* DCFR

34 The Draft Common Frame of Reference follows the continental approach. As long as the loss from an infringement of personality rights is legally relevant damage, the injured party can claim compensation.[133] In art VI–2:203 DCFR it is expressly stated that infringements of dignity, liberty and privacy lead to legally relevant damage. However, loss caused to a person as a result of injury to that person's reputation and the injury as such are only legally relevant damage if the national law so provides.[134]

35 Insofar as para 1 of the provision is concerned, the comments to the DCFR specify that this protection also includes the privacy of celebrities. Their private sphere does not only cover a private dwelling, but also the outside of a home if a celebrity, for example, wishes to eat in a restaurant alone. The existence of a private sphere is quite independent of whether the person is or is not of current notoriety.[135]

36 The different approach between para 1 concerning various personality interests and privacy and para 2 concerning reputation and defamation is explained in the comments. The extent to which honour, reputation, good standing or status in society, or similar attributes of a person should be protected by the legal system is a matter of controversy among the various European jurisdictions, not least because of the correlative limitation of freedom of expression. Consequently, the DCFR make no attempt to directly protect such attributes. Therefore, an injury to reputation is only legally relevant damage if this is envisaged by the applicable national law. However, it needs to be borne in mind that a claim might succeed on the basis of art VI–2:204 DCFR if the case involves communication of false information for which the responsible person is accountable.[136]

---

132 *Koziol* (fn 130) 45.
133 Articles VI–1:101 and VI–2:101 together with art VI–2:203 DCFR. Cf *C von Bar/E Clive*, Principles, Definitions and Model Rules of European Private Law, Draft Common Frame of Reference (DCFR) (full edn 2009) 3083 ff, 3139 ff, 3253 ff. Cf also *Brüggemeier* (fn 1) 30 f.
134 Cf *von Bar/Clive* (fn 133) 3253 ff. Cf also *Brüggemeier* (fn 1) 30 f.
135 Cf *von Bar/Clive* (fn 133) 3257.
136 Cf *von Bar/Clive* (fn 133) 3259.

F   *Conclusion*

37 Medieval law in most European countries included protection of honour through the *actio iniuriarum* which was adopted from Roman law.[137] *Germany*, however, had a very specific development, where this particular claim was abolished in the nineteenth century and later left out of the BGB.[138] Dissent was formulated by some scholars, most importantly by *Otto von Gierke*, who was one of the first to formulate a thesis of a general personality right. As an example he cited the publishing of letters as a violation of a personality right, even if no copyright on those letters existed.[139] Only after World War II did the passing of the GG with its enforceable individual rights change the course of German legal development.[140] Similarly to Germany in the early days of the BGB, Sweden provides protection of personality interests such as honour and reputation through criminal law. Civil personality rights are not acknowledged between private parties. Recently, again somewhat parallel to the development in 1950s Germany but also France in the 1970s, under the influence of fundamental rights and in Sweden's case more importantly of the ECHR, the legal protection of the personality seems to have started to develop further, especially if the State is the tortfeasor.[141]

38 In other jurisdictions, which followed the path of Natural law with its general clause of the law of delict (*neminem laedere*) together with the heritage of the *actio iniuriarum* of the *ius commune,* the development of tort protection of personality rights was easier.[142] For example in France, the protection of honour was covered under general clauses of protected interests in tort law, despite not being mentioned explicitly.[143] A particular example of this approach is Austria, which protected a right to personality from 1812 onwards in § 16 ABGB. The particular interpretation of the provision was contested for a part of its 200-year-old history; however, the current interpretation as the basis of personality rights protection seems in line with the historical intention of the drafters.

---

137   *Kern* (fn 4) 84.

138   § 1300 BGB in 1900 protected the sexual honour of women. *Kern* (fn 4) 84 ff with further references. Some scholars had wanted protection for personality rights. The discussion was mainly focused on copyright law. Cf the *actio iniuriarium* in RGZ 41, 43, 49 f.

139   *Gierke* (fn 77) 260, 702 ff. Cf for further references and details no 18 and fn 77 above.

140   Cf under III (no 41 below).

141   *Brüggemeier* (fn 1) 9 with further references.

142   *Brüggemeier* (fn 1) 8 with further references.

143   *Kern* (fn 4) 84 f. Especially in jurisdictions that followed Natural law and its idea that every person was born with a certain set of rights (*iura connata*), cf the chapter on Austria.

39   In the English common law of torts, the protection of a person's honour and reputation by the law of defamation has had a long but intricate history. Beyond defamation law, other personality interests such as dignity, autonomy and privacy are protected by a legal patchwork of common law, equity law and statutory law; however, not all interests that other jurisdictions protect are covered and this seems to be intentional. English common law has not yet formally recognised a tort of violation of privacy.[144]

40   Due to the jurisprudence of the ECtHR, the ECHR has mostly led to a development of similarities in the protection of personality interests in Europe, despite the completely different historical approaches.[145] This development is expected to continue in the future. Despite the newly developed similarities, the differences still seem to be vast, as is evidenced by the harmonisation efforts of the PETL and the DCFR. Both opted for a very flexible system – the DCFR even left liability for reputation to the national systems – in my view because of the difficulty of finding a common rule on the protection of personality interests in Europe. In future, if the influence of the ECtHR continues, finding more common ground might become easier.

III   Systematic Approach: General Right to Personality or Various Individual Personality Rights

A   *Single Right vs Bundle of Rights Approach*

41   The main issue with the systematic view of personality rights is whether or not one all-embracing personality right exists or if there is a multitude of various individual personality rights.[146] The differences between these two approaches will be discussed below.

1   Single Right

42   The law in Germany follows the view that one general underlying personality right exists, which includes all protected personality interests.[147] The BGH defines this general right as a right of every individual to the respect of their human dignity and the development of their individual personality, which

---

144   Cf above no 24 and fn 106.

145   Cf *von Bar* (fn 1) § 1 no 85.

146   *Kern* (fn 4) 83 ff.

147   It is sometimes discussed as a *Rahmenrecht* (frame right); cf *G Wagner* in: M Habersack (ed), Münchener Kommentar zum BGB, (6th edn 2013) § 823 no 242 with further references; Palandt/*Sprau* (fn 91) § 823 no 84 ff; *Kern* (fn 4) 83 ff, 93.

is not only protected *vis-à-vis* the State but also *vis-à-vis* other citizens.[148] It needs to be stressed at this point that the concept of a general personality right in Germany goes back to the influence of the Constitution and might be misleading.[149] The general right to personality in Germany covers a collection of diverse areas of protected personality interests, which differ in their preconditions and their sub-categories.[150] Unlike in cases of infringements of bodily integrity and damage to property, so far only severe violations of the personality right which cannot be remedied otherwise allow an award of monetary compensation of non-pecuniary damage.[151] Italy also seems to follow the view that there is one general right of personality – the *teoria monistica* – even though this view is contested.[152] The basis for this view can be found in art 2 *Costituzione*.[153] In Austria as mentioned the protection of personality rights is based on § 16 of the ABGB, which was already introduced in the Code's original version from 1812. Nevertheless, it was only in 1978 that the Austrian Supreme Court (*Oberster Gerichtshof,* OGH) first used this provision to establish a general personality right.[154] However, recently the Supreme Court seems to have started to waver on this position as there are judgments which state that § 16 ABGB covers a wide array of individual personality rights, not one general personality right.[155] For scholars it is not clear if § 16 ABGB really introduces a

---

148   Palandt/*Sprau* (fn 91) § 823 no 84; BGHZ 24, 72, 76.

149   On the one hand, it stems from the pre-constitutional legal expressions based on subjective property rights – § 823 para 1 BGB – and on the other hand, it is influenced by the constitutional language of fundamental rights. Cf *Brüggemeier* (fn 1) 24.

150   *Brüggemeier* (fn 1) 24 f with further references; *Larenz/Canaris* (fn 25) 491 ff; Palandt/*Sprau* (fn 91) § 823 no 84 ff.

151   *Larenz/Canaris* (fn 25) 495 f; *Brüggemeier* (fn 1) 25; Palandt/*Sprau* (fn 91) § 823 no 84 ff.

152   G Pino, The Right to Personal Identity in Italian Law: Constitutional Interpretation and Judge-Made-Rights, in: M van Hoecke/F Ost (eds), The Harmonisation of European Private Law (2000) 230 ff; *Warzilek* (fn 10) 616 f; *Kern* (fn 4) 83 ff.

153   *Pino* (fn 152) 230 ff; *Kern* (fn 4) 83 ff.

154   OGH 4 Ob 91/78 SZ 51/146 = RdA 1979/24 (*Reischauer*) = ZAS 1979/24 (*Marhold*); the following case law speaks of a general personality right OGH 1 Ob 536/88 jbl 1988, 577; 4 Ob 227/04t Medienrecht (MR) 2005, 49. Rummel/*Aicher* (fn 7) § 16 no 12 ff with further references; Kletečka/Schauer/*Schauer* (fn 43) § 16 no 12 ff; *Karner* (2013) öjz 906, 907. Some scholars do not see the Supreme Court's rhetoric as proof the Court means a general right exists, cf Schwimann/Kodek/*Posch* (fn 44) § 16 no 12; *Canaris* (1991) jbl 205, 211 ff. Dignity and honour are protected through other rules as well, in tort law this is mainly §§ 1328a and 1330 ABGB, protecting privacy and dignity and honour respectively. Cf *Koziol/Warzilek* (fn 128) 7 ff, 15.

155   OGH 4 Ob 59/00f und 4 Ob 64/00s MR 2000, 145; cf H Koziol/A Warzilek (eds), Persönlichkeitsschutz gegenüber Massenmedien (2005) 3 f. See however OGH 4 Ob 227/04t MR 2005, 49.

general right or particular individual personality rights.[156] Other countries in continental Europe had consistently protected honour as a personality right and added other personality rights when they emerged; the idea of a general all-encompassing personality right was not expressed until later than in Germany, mostly because there seemed to be no need.[157]

43   The advantage of a general, single, all-encompassing personality right lies mostly in the avoidance of contradictions in approach and gaps in protection. A single right can be further developed according to changes in technology and society.[158] However, critics state it is not clearly enough contoured and can cause legal uncertainty.[159]

2   Bundle of Rights

44   As was shown above, France started very early to protect certain personality rights based on arts 1382 and 1383 *Code Civil*. One of the first decisions of this kind concerned the right to one's image in the famous *Rachel* case from 1858.[160] Articles 1382 and 1383 were not seen as protecting one all-encompassing personality right, but a diverse field of personality interests.[161] Similarly, the Swedish legislature does not protect one general right of personality but a bundle of individual rights through criminal law.[162]

45   England also follows the bundle of rights approach.[163] The distinction in English law is not according to the right or interest harmed, but according to the nature of the violation, which must fulfill the prerequisites of an existing tort.[164] It is therefore necessary to find a tort or equitable institute, for example, libel,

---

156   *Karner* (2013) ÖJZ 906, 908. Historically, a general right as a framework right with a variety of individual rights seems to have been what the drafters of the Austrian Code had in mind, cf *Zeiller*, Privatrecht (fn 57) 64 ff; cf *Wellspacher* (fn 49) 187 f. For the general right as a framework right which is not absolute cf Rummel/*Aicher* (fn 7) § 16 no 13 f; Kletečka/Schauer/*Schauer* (fn 43) § 16 no 13. For individual single rights cf *Koziol* (fn 2) 6; seemingly also *Koziol/Warzilek* (fn 155) 3 f.

157   *Kern* (fn 4) 92 ff. Cf for other jurisdictions which follow the general single right approach *von Bar* (fn 1) § 1 no 81 fn 502 f.

158   *Gierke* (fn 77) 260, 702 ff. Cf *Kern* (fn 4) 87; *Koziol/Warzilek* (fn 155) 3 f; *Karner* (2013) ÖJZ 906, 908.

159   *Warzilek* (fn 10) 616.

160   Trib Civ Seine, 16 June 1858, 3, 62; *Karner* (2013) ÖJZ 906, 907.

161   *Brüggemeier* (fn 1) 13 and *Thiede* (fn 28) 89 with further references.

162   Cf II (no 3 above) and IV (no 48 below).

163   *Wainwright v Home Office* [2003] 4 All ER 969; *Deakin/Johnston/Markesinis* (fn 31) 706 ff; *Lunney/Oliphant* (fn 31) 781 ff. *Warzilek* (fn 10) 618 sees English and US law as outside of the categories for single or general right.

164   *Deakin/Johnston/Markesinis* (fn 31) 706 ff; *Karner* (2013) ÖJZ 906, 907 f; *idem* (fn 87) 26 f. *H Stoll*, Haftungsfolgen im bürgerlichen Recht (1993) 364 f. *Canaris* (1991) JBl 205, 206 ff

slander, trespass, nuisance, breach of confidence or unauthorised disclosure of private information, which fits the particular conduct.[165] However, English law recognises privacy as a value underlying specific liabilities.[166] Some still criticise the fact that this has led to a kind of patchwork system and gaps in protection, although most of those seem to be intentional and based on policy reasons.[167] It appears that English scholars see the described approach as the preferred way of dealing with infringements of personality rights.[168]

46 The advantage of protection through individual rights lies in the differences between the single acknowledged 'rights' or 'scopes' of protected personality interests, partially described below. Some enjoy stronger protection, some are not protected at all, for example, causing someone pure aggravation; covering them under a general right therefore does not appear to honour these differences sufficiently. Furthermore, so far, few very clearly defined singular rights have been accepted and the protection of these rights and interests is not always the same.[169] However, specific rules can leave gaps in protection and contradictions in values, which can be avoided through the acceptance of a general personality right.[170]

B   *Conclusion*

47 Many scholars agree that the difference in approach of general vs individual personality rights does not matter much in practice. Even when discussing an all-encompassing right, one has to painstakingly check whether the interest in

---

suggests this approach should also be followed in Austria and Germany. *von Bar* (fn 1) § 1 no 82 ff follows this approach in his discussion of the topic.

165   *Deakin/Johnston/Markesinis* (fn 31) 706 ff; *Thiede* (fn 28) 68 ff.

166   *Wainwright v Home Office* [2003] 4 All ER 969; *Deakin/Johnston/Markesinis* (fn 31) 706 ff; *Lunney/Oliphant* (fn 31) 781.

167   Cf *Wainwright v Home Office* [2003] 4 All ER 969; *Mosley v News Group Newspapers* [2008] EWHC 1777 (QB); *Lunney/Oliphant* (fn 31) 781 ff. Cf the criticism by *Deakin/Johnston/ Markesinis* (fn 31) 706 ff; *Zimmermann* (fn 4) 1074 ff (critical of defamation law in particular); *von Bar,* Deliktsrecht II (fn 32) § 3 no 272 f and *idem* (fn 1) § 1 no 92, 94, 104 (missing is in his view for example protection of personality rights *post-mortem*). Cf also *Kaye v Robertson* [1991] Fleet Street Reports (FSR) 62 (CA): 'It is well known that in English law there is no right to privacy.' Completely different is the situation in the US, cf *S Warren/ld Brandeis,* The Right of Privacy (1890) 4 Harvard Law Review (Harv L Rev) 193.

168   Cf *Wainwright v Home Office* [2003] 4 All ER 969; *Mosley v News Group Newspapers* [2008] EWHC 1777 (QB); *Deakin/Johnston/Markesinis* (fn 31) 706 ff; *Lunney/Oliphant* (fn 31) 781 ff. For criticism of the legal protection at least before the decision in *Mosley* cf *Karner* (2013) ÖJZ 906, 907 f.

169   *Koziol/Warzilek* (fn 155) 3 f; *Karner* (2013) ÖJZ 906, 908.

170   *Warzilek* (fn 10) 616.

question is covered by the protection and to what extent. The scope of protection differs largely from right to right and the theory of the bundle of personality rights only chooses to underline this difference[171] and the need to analyse the scope in question.[172]

IV   Scope of Protection[173]

A   *Dignity, Honour and Reputation*

48 The development of personality rights started in most countries with the rights to dignity, honour and reputation.[174] In Europe a reason for this might be that they were already recognised as legally protected interests, *dignitas* and *fama*, in Roman law.[175] As far as current multi-national law is concerned, these interests do not fall under the protection of art 8 ECHR according to the prevailing view.[176]

49 In most jurisdictions these personality interests offer protection against statements which could have a detrimental effect on a person's dignity and honour in the eyes of others and could potentially lead to ostracizing or humiliation by the public.[177] This is judged based on an objective standard – the ordinary fair-minded reader – and covers prestige and reputation.[178] Some jurisdictions, however, differentiate between honour and reputation and see them as covering two different interests. In French law, for example, honour is violated if it is

---

171   *Edlbacher* (1983) ÖJZ 423, 428; *Brüggemeier* (fn 1) 6 with further references; Rummel/*Aicher* (fn 7) § 16 no 14; Schwimann/Kodek/*Posch* (fn 44) § 16 no 13 f; *Koziol/Warzilek* (fn 155) 3 f; *Karner* (2013) ÖJZ 906, 908.

172   *Koziol/Warzilek* (fn 155) 3 f; *Karner* (2013) ÖJZ 906, 908; *Canaris* (1991) JBl 205, 210 seems to argue that some differences in practice should be at least seen as possible. *Warzilek* (fn 10) 618 sees most European systems as following a 'hybrid' approach anyway.

173   Cf for a discussion according to the nature of the violation and not the violated interest, *von Bar* (fn 1) § 1 no 81 ff. Cf for the historical roots of personality rights, II (no 3 above).

174   *Brüggemeier/Colombi Ciacchi/O'Callaghan* (fn 1) 567 with further references; *Warzilek* (fn 10) 620 ff; *von Bar* (fn 1) § 1 no 81.

175   *Brüggemeier/Colombi Ciacchi/O'Callaghan* (fn 1) 568 with further references. Cf II.A (no 4 above).

176   *W Berka*, Persönlichkeitsschutz und Massenmedien im Lichte der Grundfreiheiten, in: H Koziol/A Warzilek (eds), Persönlichkeitsschutz gegenüber Massenmedien (2005) 510 ff with further references.

177   Cf *Thiede* (fn 28) 189 ff with further references.

178   *Thiede* (fn 28) 190; *Brüggemeier/Colombi Ciacchi/O'Callaghan* (fn 1) 568 with further references. A subjective test exists in Spain and Switzerland, *Warzilek* (fn 10) 620 f with further references.

implied that a person committed a crime or an immoral act, behaved without virtue or breached duties to the mother country or his family.[179] Reputation meanwhile covers the estimation of a person in society and the opinion that third parties have of the life of the person.[180] The difference seems to be based on the viewpoint – the internal view is the honour of the person or the external view is their reputation.[181]

50 Most jurisdictions, like Germany and Austria, differentiate between violations of dignity and honour by statements of fact and statements of opinion. The difference between the two lies in the possible defences. A statement of fact does not in most jurisdictions lead to liability if it can be proven as true and additionally in some legal systems is also not worded in an insulting way or the tortfeasor was justified in making the information public.[182] In Norway the statement has to be unlawful and untrue.[183] In Sweden it is also seen as a sufficient defence if the tortfeasor had good reasons to think his statement was true.[184] In England the defamatory statement does not have to be untrue. However, proving the truth of the statement is a defence.[185] In most jurisdictions an opinion, however, is justified as long as it is covered by freedom of speech or freedom of expression, meaning that it can be seen as valid criticism and not merely an insult.[186] In England, for example, it is a defence if the statement

---

179   Cour de cassation, Chambre criminelle (Cass crim) D 1934, 382; Tribunal de grande instance (TGI) Paris, D 1974, jur 697; *B Beignier*, L'honneur et le droit (1995) 154; *Thiede* (fn 28) 93 f with further references.

180   *E Derieux*, Droit de la communication (1991) 395; *Beignier* (fn 179) 153; *Thiede* (fn 28) 94 f.

181   *Thiede* (fn 28) 94 f.

182   English law for example does not require the second requirement. Under sec 4 of the Defamation Act 2013 it is, however, a defence if the publication was in the public interest. *Lunney/Oliphant* (fn 31) 739 ff. Cf for the common law *Flood v Times Newspapers Ltd* [2012] 2 AC 273 at [27] per Lord *Philips*; *Deakin/Johnston/Markesinis* (fn 31) 632 ff. For Austria for example cf *Koziol/Warzilek* (fn 155) 10 f; *Berka* (fn 176) 520 f; for a comparative analysis *Warzilek* (fn 10) 621 f. For Sweden and public interest *Lindell-Frantz* (fn 74) 54 ff.

183   *HJ Mæland*, Libel and the Respect for Privacy in Mass Media, in: A Beater/S Habermeier (eds), Invasions of Personality Rights by the Media (2005) 70, 71 ff. He also makes it seem that value judgements do not lead to liability, only factual statements do in Norway.

184   *Lindell-Frantz* (fn 74) 54 ff.

185   Cf *Deakin/Johnston/Markesinis* (fn 31) 661 ff; *Lunney/Oliphant* (fn 31) 718 ff; *Thiede* (fn 28) 62 f, 76 f. Cf also now sec 2 of the Defamation Act 2013 and *Lunney/Oliphant* (fn 31) 721 ff.

186   Similarly, in England a written defamation leads to strict liability subject to defences, one of which is proving the truth of a statement; *Jansen* (fn 23) 492; *C Sappideen/P Vines*, Fleming's The Law of Torts (10th edn 2011) 600 ff; *Deakin/Johnston/Markesinis* (fn 31) 604 ff. Cf above. However, not all jurisdictions draw this line, cf *Jansen* (fn 23) 489; *Thiede* (fn 28) 190 f

was an honest opinion (now sec 3 of the Defamation Act 2013).[187] In Sweden
in most cases the freedom of the press and expression is regarded as very important and courts often do not see a violation of the Penal Code if the statement was a joke or an opinion.[188] It becomes a balancing act in which persons
in official functions in particular have to accept more intense criticism than
others.[189]

51 In England most violations of honour, dignity and reputation are protected through the tort of defamation.[190] It is not necessary in English law that
the tortfeasor knew or could have known that his statement was defamatory.[191] However, some scholars argue that, due to defamation only covering
statements, there is a gap in protection compared to other European jurisdictions.[192] Violations of honour, dignity and reputation are, however, also protected (directly or indirectly) by the above-discussed breach of confidence and
the new tort of unauthorised disclosure of private information.[193] Additionally
the tort of malicious falsehood could also be applicable if the non-defamatory
statement is untrue. This tort mostly protects economic interests, but also personality interests, as it protects an individual from being shown in an untrue
light.[194] The statement needs to be false and the tortfeasor had to have acted

---

with further references. In Germany these limits are based on art 5 GG. Austria protects
honour in § 1330 ABGB, cf *R Reischauer* in: P Rummel, Kommentar zum ABGB (3rd edn
2004) § 1330 no 1 ff; Kletečka/Schauer/*Kissich* (fn 59) § 1330 no 1 ff; *E Karner/H Koziol*,
Der Ersatz ideellen Schadens im österreichischen Recht und seine Reform ÖJT ii/1 (2003)
98 ff. An opinion can be insulting to some degree without triggering liability; *Berka*
(fn 176) 522 f.

187   *Esher* in *Merivale v Carson* [1887] QB 275 (290); cf *Lunney/Oliphant* (fn 31) 725 ff. Cf also
now sec 3 of the Defamation Act and *Lunney/Oliphant* (fn 31) 726 ff.

188   *Lindell-Frantz* (fn 74) 58 ff.

189   *Brüggemeier/Colombi Ciacchi/O'Callaghan* (fn 1) 568 with further references. For Sweden
see *H Strömberg/H-G Axberger*, Yttrandefrihetsrätt (2004) 77; *Lindell-Frantz* (fn 74) 59.

190   *Sappideen/Vines* (fn 186) 600 ff; *Deakin/Johnston/Markesinis* (fn 31) 604 ff.

191   *Deakin/Johnston/Markesinis* (fn 31) 658 ff also regarding the possibility of an offer to make
amends in cases when the tortfeasor did not know his statement was defamatory; for an
overview of the historical development regarding *animus iniuriandi* from an outsider's
perspective *Zimmermann* (fn 4) 1074 ff.

192   *Brüggemeier/Colombi Ciacchi/O'Callaghan* (fn 1) 569 with further references. This gap
seems intentional, see *Wainwright v Home Office* [2003] 4 All ER 969.

193   Cf above.

194   Cf *Lunney/Oliphant* (fn 31) 776; *Deakin/Johnston/Markesinis* (fn 31) 699; also *Grappelli and
Another v Derek Block (Holdings) Ltd and Another* [1981] 2 All ER 272.

with *malice*.[195] Both facts have to be proven by the claimant.[196] It is not sufficient if a negative interpretation might only be inferred from the statement; innuendo is not enough to trigger liability.[197]

52 Nevertheless, compared to systems which have a Natural law clause of *neminem laedere*, such as the Roman law traditions, along with Austria and Switzerland, some injuries seem at first glance to be covered by the rules of the latter while not leading to liability in the English law system.[198] In my opinion, the end result might in most cases be similar because, simply put, even in systems which have a Natural law clause at first every wrongful infringement of privacy is in theory covered, but many exceptions and defences might exist. Additionally, English legal scholars might see the differences which can be perceived from a comparative point of view as potential gaps as intentional.[199]

53 Regarding the applicable torts in detail, the latest development in English law regarding defamation – the Defamation Act 2013 – has to be mentioned.[200] The purpose of this Act is to find a better balance between a person's reputation and freedom of speech while avoiding the potential chilling effect liability might have on the freedom of expression.[201] According to sec 1, a statement is not defamatory unless its publication has caused or is likely to cause serious harm to the reputation of the claimant.[202] The threshold test seems to blur the distinction between the questions of whether a statement is defamatory and the damage flowing from it. As formulated in the Act, the threshold seems to apply, according to English scholars, to the harm caused or likely to be caused by the statement, and not the seriousness of the statement itself.[203] The

---

195 Cf *Deakin/Johnston/Markesinis* (fn 31) 699; *Lunney/Oliphant* (fn 31) 776; *Thiede* (fn 28) 67. A 'calculated, reckless indifference to the truth or falsity of the allegations' is sufficient as 'malice is to be inferred from the grossness and falsity of the assertions and the cavalier way they were published.' *Joyce v Sengupta and Another* [1993] 1 All ER 897.

196 *Deakin/Johnston/Markesinis* (fn 31) 699.

197 Cf *Deakin/Johnston/Markesinis* (fn 31) 699; *Thiede* (fn 28) 67.

198 *Brüggemeier/Colombi Ciacchi/O'Callaghan* (fn 1) 569 with further references.

199 Cf *Wainwright v Home Office* [2003] 4 All ER 969, which seems to imply the 'gap' in protection in English law is intentional.

200 Cf *Lunney/Oliphant* (fn 31) 686 ff.

201 *Lunney/Oliphant* (fn 31) 686.

202 Cf for the definition prior to the Defamation Act 2013 Report of the Committee on Defamation, HMSO, Cmnd 5909 (1975) no 65; *WVH Rogers*, Winfield & Jolowicz on Tort (17th edn 2006) no 12-2; *Youssoupoff v Metro-Goldwyn-Mayer Pictures Ltd* [1934] 50 Times Law Reports (TLR) 581. Cf *Deakin/Johnston/Markesinis* (fn 31) 632 ff; *Lunney/Oliphant* (fn 31) 692 ff; *Thiede* (fn 28) 60 f. According to some scholars, the previous law was quick to find a defamatory statement, cf *von Bar* (fn 1) § 1 no 88.

203 Cf for the criteria to be taken into account *Lunney/Oliphant* (fn 31) 699.

adoption of the threshold requirement, and its enactment in statutory form, nevertheless seems a proper development of the law that strikes an appropriate balance between the Convention rights to freedom of expression (art 10) and respect for private life (art 8).[204]

54 As mentioned above, Sweden has, as far as Europe is concerned, very specific rules that protect personality rights. A closer look is therefore also warranted. § 1 of the Swedish Tort Liability Act provides for liability for negligent acts and is only applicable to personal or property damage, the former seemingly excluding personality rights that do not concern health and life. Civil personality rights therefore do not seem to be acknowledged and private liability in personality interest cases is dependent on criminal law according to the principle of accessory.[205] Additionally, according to § 2 of the Swedish Tort Liability Act, non-pecuniary loss is only to be compensated if it was caused through a crime.[206]

55 The Penal Code states that defamation is a criminal act if a person who has provided the information did so with the intent that it should be known to others that the person in question is in some way immoral.[207] Furthermore, an insult is also a crime. This is the case when someone is verbally abused as well as when someone is accused of something blameworthy. Insult is a milder form of violation than defamation.[208] Additionally, for a tort law claim, the violation

---

204 *Lunney/Oliphant* (fn 31) 699.

205 Although specific provisions apply for use of pictures and names in advertising and for the media (Law concerning Name and Picture Advertising, The Freedom of the Press Act, The Fundamental Law on the Freedom of Expressions), cf *Lindell-Frantz* (fn 74) 51 f, 54 ff; *Brüggemeier* (fn 1) 28 f with further references; and in this direction *Lauer/Colombi Ciacchi* (fn 74) 690 f. However, according to most scholars and the jurisprudence, a criminal conviction is not a prerequisite. It is sufficient, at least in cases that do not concern the media, for the civil court to decide whether a criminal act took place. *Lindell-Frantz* (fn 74) 51 f. *J Hellner/S Johansson,* Skadeståndsrätt (6th edn 2000) 405 ff, Statens Offentliga Utredningar (SOU) 1992:84; *von Bar* (fn 1) § 1 no 89, 91 with further references in particular in regards to the media infringing on personality rights.

206 *Lindell-Frantz* (fn 74) 51 f; *Brüggemeier* (fn 1) 28 f with further references; and in this direction *Lauer/Colombi Ciacchi* (fn 74) 690 f.

207 *Lindell-Frantz* (fn 74) 55 ff. Already in 1988 the Swedish courts awarded damages to a doctor whose name was used in a published letter, as it was used for marketing purposes and the use was not covered by the freedom of the press. Rattsfall fran Hovratterna (RH) 1988:107; and with horizontal effect of fundamental ECHR rights regarding a published picture cf NJA 1999, 749; *Lauer/Colombi Ciacchi* (fn 74) 678 f, 685.

208 *Lindell-Frantz* (fn 74) 60 f. There are only a few cases concerning insult in Swedish case law.

also has to be a grave violation. This is assessed on objective grounds.[209] Whenever the violation was committed by the media, the Freedom of Press Act is seen as exclusively applicable. It regulates which behaviour by media constitutes a crime and emphasises the protection of the freedom of speech to an (in comparison to other jurisdictions) far reaching degree through safe guarding whistle blowers from responsibility with only a few exceptions; child pornography or espionage, for example, are seen as crimes.[210]

56 Due to the fact that general tort law is not applicable, remarkable gaps still remain in the protection of personality interests in Sweden. As mentioned above, in general the Swedish judiciary is very hesitant to develop law independently where there are gaps in protection left by the legislator. Instead, another mechanism of dispute regulation was introduced which is deeply rooted in the culture of the Nordic countries: private voluntary self-regulation. This mainly includes specific self-regulatory institutions with codes of conduct for the media.[211] It remains in doubt if this system, coupled with the protection of the Penal Code, meets the standards set out by the ECtHR.[212]

57 The personality rights of honour and dignity can also be distinguished in Europe by the type of injury, mainly disparaging remarks on the one hand and degrading treatment on the other hand.[213] Examples of degrading treatment which violates dignity include body searches, where persons are seen naked by third parties in inspection rooms or degrading treatment and accommodation of detainees in prison.[214] Dignity exists by virtue of being human and is covered by art 3 ECHR, which prohibits torture, and inhuman or degrading treatment or punishment.[215] In my view, the protection under the heading of

---

209 *Lindell-Frantz* (fn 74) 60 f. Some professions have to expect violations and therefore the graveness has to be greater. Violations by the media seem to imply a sufficient graveness as the statement is so widely spread.

210 *Schultz* (2009) 6 ERPL 326 f.

211 *Brüggemeier* (fn 1) 30 with further references.

212 *Lindell-Frantz* (fn 74) 66 ff.

213 *Brüggemeier/Colombi Ciacchi/O'Callaghan* (fn 1) 568 with further references.

214 *Brüggemeier/Colombi Ciacchi/O'Callaghan* (fn 1) 568 with further references. Cf *Wainwright v Home Office* [2003] 4 All ER 969; BGH BGHZ 161, 33; BVerfG, NJW 2006, 1580; BVerfG, 1 BvR 1807/07.

215 ECtHR *Valasinas v Lithuania*, 24.7.2001, no 44558/98 (unreported – applicant made to strip naked and have his sexual organs touched in front of a woman); ECtHR *Iwanczuk v Poland*, 15.11.2001, no 25196/94 (unreported – applicant ordered to strip naked and subjected to humiliating abuse by guards when he tried to exercise his right to vote in facilities provided in prison); ECtHR *Lorsé v The Netherlands*, 4.2.2003, no 52750/99

personality rights should go further and include treatment which does not yet trigger art 3 ECHR.[216]

B   *Privacy*

58 The protection of privacy is in my view the overarching category including violations discussed under other headings which have in common an intrusion into the private life of an individual that do not belong under the title of protection of honour, dignity and reputation.[217] At the core of this right is the interest in being left alone.[218] In Europe, as will be discussed in detail later, art 8 para 1 ECHR covers the right to respect for private and family life, home and correspondence, and, therefore, in this regard an overarching basis for protection exists.

59 As far as the national systems are concerned, in France and Portugal, the civil codes expressly provide for protection.[219] The case law in Sweden uses the law of defamation described above also to protect against violations of privacy;[220] however the protection offered lags behind the protection provided by the ECHR and the standard of protection provided by other European countries.[221]

(unreported – applicant strip searched weekly over 6 years in high security wing without sufficient security justification). Cf also *Wainwright v Home Office* [2003] 4 All ER 969 where an invasion of privacy took place but art 3 of the ECHR was not infringed. Dignity is seen as an absolute right by scholars, *Brüggemeier/Colombi Ciacchi/O'Callaghan* (fn 1) 568 f with further references.

216   Whether or not this protection should also entail the award of damages, or whether in some cases a judgment stating the unlawfulness of the violation should be seen as sufficient, is a different topic of discussion. Cf the approach in Germany BGH BGHZ 161, 33; BVerfG, NJW 2006, 1580; *Brüggemeier/Colombi Ciacchi/O'Callaghan* (fn 1) 569 with further references.

217   Cf, however, *Zimmermann* (fn 4) 1084, who sees dignity at least in South African and Roman Dutch common law as the overarching category which includes privacy and is the third category next to *fama* (defamation) and *corpus* (material personality rights).

218   *Von Bar* (fn 1) § 1 no 102; *Brüggemeier/Colombi Ciacchi/O'Callaghan* (fn 1) 569 with further references; see also *Warren/Brandeis* (1890) 4 Harv L Rev 193. Cf also a seemingly different definition in *Warzilek* (fn 10) 622 ff.

219   In art 9 French Civil Code and art 79 Portuguese Civil Code and art 26 para 1 Portuguese Constitution. See also *Brüggemeier/Colombi Ciacchi/O'Callaghan* (fn 1) 569 with further references. Cf above.

220   *M Schultz*, The Responsible Web: How Tort Law Can Save the Internet (2014) 2 Journal of European Tort Law (JETL) 4, 12; Swedish Supreme Court NJA 1992, 594 and comments in *M Schultz*, Förtalochintegritet (2012) Juridisk Publikation 221 ff.

221   *Schultz* (2009) 6 ERPL 329 ff.

In England, the equitable doctrines of breach of confidence and unauthorised disclosure of private information serve to protect some aspects of privacy.[222] In most other European jurisdictions written or unwritten rules of general tort law are interpreted as protecting privacy.[223] In Austria protection of privacy is based on the specific tort law provision of § 1328a ABGB, which protects against intrusions into private spheres or use of private information, and the general provision of § 16 ABGB.[224] The Austrian system as a special example of the European jurisdictions acknowledges in § 16 the rational freedom of a person to make decisions about their life which is inherent to every human being and the inborn rights needed to protect this freedom.[225] This protection includes the protection of life, liberty and health as well as privacy and dignity.[226]

60   It is in particular the phrasing as a general provision instead of an enumeration which allows § 16 ABGB to recognise new personality rights and interests as they emerge.[227] Additionally, if special provisions fail to provide protection for certain personality rights or a specific violation of a personality right, § 16 ABGB is seen as providing a blanket protection against invasions of privacy and other personality interests based on a balance of the affected interests.[228] The interpretation of this provision, and therefore the protection of personality interests in private law, is influenced by their protection under the fundamental

---

222   *Brüggemeier/Colombi Ciacchi/O'Callaghan* (fn 1) 569 with further references. Cf above.

223   *Brüggemeier/Colombi Ciacchi/O'Callaghan* (fn 1) 569 with further references. Cf above.

224   *Koziol/Warzilek* (fn 155) 15; *M Hinteregger* in: A Kletečka/M Schauer (eds), ABGB-ON (1.01 edn 2014) § 1328a no 1 ff.

225   Kletečka/Schauer/*Schauer* (fn 43) § 16 no 1.

226   As far as liberty is concerned, it is argued that § 16 not only protects physical liberty, but also the freedom to make up your own mind and act accordingly, however in a more limited scope than physical liberty. The former includes medical decisions and freedom of speech and is only protected against intent. *Koziol* (fn 2) 7 f; Schwimann/Kodek/*Posch* (fn 44) § 16 no 20 ff; Rummel/*Aicher* (fn 7) § 16 no 17; *Adler* (fn 2) 189 ff.

227   The provision also aids in the analogous application of existing provisions covering single specific personality rights, cf Schwimann/Kodek/*Posch* (fn 44) § 16 no 6; Koziol/P Bydlinski/Bollenberger/*Koch* (fn 46) § 16 ABGB no 8. During its application, the interests which were covered have changed, cf for the old view of when honour is protected *Adler* (fn 2) 193 ff, 199 ff which is in some details very different to the current view described here.

228   *Mauczka* (fn 3) 240 ff; *Koziol* (fn 2) 15; *Koch* (fn 44) 224; OGH 10 ObS 40/90 SZ 63/32; RIS-Justiz RS0115391. Cf Schwimann/Kodek/*Posch* (fn 44) § 16 no 3, 30; Rummel/*Aicher* (fn 7) § 16 no 10; Koziol/P Bydlinski/Bollenberger/*Koch* (fn 46) § 16 ABGB no 8, 10 with further references.

freedoms.[229] In general § 16 ABGB protects all rights which preserve a person in their physical, psychological and mental uniqueness.[230]

61 Which concrete interests are protected has to be determined after a careful examination, both of other existing rights in the legal system, national laws or fundamental freedoms, and of the hypothetical will of the legislator, if applicable in the jurisdiction.[231] The right to privacy as well as other personality rights is in some jurisdictions seen as an absolute right in as far as it should be protected against violations by third parties;[232] however, not all behaviour against a right protecting personality rights or privacy is automatically seen as wrongful. Sometimes the behaviour of someone exposing secrets of a person is seen as not wrongful, for example under Austrian law.[233] The concrete scope of the right to privacy has not yet been determined.[234] In general it is the case in European jurisdictions that for example a right to anonymity and the right to privacy have to be balanced against the freedom of speech and interests

---

229 This is seen as the *'mittelbare Wirkung der Grundrechte,'* cf *F Marhold*, Kommentar zu OGH 24.10.1978, 4 Ob 91/78 (1979) ZAS 177, 178; Schwimann/Kodek/*Posch* (fn 44) § 16 no 4; Koziol/P Bydlinski/Bollenberger/*Koch* (fn 46) § 16 ABGB no 10; *Koch* (fn 44) 224 f, 228 ff; Rummel/*Aicher* (fn 7) § 16 no 30 ff with further references. Fundamental freedoms do not have a direct application in private law, but they can influence the interpretation of existing private law rules.

230 *Edlbacher* (1983) ÖJZ 423, 425.

231 For Austria see Schwimann/Kodek/*Posch* (fn 44) § 16 no 12.

232 In Austria for example the courts have agreed with this view since 4 Ob 91/78 SZ 51/146 = ZAS 1979,176 (*Marhold*) = drdA 1979,394 (*Raschauer*), cf RIS-Justiz rs0008999; cf Schwimann/Kodek/*Posch* (fn 44) § 16 no 38; Koziol/P Bydlinski/Bollenberger/*Koch* (fn 46) § 16 ABGB no 4, 9; Rummel/*Aicher* (fn 7) § 16 no 18; for other personality rights in general cf Schwimann/Kodek/*Posch* (fn 44) § 16 no 12; *Koziol* (fn 2) 6.

233 In this particular case the claimants before an administrative authority had submitted documents which included personal information of others to back their claim, which ironically enough was that the documents and their publication to certain individuals constituted a breach of a duty of confidentiality by the workers' council. The administrative authority chose to read out the documents in the hearing. The interest to be able to prove your rights and the right of the deciding body on how they conduct the search for evidence was in this particular case seen as greater than the interest of the other workers to keep their school records from being read in a hearing. 4 Ob 91/78 SZ 51/146 = ZAS 1979, 176, 177 ff (*Marhold*) = drdA 1979,394 (*Raschauer*), cf RIS-Justiz rs0008999. Cf Schwimann/Kodek/*Posch* (fn 44) § 16 Rz 38; Koziol/P Bydlinski/Bollenberger/*Koch* (fn 46) § 16 ABGB no 4; Rummel/*Aicher* (fn 7) § 16 no 18; for other personality rights in general cf Schwimann/Kodek/*Posch* (fn 44) § 16 no 12; Koziol/P Bydlinski/Bollenberger/*Koch* (fn 46) § 16 ABGB no 9; *Koziol*, Haftpflichtrecht II (fn 2) 6; *Canaris* (1991) JBl 205, 211 ff.

234 For Austria see Schwimann/Kodek/*Posch* (fn 44) § 16 no 38.

of the public to be informed in certain cases.[235] The protection of the private sphere might have to give way, in particular if the protection of public interests, for example State security or information accessible to the public about possible criminal dealings of a politician, are in danger.[236] A recent case which has influenced the discussion in Europe and the US is the Prism scandal, where *Edward Snowden*, a former National Security Agency (NSA) employee, revealed secret NSA files to show how the agency was intruding on civilians' privacy, which had the potential to be harmful for State security.[237] Some scholars, however, suggest that there is an absolute protected core area of privacy, which may never be intruded upon.[238]

62 In France a specific legal situation has existed since the Act of 17 July 1970, which introduced art 9 *Code Civil*. From a content point of view, this Act is seen as merely codifying the previous case law regarding the protection of privacy. Article 9 is therefore interpreted in line with the preceding jurisprudence to arts 1382 and 1383 *Code Civil*; however, it is seen as providing for a strict liability for infringements of an individual's private life.[239] Therefore, the legislature chose to strengthen the privacy protection compared to the situation before the Act came into force, which also marks a difference to the other Europen jursdictions which require fault. However, other infringements of personality interests in France have to be based on arts 1382 and 1383 where fault is still seen as a necessary condition, although, due to the influence of art 9, a violation as such is in most cases seen as *fautif*.[240] The protection of personality interests in France has therefore been overall strengthened through the new Act also compared to other European legal systems. England is partially on the other side of the spectrum as other privacy interests apart from reputation and honour are at present protected through a legal patchwork of common law, statutory law and equitable remedies, aided by self-regulatory mechanisms. In English law the doctrines of malicious falsehood, passing-off, breach of

---

235   Rummel/*Aicher* (fn 7) § 16 no 27; Schwimann/Kodek/*Posch* (fn 44) § 16 no 25.

236   *Brüggemeier/Colombi Ciacchi/O'Callaghan* (fn 1) 570 f; *von Bar* (fn 1) § 1 no 101; *Thiede* (fn 28) 17 f; cf for public figures *Warzilek* (fn 10) 632 ff and ECtHR *Caroline von Hannover v Germany*, 24.6.2004, no 59320/00, 2004-VI = EuGRZ 2004, 404.

237   Cf for example <http://www.theguardian.com/world/2013/aug/21/edward-snowden-nsa-files-revelations> (last access: 19.2.2016). Also cf <wikileaks.org> (last access: 19.2.2016).

238   Disagreeing *Brüggemeier/Colombi Ciacchi/O'Callaghan* (fn 1) 570.

239   *Kern* (fn 4) 92 f; *Brüggemeier* (fn 1) 14 f and *Thiede* (fn 28) 89 f with further references. Additionally, revelations concerning the intimate core of private life justify pre-trial interdictal/injunctive relief.

240   *Derieux* (fn 180) 459; *R Linden*, Une creation prétorienne: Les droits de la personnalité (1974) 86 ff; *Thiede* (fn 28) 103, 116 f; Cour de cassation, Juris Classeur Périodique (JCP) 1997, II 22805; Cour de cassation, JCP 1997, II, 22873.

confidence and unauthorised disclosure of personal information; occasionally trespass and nuisance are used in cases of violations of personality rights.[241] In cases concerning the media, freedom of the press is an important factor to consider.[242] A general right to privacy does not exist and some believe therefore that there are gaps in protection.[243]

63   Norway, in contrast, protects the 'peace of private life' in para 3–6 of the Norwegian Compensation Act 1969.[244] According to this para, the offender may be required by the court to pay compensation for the injury sustained, for loss of future earnings and for non-financial injury – as the court finds reasonable, if he acted negligently.[245] In as far as interpretation of this provision by the courts is concerned, the courts have started to decide cases regarding freedom of the press and the right to privacy according to the balance of art 8 (privacy) and art 10 (freedom of speech) of the ECHR as struck by the ECtHR,[246] although in recent years some judgments imply a heavy protection of the freedom of speech.[247] However, the privacy of persons of no interest to political discussions within society must be respected, even if the persons in question are 'celebrities.'[248] It seems that, even in the Nordic countries, the jurisprudence of the ECtHR leads to at least partial harmonisation and development of the law.[249]

64   In most European countries the protection usually covers the private and intimate spheres, which may not be intruded upon without consent.[250] The core

---

241   *Khorasandijian v Bush* [1993] QB 727. Cf *Deakin/Johnston/Markesinis* (fn 31) 701 ff, 706 ff; *Brüggemeier* (fn 1) 8, 26.

242   Cf *Deakin/Johnston/Markesinis* (fn 31) 763 ff; *R Parkes*, Privacy, Defamation and False Facts, in: M Warby QC/N Moreham/I Christie (eds), The Law of Privacy and the Media (2nd edn 2011) no 7.50 ff, 7.65 ff; *Brüggemeier* (fn 1) 26.

243   Cf for references of the 'gaps' no 45 fn 168.

244   *Mæland* (fn 183) 70 ff; *B Askeland*, Norway, in: H Koziol/bc Steininger (eds), European Tort Law (hereinafter ETL) 2007 (2008) 440, no 5 ff.

245   *Mæland* (fn 183) 71 ff.

246   Cf above for the *Caroline of Hannover* case. *Mæland* (fn 183) 71 f; *Askeland* (fn 244) 441 f. Norway had been previously judged by the ECtHR as having set the freedom of expression threshold too low. It seems that now the courts have gone the other way and protect the freedom of expression of the media too much.

247   *Mæland* (fn 183) 72 ff.

248   Høyesterett (Supreme Court, Hr) Norsk Retstidende (Rt) 2007, 687; cf *Askeland* (fn 244) 441 f.

249   *K Oliphant*, Comparative Remarks, in: H Koziol/BC Steininger (eds), ETL 2008 (2009) no 2, 15 f.

250   Cf for the definition of the private sphere in German law *Thiede* (fn 28) 15 ff and in general *Warzilek* (fn 10) 623. Cf also *Brüggemeier/Colombi Ciacchi/O'Callaghan* (fn 1) 569 f; *von Bar* (fn 1) § 1 no 102 ff.

of this right has been identified as the sphere regarding health, sexuality and
family life – the intimate sphere which is protected in an absolute way.[251] Outside of this intimate sphere, a possible violation has to be judged according
to the balance of interests on a case-by-case basis.[252] There are various forms
of possible infringement, for example photographing and filming, publishing
private diaries or correspondence or online searches of private electronic information systems.[253] The Austrian Supreme Court for example considers a
systematic, hidden and identifying video surveillance with a retrievable image
recording as a violation of § 16 ABGB in combination with art 8 ECHR and the
herein encoded right to privacy, so that the party using the recording equip-
ment carries the burden of proof that he was protecting his own valid interests
with appropriate measures.[254] Another example of violations of § 16 ABGB is
spam, as well as certain types of suggestive advertisements hidden as private
mails.[255] It is unclear whether business affairs can be protected under the right
to privacy.[256]

65   The right to privacy in some jurisdictions also includes the interest in anonymity, also in the sense that a person has an interest not to have their affairs made
public against their will.[257] A variation of these interests is the *droit à l'oubli* –
the right to be forgotten.[258] The European Court of Justice has in a recent judgment acknowledged that, according to European Union law and in particular
also the Charter of Fundamental Rights of the European Union, a person has a
right to demand their old data be removed from databases and search engines,

---

251   For Austria for example cf Schwimann/Kodek/*Posch* (fn 44) § 16 no 39 with further references; for example see OGH 6 Ob 103/07a; 4 Ob 150/08z MR 2008, 346; RIS-Justiz rs0122148.
For other examples cf also Rummel/*Aicher* (fn 7) § 16 no 24 ff.

252   For Austria for example cf Schwimann/Kodek/*Posch* (fn 44) § 16 no 39; Rummel/*Aicher*
(fn 7) § 16 no 24 ff. For a differentiation according to spheres cf *A Heldrich*, Persönlichkeitsschutz und Pressefreiheit (1998) 16 ff.

253   Cf *von Bar* (fn 1) § 1 no 93 ff; *Brüggemeier/Colombi Ciacchi/O'Callaghan* (fn 1) 569 f with
further references; BVerfG NJW 2008, 822.

254   Schwimann/Kodek/*Posch* (fn 44) § 16 no 39 with further references; OGH 8 Ob 108/05y
Evidenzblatt (EvBl) 2006/67. For other examples cf also Rummel/*Aicher* (fn 7) § 16 no 21 ff.

255   4 Ob 59/00f Entscheidungen des OGH in Zivil- und Justizverwaltungssachen (SZ) 73/47; cf
Schwimann/Kodek/*Posch* (fn 44) § 16 no 39 with further references. For other examples cf
also Rummel/*Aicher* (fn 7) § 16 no 21 ff.

256   Schwimann/Kodek/*Posch* (fn 44) § 16 no 40; Rummel/*Aicher* (fn 7) § 16 no 21 ff.

257   *Brüggemeier/Colombi Ciacchi/O'Callaghan* (fn 1) 570; *von Bar* (fn 1) § 1 no 93 ff.

258   *Brüggemeier/Colombi Ciacchi/O'Callaghan* (fn 1) 570 with further references.

unless there is an interest of the public to be informed even after some time has passed.[259]

C   *Right to One's Image and Likeness*

66 The right to one's image was an issue even before the emergence of photography, although the latter certainly exacerbated the problem.[260] It became one of the main issues regarding personality rights which influenced the overall discussion of the protection of all personality interests.[261]

67 The extent of the right to one's image is in general the same in most European jurisdictions. It is a violation of this right if an image is published – or in some specific instances also simply taken – without the express agreement of the person pictured and if he or she is clearly recognisable.[262] The discussion regarding the protection distinguishes different categories. On the one hand whether or not the person depicted is famous is regarded in some jurisdictions as influencing the degree of protection. On the other hand pictures taken in public spheres are distinguished from pictures taken in the private sphere of life.[263] As far as the private sphere is concerned, it has to be borne in mind that

---

259 ECJ 13.5.2014, C-131/12, *Google Spain, Google Inc v Agencia Española de Protección de Datos* [2014] ECLI:EU:C:2014:317; cf *T Thiede/BA Koch*, European Union, in: E Karner/BC Steininger (eds), ETL 2014 (2015) 660, no 40-44 and *LE Weissel*, Personality Rights and the Internet in Europe, in this volume. Cf *M Schmidt-Kessel/C Langhanke/I Gläser/HK Herden*, Recht auf Vergessen und piercing the corporate veil (2014) Zeitschrift für Gemeinschaftsprivatrecht (GPR) 192 ff; *BA Koch*, Cyber Torts: Something Virtually New? (2014) 2 JETL 6.

260 Cf no 13 above, *Rachel* case, Trib civ Seine, D 1858, 3, 62 (distribution of sketches of a photograph); *Prince Albert v Strange* (1849) 1 Mac & G 25, 64 ER 293 (distribution of drawings); *Brüggemeier/Colombi Ciacchi/O'Callaghan* (fn 1) 570.

261 Cf above in II: France, England and also Germany. The influence was different in each jurisdiction.

262 Cf *Brüggemeier/Colombi Ciacchi/O'Callaghan* (fn 1) 570. As far as photographs simply taken are concerned, in most jurisdictions either the way of taking the photograph – in secret for example – or the content of the picture have to add to the wrongfulness of the act, for Austria see OGH 6 Ob 256/12h (2013) ÖJZ 732, 735 (*Karner*); cf *Karner* (2013) ÖJZ, 906, 910 for the problematic relationship with § 78 *Urheberrechtsgesetz* and the legislator's will behind the latter. § 78 *Urheberrechtsgesetz* requires the picture to have violated interests of the pictured person, cf *Koziol/Warzilek* (fn 155) 19 ff; *Koziol* (fn 2) 11 f.

263 For the different protection according to the spheres touched cf above. The underlying reason for this protection is the violation of privacy through the image, cf also Case 7, *G Brüggemeier/A Colombi Ciacchi/P O'Callaghan* (eds), Personality Rights in European Tort Law (2010) 275 f.

the overall issue of a violation of privacy also plays a role in these instances. Most jurisdictions therefore protect the right to one's image when the picture shows a person in the private areas of their life. Whether this person is famous plays no role in the protection in these cases. The differences between jurisdictions start cropping up once the picture in question was taken in the workplace,[264] in public places[265] or depicts a famous person.[266] In the latter case, different positions were taken, mainly by Belgian and French law on the one hand and German law on the other. Belgian and French law require the consent of the public figure even if the photograph is taken in a public sphere, while certain exceptions are made.[267] German law, however, allowed the secret taking and publication of photographs by the press in principle but there were some exceptions.[268] The case-law regarding the statute took the view that photographs of 'public figures' could be taken and published without the consent of the pictured person and on any occasion, unless there was an intrusion into the person's private domestic sphere such as their house, etc.[269] This case law was later criticised by the ECtHR.[270]

68 As regards the German position on famous persons, the European Court of Human Rights made it clear in the case regarding *Caroline von Hannover* that solely the French and Belgian position is compatible with art 8 para 1 ECHR.[271] Paparazzi had taken pictures without Caroline's express consent, for example while out eating at a restaurant or otherwise going about her daily life in public places, and these pictures were published in magazines. The German BGH did not consider this a violation of art 8 ECHR, because it was covered by art 10 ECHR, the freedom of speech. The European Court of Human Rights, however, took a different approach. It differentiated between information which is

---

264   Most jurisdictions lessen the protection in the workplace, cf Case 7 *Brüggemeier/Colombi Ciacchi/O'Callaghan* (fn 263) 275 ff; see, however, France 285. Cf also *Warzilek* (fn 10) 616.

265   Most jurisdictions lessen the protection in public places, cf Case 7, *Brüggemeier/Colombi Ciacchi/O'Callaghan* (fn 263) 275 ff; see, however, France, unless the presence in the photograph is a mere coincidence 285.

266   *Warzilek* (fn 10) 632 ff *Brüggemeier/Colombi Ciacchi/O'Callaghan* (fn 1) 571.

267   *Warzilek* (fn 10) 633; *Brüggemeier/Colombi Ciacchi/O'Callaghan* (fn 1) 571.

268   *Brüggemeier/Colombi Ciacchi/O'Callaghan* (fn 1) 571. Cf the *Kunsturhebergesetz* under II.C (no 26 above).

269   *Brüggemeier* (fn 1) 21 with further references.

270   ECtHR *Caroline von Hannover v Germany*, 24.6.2004, no 59320/00, 2004-VI = EuGRZ 2004, 404. Cf *Brüggemeier/Colombi Ciacchi/O'Callaghan* (fn 1) 571; *Thiede* (fn 28) 17 f; above II.B.

271   *Caroline von Hannover*, no 59320/00, 2004-vi = EuGRZ 2004, 404. Cf *Brüggemeier/Colombi Ciacchi/O'Callaghan* (fn 1) 571; *Thiede* (fn 28) 17 f; *Warzilek* (fn 10) 634.

merely entertainment for a certain group of readers concerning persons not fulfilling official functions and information which is necessary for public debate, in particular concerning persons when they perform an official function. This case fell under the first category and was therefore not covered by the freedom of speech.[272]

69 Despite the parallels in the extent of the protection, the development of the right to one's image differed from country to country.[273] In some jurisdictions the legislator introduced statutory rules to deal with the issues concerning the distribution of photographs and the rights of the depicted persons, as for example in Germany, Spain and partially in Austria.[274] In the latter jurisdiction for example the right to one's image is in part based on § 16 ABGB together with art 8 ECHR and in part protected by §§ 78, 87 para 2 *Urheberrechtsgesetz* (Copyright Law).[275] In some jurisdictions no specific regulation exists and courts were left to deal with the issue, most notably France and Switzerland.[276] In English law the right to one's image was previously only covered by breach of confidence or in some cases based on trespass or the violation of a specific statutory right (eg sec 85 Copyright Designs and Patents Act 1988). Now the new tort of unauthorised disclosure of private information also offers more protection.[277] The law in Sweden as shown above is a notable exception

---

272 ECtHR *Caroline von Hannover*, no 59320/00, 2004-VI = EuGRZ 2004, 404. Cf *C Grabenwart-er*, Schutz der Privatsphäre versus Pressefreiheit: Europäische Korrektur eines deutschen Sonderwegs (2004) Archiv für Presserecht (AfP) 209 ff; *idem*, Medienfreiheit und Bildnissc-hutz nach der Menschrechtskonvention, FS Ress (2005) 979 ff; *Brüggemeier* (fn 1) 17, 34 ff; *Thiede* (fn 28) 180 ff. The Austrian OGH followed this approach, OGH 4 Ob 121/08k; 4 Ob 165/08f. The German BVerfG and BGH seem to also be moving tentatively in this direction, cf BVerfG 1 BvR 1602, 1606, 1626/07; BGH NJW 2007, 1977/1982; Gewerblicher Rechtsschutz und Urheberrecht (GRUR) 2007, 902. Cf in detail *T Thiede*, Personality Rights, the Mass Media and the European Convention on Human Rights, in this volume.

273 *Brüggemeier/Colombi Ciacchi/O'Callaghan* (fn 1) 570 f.

274 *Brüggemeier/Colombi Ciacchi/O'Callaghan* (fn 1) 570 f. In Austria this issue is dealt with in §§ 78, 87 para 2 *Urheberrechtsgesetz*. Cf *Karner/Koziol* (fn 186) 100 f; *Koziol/Warzilek* (fn 128) 19 f; *GE Kodek* in: G Kucsko (ed), urheber.recht, Systematischer Kommentar zum Urheberrechtsgesetz (2007) § 78 no 1 ff. For details cf II (no 3 above).

275 OGH 6 Ob 256/12h; *Karner* (2013) ÖJZ 906, 910. Cf for details of the Austrian position *Kozi-ol/Warzilek* (fn 128) 19 f. Similarly in Italy and the common law system of England the dissemination of photographs portraying individuals is regulated by both tort or delict and statutory law, cf *Brüggemeier/Colombi Ciacchi/O'Callaghan* (fn 1) 571.

276 *Warzilek* (fn 10) 625.

277 Cf II (no 3 above).

in Europe as the legal protection requires a crime.[278] Additionally in the EU
Member States, EU data protection law can offer remedies.[279]

D   *Commercial Appropriation of Personality*

70 Under this heading, scholars discuss a sub-category of the right to one's image:
the commercial value of photographs of famous persons and their unauthorised use for advertising purposes as well as the commercial unauthorised use
of other aspects of a famous person, such as voice, are covered here.[280] The
sub-category is in most jurisdictions seen as covering mostly economic interests of public figures and famous persons. As far as the unauthorised use of a
picture or other aspect of an unknown person for advertising purposes is concerned, most jurisdictions only offer the general protection of image, privacy
or dignity, honour and reputation.[281] Especially in light of the proposed and
then dropped changes to the terms of use by Instagram – a social network-
ing site which allows the posting and sharing of pictures – which seemed to
imply a right of Instagram and its affiliated partners to use any picture up-
loaded to their site for any purpose including advertisements,[282] it might be
necessary to consider including non-famous persons under this heading too,
especially since the type of recoverable damage seems to be different in some

---

278   *Brüggemeier/Colombi Ciacchi/O'Callaghan* (fn 1) 571. Cf II.B (no 8 above) for further
        references.
279   Directive 95/46/EC of the European Parliament and of the Council of 24 October 1995 on
        the protection of individuals with regard to the processing of personal data and on the
        free movement of such data, Official Journal (OJ) L 281, 23.11.1995, 31–50 and Directive
        2002/58/EC of the European Parliament and of the Council of 12 July 2002 concerning
        the processing of personal data and the protection of privacy in the electronic communi-
        cations sector (Directive on privacy and electronic communications) OJ L 201, 31.7.2002,
        37–47; cf *C Kuner*, European Data Protection Law: Corporate Compliance and Regula-
        tion (2007) 1 ff. Cf for a short overview of the European Directives – which will not be
        discussed in this paper – relevant to violations of personality rights cf *R Perry/TZ Zarsky*,
        Liability for Online Anonymous Speech (2014) 2 JETL 15 ff.
280   *Brüggemeier/Colombi Ciacchi/O'Callaghan* (fn 1) 572 f; *Brüggemeier* (fn 1) 35 f. Cf
        H Beverly-Smith/A Ohly/A Lucas-Schloetter, Privacy, Property and Personality. Civil Law
        Perspectives on Commercial Appropriation (2005) 1 ff.
281   Of course only if the person is even recognisable and the association with the product
        advertised either violates their dignity or the used aspect stems from the private sphere
        and therefore violates privacy. For images of non-famous persons cf *Roberson v Rochester
        Folding Box Co*, 64 North Eastern Reporter (NE) 442 (NY 1902); *Pavesich v New England
        Life Insurance Co*, 50 South Eastern Reporter (SE) 68 (Ga 1905) and BGH BGHZ 26, 349
        (*Herrenreiter*). *Brüggemeier/Colombi Ciacchi/O'Callaghan* (fn 1) 572.
282   <http://www.huffingtonpost.com/2012/12/20/instagram-terms-of-service-change_n
        _2333284.html> (last access: 19.2.2016).

jurisdictions in this sub-category compared to the right to one's image; the latter does not take regard of a possible commercial value of the photograph in all jurisdictions and economic loss may not be recoverable.[283]

71 This issue could possibly be dealt with through a concurrent claim under the law of unjust enrichment, which is what the law in Germany seems to do. The BGH accepted that a right to personality also includes an allocation of authority to the person in question and this seems to include non-famous persons as well. This means that an economic right is included too and therefore, especially in cases of commercial appropriation of personality or the right to one's image, a claim exists not only in tort law but also under the law of unjust enrichment.[284]

E   *Right to Personal Identity*

72 One of the important interests regarding the protection of personality is the right to authentic representation in public;[285] the discourse about this interest is connected to the discussion about dignity, honour and reputation in as far as statements are concerned which give a wrong impression of a person.[286] The difference is that, under this heading, the statement does not have to be defamatory; it just needs to be a false, non-authentic portrayal of the person.[287] Some jurisdictions stress this distinction and treat the right to not be portrayed in a false, non-authentic light as a sub-category of the overarching principle of personality: the right to freely represent and define oneself[288] and as such a separate category to the right to dignity, honour and representation.[289] In England this interest is covered under the tort of malicious falsehood.[290] Examples include quotes that were actually not made by the person or are

---

283 *Brüggemeier/Colombi Ciacchi/O'Callaghan* (fn 1) 572.

284 BGHZ 143, 214, 225; cf for further details and further references *Jansen* (fn 23) 487 f. The cases in question regard famous persons; however, the language of the court and scholars seems to imply the same protection for non-famous individuals. Cf for a similar protection of famous and non-famous persons *von Bar* (fn 1) § 1 no 86.

285 Cf *von Bar* (fn 1) § 1 no 92 with further references; for Italy cf *Pino* (fn 152) 225 ff.

286 See above.

287 *Brüggemeier/Colombi Ciacchi/O'Callaghan* (fn 1) 573; *von Bar* (fn 1) § 1 no 92. This right has different practical importance in different countries, cf for Germany and Austria *Koziol/Warzilek* (fn 155) 15 f.

288 Cf already *Mauczka* (fn 3) 279; see also currently *Brüggemeier/Colombi Ciacchi/O'Callaghan* (fn 1) 573.

289 Cf *Brüggemeier/Colombi Ciacchi/O'Callaghan* (fn 1) 573.

290 Cf under II.B (no 8 above). Cf however *von Bar* (fn 1) § 1 no 92 who sees the protection in English law in this regard as unsatisfactory, although he seems to only consider breach of confidence and defamation.

misused in a different context and imply a political opinion the person actually does not hold.[291] One early example of cases under this personality right is the *Schacht-Leserbrief* judgment of the BGH, which was discussed in detail above under II.[292] Of interest is also a case from Italy.[293] The Church campaigned at the beginning of the 1970s to abolish divorce law and used a photograph for this purpose supposed to evoke the 'traditional' Catholic family. It showed a man and a woman working in a field. The problem was that these persons were neither married nor did they agree with the campaign to abolish divorce law. The Court of First Instance in Rome awarded compensation because of the injury to the right to image and the right to personal identity.[294]

73 In this context, the adaptation of a person's life story in novels or films needs to be considered, as it often – due to artistic licence – includes depicting the person in question in a false light. In these cases complex issues arise, as the freedom of art needs to be balanced with the protection of personality.[295] It seems that in some jurisdictions the freedom of art would prevail, unless a direct insult to the person was involved; in other words, a simple violation of the right to personal identity would not suffice.[296] Other jurisdictions offer stronger protection, in particular if the depicted person's real name was used or the person was very easily identifiable.[297]

F   *Self-determination*

74 Under this heading a variety of interests is discussed.[298] The starting point can be seen in the right to self-determination over one's own body connected to the entire law regarding medical treatment and patient information. Traditionally, such cases have been discussed under the title 'unlawfulness of

---

291 BVerfG BVerfGE 54,208 – *Böll/Walden*; BVerfG BVerfGE 54, 148 – *Eppler*; for further examples cf *von Bar* (fn 1) § 1 no 92.

292 Cf II (no 3 above) Germany.

293 Pretura Roma, Giurisprudenza Italiana (Giur It) 1975, 1, 2, 514; cf *Pino* (fn 152) 232 f; *Kern* (fn 4) 93 with further references; *Brüggemeier/Colombi Ciacchi/O'Callaghan* (fn 1) 573.

294 The picture was also taken without the consent of the depicted persons. Pretura Roma, Giur It 1975, 1, 2, 514.

295 *Brüggemeier/Colombi Ciacchi/O'Callaghan* (fn 1) 574.

296 Case 4, *Brüggemeier/Colombi Ciacchi/O'Callaghan* (fn 263) 206 ff; OLG Wien MR 1995, 52; MR 1985/1 A 9 for Austria; 210 for England and 210 ff for Finland.

297 Cf for example Case 4, *Brüggemeier/Colombi Ciacchi/O'Callaghan* (fn 263) 208 ff for Belgium; 213 f for France.

298 One could also include the right not to have true private facts dragged into the public under this heading, cf *von Bar* (fn 1) § 1 no 101.

bodily injury.'[299] In most cases the right to self-determination is connected to information, for example the right to be informed or not to be informed over one's genetic origins or one's descendants is a right of access to certain types of information. One of the other more prominent issues in current times is the right to determine which information is stored and accessible to others, in other words the power to decide what happens with one's own personal data. In most European states, EC directives and national data protection laws regulate the area connected to self-determination of the personal data stored or accessible in various databases.[300]

G   *Conclusion*

75 The jurisdictions in Europe cover a wide array of interests under the heading of personality rights. The protection can be divided into two categories: privacy on the one hand and dignity, honour and reputation on the other hand. Privacy covers many individual interests, such as the right to one's image, commercial appropriation of personality, the right to personal identity and self-determination. The jurisdictions adopt a similar approach in the protection of many of these issues; however, differences in the details remain.

V   Overall Résumé

76 Overall, the protection of personality rights has a long history in most jurisdictions in Europe, in particular due to the influence of Roman law and the *actio iniuriarum*. This common history of Roman law has still left room for a diverse development, especial in Austria, which followed the Natural theory approach, in Germany, where the *actio iniuriarum* was formally repealed in 1879, and in Sweden, where personality rights are for the most part only protected through

---

299 *Brüggemeier/Colombi Ciacchi/O'Callaghan* (fn 1) 574 f. The Netherlands and France also discuss under this heading the right of women or both parents to freedom of choice, which leads to cases where a doctor does not inform the pregnant woman of a possible disability of her foetus being seen as an infringement of personal self-determination. In France the doctrine of *perte d'une chance* is applied. Cf Hoge Raad Rechtspraak van de Week (RvdW) 2005, 42 (*Kelly*) (Netherlands); Cass civ, JCP 1991, IV 336 (France).

300 *Brüggemeier/Colombi Ciacchi/O'Callaghan* (fn 1) 574. Most interesting in this regard was the Case ECJ 13.5.2014, C-131/12, *Google Spain and Google Inc* [GC] ECLI:EU:C:2014:317 in which the court stated that individuals indeed do have a right against search engines to have links to websites removed when the individual's name is used as a search query. Cf in detail with further references *Thiede/Koch* (fn 259) no 40-44 and *Weissel* (fn 259). Cf for the EC directives above.

the Penal Code and tort law claims for a long time only existed according to the principle of accessory.

77 Due to the influence of constitutional human rights and the ECHR, in particular after World War II, most jurisdictions have started to develop in a common direction. The jurisdiction of the ECtHR is the driving force behind some of the changes in the protection of personality rights and has led to some unification in this field. Nevertheless, the PETL and DCFR seemed to struggle to find common principles in their model rules as they included personality rights in the tort law protection but left the scope of protection open to the national systems. It might be that if the current common development through the jurisprudence of the ECtHR continues, a new attempt at model rules could already lead to different results.

78 One of the differences in the various jurisdictions that seems to remain is that some see a bundle of specific personality rights while others argue for a general right that protects various personality interests. The difference in approach makes very little difference in practice as each protection of a personality interest has to be based on a careful balance of interests.

79 As far as the scope of protection is concerned, most jurisdictions protect dignity, honour and reputation by differentiating between statements of fact and statements of opinion. Privacy as the overarching category covering all other personality interests means the private and intimate sphere of a person which also includes the right to one's image and likeness, commercial appropriation of personality, right to personal identity, self-determination and others. Some jurisdictions protect a wider scope of these interests and, although some common ground and common principles can be found, differences in the details remain.[301]

80 It will be very interesting to see how the future jurisprudence of the ECtHR will continue to influence the protection of personality rights in Europe and if in the future the law in this field will be even more harmonised.

---

301 Cf *von Bar* (fn 1) § 1 no 81 ff, 85 with further references already described that the European jurisdictions show a wide consensus when one looks at in which cases liability is seen as justified. The reasoning and the law used might be different mostly due to historical development, but the results are comparable in practice.

CHAPTER 3

The Protection of Personality Rights in Private Law: Remedies

Monika Hinteregger

I   Introduction

1   In the following I will give a short account of the private law remedies that are available for the infringement of personality rights in Europe. The examination of the national laws concentrates on three European countries, Germany, France and England, which are the biggest European countries as regards number of inhabitants and the leading jurisdictions of three legal families, the Germanic and the Romanic legal family and the common law. It will be shown that the protection of personality rights in private law has been highly influenced by the evolution of strong and comprehensive systems for the protection of human rights after World War II both on an international and national level.

II   The Obligation of the State to Actively Protect Personality Rights

2   The interpretation and application of art 8 (respect for private and family life) and art 10 (freedom of expression) of the European Convention on Human Rights (ECHR) by the European Court of Human Rights (ECtHR) had a considerable impact on the laws for the protection of personality rights in Europe. Since 2000 another system for the protection of human rights has been starting to play an important role for the European Union and its Member States, the Charter of Fundamental Rights of the European Union (CFR).[1] The obligations of the Charter are addressed to the institutions and bodies of the Union and cover all activities of these entities whether they are of a legislative or administrative

---

1   [2012] Official Journal (OJ) C 326/391. The CFR was solemnly proclaimed on 7 December 2000 by the European Commission, European Parliament and Council of Ministers and approved by the Member States. It got full legal effect with the entry into force of the Lisbon Treaty on 1 December 2009. See *P Craig/G de Búrca*, EU Law: Text, Cases, and Materials (5th edn 2011) 394.

character. The Member States are bound by the Charter insofar as they are implementing Union law both by legislation (eg implementation of Directives) or administrative acts (art 51 CFR).[2] The Charter has the same legal value as the basic EU treaties, the Treaty on European Union (TEU) and the Treaty on the Functioning of the European Union (TFEU).[3] The relevance of the ECHR is, however, not diminished by the new system. According to art 6 (3) TEU, the fundamental rights of the ECHR constitute general principles of the Union's law and art 6 (2) TEU declares that the Union shall formally accede to the Convention.

3   The obligations to respect the rights and freedoms of both the Convention and the Charter comprise of two dimensions. The first dimension consists of the traditional function of fundamental rights which is to protect individual persons from unjustified infringements of their fundamental rights by the Union's institutions and the Member States (the negative obligation). As a second dimension, it is nowadays uncontested that fundamental rights also entail the positive obligation to ensure that the guarantees embodied by the fundamental rights are implemented. Both obligations are now clearly provided by art 51 CFR which obliges institutions and Member States to 'respect the rights, observe the principles and promote the application thereof in accordance with their respective powers.'[4] The notion that fundamental rights encompass positive obligations for the state has already been recognised in the application and interpretation of the ECHR by the European Court of Human Rights for some time.[5] According to the jurisprudence of the Court, the State must not only abstain from the infringement of fundamental rights of individuals, but must protect them with active measures. This also encompasses the protection of the fundamental rights of the individual against infringements by third parties. Accordingly, the ECtHR obliged the state, for instance, to establish and apply effectively a criminal law system punishing all forms of rape and sexual abuse,[6] to introduce regulations compelling both public and private hospitals to adopt appropriate measures for the physical integrity of their patients including adequate compensation for medical malpractice,[7] or to ensure the

---

2   *HD Jarass*, Charta der Grundrechte der Europäischen Union: Kommentar (2010) art 51 no 3.

3   Art 6 (1) TEU.

4   *Jarass* (fn 2) art 51 no 46 ff.

5   *M Holoubek*, Grundrechtliche Gewährleistungspflichten (1997) 243 ff; *P Szczekalla*, Die sogenannten grundrechtlichen Schutzpflichten im deutschen und europäischen Recht (2002); *C Grabenwarter/K Pabel*, Europäische Menschenrechtskonvention (5th edn 2012) 124 ff and 138 ff; *C Johann* in: U Karpenstein/FC Mayer, EMRK, Kommentar (2012) 39 ff.

6   ECtHR *MC v Bulgaria*, 4.12.2003, no 39272/98.

7   ECtHR *Codarcea c Roumanie*, 2.6.2009, no 31675/04.

right of the individual to control the use of one's image and to protect from abuse of the picture by others.[8]

4 These duties may derive from all the fundamental rights enshrined in the ECHR, but the ECtHR acknowledges that there is a broad discretion of the State as to the choice of means by which the State complies with this duty.[9] It may choose between different means to guarantee the protection of such rights, such as protection by criminal or administrative law or tort law liability. These principles now also apply to the CFR which provides in art 52 (3) that the meaning and scope of the rights contained in the Charter which correspond to rights guaranteed by the ECHR shall be the same as those laid down by the Convention.

5 The ECHR and the CFR contain a comprehensive catalogue of fundamental rights that all aim at the protection of the personality of the individual person and cover such fundamental freedoms as right to life and bodily integrity, personal freedom or the right to property.[10] Several of these rights, however, are of special importance for the protection of the non-physical aspects of the person like human dignity, honour or privacy. The relevant articles are

- art 1 CFR which ensures the protection of human dignity,
- arts 7 and 8 CFR and art 8 ECHR which guarantee respect for private and family life and the protection of personal data,
- art 10 CFR and art 9 ECHR (freedom of thought, conscience and religion) and
- the freedom of expression enshrined in art 11 CFR and art 10 ECHR.

These guarantees on the substance are complemented by the procedural guarantees of art 47 CFR and arts 6 and 13 ECHR, the right to an effective remedy and to a fair trial.

The European States and the EU institutions must observe both the negative and the positive obligation deriving from human rights in all their acts. This

---

8   ECtHR *Schüssel v Austria*, 21.2.2002, no 42409/98; *von Hannover v Germany*, 24.6.2004, no 59320/00.

9   *Grabenwarter/Pabel* (fn 5) 131 ff; Karpenstein/Mayer/*Johann* (fn 5) 39 ff. See the decisions of the ECtHR in the cases *Stubbings and others v the United Kingdom*, 22.10.1996, nos 22083/93, 22095/93; *Calvelli and Ciglio v Italy* [GC], 17.1.2002, no 32967/96; *Vo v France* [GC], 8.7.2004, no 53924/00.

10   Right to life: art 2 CFR and art 2 ECHR; right to liberty and security: art 6 CFR and art 5 ECHR; right to property: art 17 CFR and art 1 of Protocol 1 ECHR.

applies to their legislative as well as executive power and, hence, also to the regulation and enforcement of the protection of personality rights.

6 Personality rights already enjoy rather comprehensive protection by the private law systems of the Member States. The fact that they are protected under human rights aspects gives them on the one hand some degree of persistence and on the other hand reduces the discretion of the States or the EU institutions when dealing with them. This is now expressly reflected by art 52 (1) CFR which requires that any limitations of fundamental rights must meet several conditions. First, they must be provided for by law; second, they must respect the essence of those rights; and third, they must comply with the principle of proportionality which requires that 'limitations may be made only if they are necessary and genuinely meet objectives of general interest recognised by the Union or the need to protect the rights and freedoms of others.' Especially the last requirement is of great importance for the protection of personality rights. When dealing with such issues the State must always seek a balance between the interests of the injured person on the one hand and of the tortfeasor on the other. While the State may not, for instance, unduly restrict the right of compensation for the victim, it must take care that the liability rules do not commit the tortfeasor to pay compensation sums that are completely out of proportion. Accordingly the ECtHR held in several cases concerning Ireland and the United Kingdom that the attribution of disproportionately high awards of damages by the national court to the claimant for libel may constitute an illegal interference with the tortfeasor's right to freedom of expression and consequently a breach of art 10 ECHR.[11]

III   Private Law Remedies for the Protection of Personality Rights

A   *Recognition of the Personality and Inalienability of Personality Rights*

7 The recognition and protection of the personality of the individual is a crucial goal of all European private law systems. All the national civil codes expressly

---

11   See ECtHR *Tolstoy Miloslavsky v the United Kingdom*, 13.7.1995, no 18139/91 and the discussion of this decision by *W Berka*, Human Rights and Tort Law, in: A Fenyves/E Karner/H Koziol/E Steiner (eds), Tort Law in the Jurisprudence of the European Court of Human Rights (2011) 280 ff. Further cases are ECtHR *Steel and Morris v the United Kingdom*, 15.2.2005, no 68416/01 and *Independent News and Media and Independent Newspapers Ireland Limited v Ireland*, 16.6.2005, no 55120/00.

state that the human being is vested with legal capacity from birth[12] and no civil law system in Europe would recognise contractual stipulations which allow for any form of slavery, forced labour or servitude which are expressly prohibited by art 4 ECHR and art 5 CFR.[13] An interesting provision in this regard is art 27 Swiss ZGB which provides in its first subsection that nobody may in whole or in part renounce his right to be a subject of legal rights and duties or the legal capacity to act and, in the second subsection, that nobody can divest himself of his freedom or restrict himself in the exercise of his freedom to an extent that violates the law or morality. Swiss courts derive from this rule that contractual stipulations which affect the core area of the personality are void and cannot be enforced by means of law. Comparable rules can be found in all the European civil law systems. Void are, for example, the testamentary disposition that the heir may only marry a spouse who belongs to a certain religious group or nation,[14] the contractual stipulation not to marry or to divorce,[15] the contractual stipulation between a couple not to have children,[16] the obligation for an actor to have sexual intercourse on stage,[17] the obligation to have an operation or to donate blood or an organ[18] or the conclusion of oppressive contracts.[19]

---

12   For instance: § 16 Austrian Civil Code (Allgemeines Bürgerliches Gesetzbuch, ABGB), art 16 French Code Civil, § 1 German Civil Code (Bürgerliches Gesetzbuch, BGB), art 11 Swiss Civil Code (Zivilgesetzbuch, ZGB).

13   § 16 of the Austrian ABGB expressly prohibits slavery and serfdom.

14   Austria: Oberster Gerichtshof (Supreme Court, OGH) 8 September 1926, SZ 8/251.

15   Austria: *H Krejci* in: P Rummel, Kommentar zum Allgemeinen bürgerlichen Gesetzbuch (2000) § 879 no 74; Germany: *R Sack/PS Fischinger* in: J von Staudinger, Kommentar zum Bürgerlichen Gesetzbuch (2011) § 138 no 629; Switzerland: *C Huguenin* in: Basler Kommentar Zivilgesetzbuch I Art 1–456 ZGB (2010) art 27 no 13; *P Gauch/WR Schluep* (eds), Schweizerisches Obligationenrecht: Allgemeiner Teil (6th edn 1995) no 660; France: art 6 Code Civil; *J Carbonnier*, Droit Civil II (2004) no 984; *M Ferid/HJ Sonnenberger*, Das Französische Zivilrecht 1/1 (2nd edn 1994) no 1 F 645; Common law: *GH Treitel*, The Law of Contract (13th edn 2011) 439 ff.

16   Austria: OGH 14 April 1994, Juristische Blätter (JBl) 1995, 46; Germany: Bundesgerichtshof (Federal Court of Justice, BGH) 17 April 1986, BGHZ (Decisions of the BGH in Civil Matters) 97, 372; Switzerland: *S Hotz* in: A Büchler/D Jakob, Kurzkommentar ZGB (2012) art 27 no 5.

17   Germany: BAG (Decisions of the Federal Labour Court) 1 April 1976, Neue Juristische Wochenschrift (NJW) 1976, 1958; *T Mayer-Maly* in: Münchener Kommentar zum Bürgerlichen Gesetzbuch (2012) § 138 BGB no 53.

18   Austria: Rummel/*Krejci* (fn 15) § 879 no 72.

19   Eg France: art 1780 Code Civil does not allow the conclusion of an infinite working commitment ('On ne peut engager ses services qu'à temps, ou pour une entreprise déterminée');

B   *Tort Law Remedies*

1   General Considerations

8 An important remedy for the violation of personality rights is tort law. Tort law serves two goals which are both important for the protection of personality rights. On the one hand it ensures that the victim gets compensated for the loss suffered. This compensatory function of tort law serves the fundamental goal of corrective justice. On the other hand tort law has a preventive effect on potential tortfeasors. By making the tortfeasor pay for the loss caused to third parties, tort law ensures that a potential tortfeasor, when deciding upon the setting of an act or engaging in an activity, takes the possible detrimental effects of the action on third parties into due account. The threat with liability shall induce the potential tortfeasor to abstain from an action if the potential cost of the action outweighs the expected benefit. This preventive function of tort law is stressed by the economic theory of law which sees the role of tort law primarily in the achievement of economic efficiency and as an instrument to maximise social welfare.

9 Prevention is also achieved by other legal instruments, especially by administrative and criminal law, which are commonly used for the protection of personality rights. The application of tort law, however, has two advantages over the employment of administrative and criminal law instruments. First, it provides for a very finely tuned system of prevention. The causality requirement connects the degree of the sanction (amount of the awarded damages) with the incurred damage and is thereby able to give rather precise deterrent signals to potential tortfeasors. Tort law has a much lower risk of over- or under-deterrence than administrative or criminal law and can thus achieve better economic efficiency especially in situations where the socially desirable conduct is not apparent enough to trigger administrative or criminal sanctions. Secondly, tort law is less dependent on the initiative of public authorities because the enforcement of the violation of a personality right lies in the hands of the injured person, who has a good incentive to act, and requires only a functioning court system to be effective.

2   National Tort Law Remedies

10 In Europe the development of the protection of personality rights through tort law has been rather inconsistent and is still a diverse field. Today all the

---

Switzerland: Bundesgerichtsentscheide (Decisions of the Suisse Federal Court, BGE) 23 May 1978, 104 II 108 p 118 (invalidity of a contract between a young singer and her manager which gave the manager the right to decide over all aspects of the singer's professional activities).

European states provide for tort law remedies for the violation of personality rights, but they do not cover every aspect of the personality and there are differences with respect to the types and extent of recoverable damages.

11 German law was originally rather reluctant to grant monetary compensation for the violation of personality rights. The protection of the personality was to a large extent submitted to criminal law.[20] Compensatory damages could only be obtained in connection between such criminal provisions and § 823 (2) BGB which provides for compensation for the breach of a statutory duty (*Schutzgesetzverletzung*). The German BGB itself only recognised the right to one's name (§ 12 BGB) and the right to sexual self-determination (§ 825 BGB). The right to one's image (§ 22 *Kunsturhebergesetz*)[21] was regulated outside the BGB. It was only after World War II when the courts, under the influence of the 1949 German Constitution (*Bonner Grundgesetz*), which declared in art 1 that human dignity is inviolable and that it is the duty of all public authority to protect and respect it, started to use tort law for the protection of personality rights in a more comprehensive way. Since the landmark decision of the BGH in the *Schacht* case in 1954,[22] German law recognises a general personality right as an 'other' right in the sense of § 823 (1) BGB and thus puts the infringement of the personality of a person on the same level as violations of life, body, health, freedom or property which are expressly mentioned in § 823 (1) BGB as rights protected by tort law. Today the protective scope of the general personality right is rather broad. It covers the protection of privacy, the right to one's image, name and likeness, the right to identity, the right of informational self-determination and the protection of dignity, honour and reputation.[23]

12 In Germany liability for the infringement of the general personality right is fault-based. It entitles the victim to compensation for pecuniary loss which covers compensation for bodily injury, loss of earnings and compensation for expenses incurred to prevent the damage, such as the cost of an advertisement in the media to rectify an incorrect statement by the tortfeasor.[24] In cases of

---

20   *G Wagner*, The Protection of Personality Rights against Invasions by Mass Media in Germany, in: H Koziol/A Warzilek (eds), Persönlichkeitsschutz gegenüber Massenmedien (2005) 137; *G Brüggemeier*, Protection of Personality Rights in the Law of Delict/Torts in Europe: Mapping out Paradigms, in: G Brüggemeier/A Colombi Ciacchi//P O'Callaghan, Personality Rights in European Tort Law (2010) 6 ff.

21   § 22 *Kunsturhebergesetz* was introduced as a legislative reaction to the famous *Bismarck* case of 1899 (Reichsgericht [RG] 28 December 1899, Decisions of the RG [RGZ] 45, 170).

22   BGH 25 May 1954, BGHZ 13, 334.

23   *Brüggemeier* (fn 20) 25.

24   *R Rixecker* in: Münchener Kommentar zum Bürgerlichen Gesetzbuch (hereinafter MünchKomm) (2012) Anhang § 12 no 232 ff.

commercial exploitation of the personality, eg the unauthorised use of a celebrity's name or image, the incurred damage may also be determined in an abstract way according to the licence fees in intellectual property law.[25] With the violation of personality rights special focus lies on the availability of non-pecuniary damages. In Germany damages for non-pecuniary loss, such as compensation for pain and suffering, are restricted to cases where the personality right was gravely infringed and where the detrimental effects of the infringement cannot be compensated otherwise. This rule was first established in two cases concerning the unauthorised use of photographs of private persons for the marketing of sexual stimulants: the *Herrenreiter*[26] and the *Ginseng*[27] cases in 1958 and 1961. The German BGH derives this rule directly from the right to human dignity and self-determination established by the German Constitution, setting aside § 253 BGB which allows compensation for non-pecuniary loss only for infringements of physical personality rights (injury to body, health, freedom or sexual self-determination) and in cases explicitly provided by law. German law does not accept punitive damages, but with respect to compensation for the violation of personality rights the deterrent effect of tort liability is of high importance. This was made explicit by the BGH in the *Caroline von Monaco* case[28] – the publication of a fictitious interview by a journal – where it found that a retraction alone is not sufficient when the attack is aimed at the very essence of the victim's personality. Given the contents of the publications, their distribution numbers, and the defendant's motives and degree of culpability, the infringement, according to the BGH, warrants the attribution of a considerable amount of money, because monetary compensation for an infringement of the general right of personality shall not only compensate for the incurred immaterial loss but must also serve the victim's satisfaction and the purpose of prevention. *Wagner*[29] rightly indicates that the comparatively huge compensation amount awarded to the plaintiff could also be explained as pecuniary compensation for the unauthorised exploitation of a patrimonial right of personality: the benefit of a famous name, image and personality.

13   French law has a long tradition in the protection of personality rights by civil law remedies. Like in Germany the development of the protection of personality

---

25   MünchKomm/*Rixecker* (fn 24) Anhang § 12 no 234.

26   BGH 14 February 1958, BGHZ 26, 349 (*Herrenreiter*).

27   BGH 19 September 1961, BGHZ 35, 363 (*Ginseng*).

28   BGH 15 November 1994, NJW 1995, 861. The total compensation sum attributed by the BGH and the OLG Hamburg (25 July 1996, NJW 1996, 280) amounted to DEM 140,000 (€ 71,580).

29   *Wagner* (fn 20) no 109.

rights is characterised by landmark decisions.[30] Since the *Rachel* case,[31] decided in 1858, French civil law started to recognise a person's image, name and likeness and the confidentiality of correspondence as exclusive rights protected by civil law. Violations entitle the victim to seizure, interdict and damages. Protection of the private life was first granted in the *Marlene Dietrich* case in 1955,[32] where the courts awarded the German actress *Marlene Dietrich* a considerable amount of money (FRF 1.2 million) as compensation for the unauthorised publication of a fictitious interview with the actress telling her memoirs in a French journal. When assessing the compensation amount the court considered the immaterial damage caused to the actress but also her pecuniary interest in the publication of her memoirs. In the *Philipe* case[33] in 1966, the *Cour de Cassation* granted injunctive relief in interlocutory proceedings to stop the publication of photographs of the young son of the French actor *Gérard Philipe*, illegally taken in a hospital, and the dissemination of information concerning his disease and details of his medical treatment. The courts ordered the seizure of copies of all newspapers and posters because of this 'intolerable intrusion into private life.' In 1970 the protection of private life was included in the *Code Civil*. The French legislature introduced a new art 9 into the *Code Civil*[34] which establishes that everyone has the right to respect for his private life and provides that, in addition to the adjudication of damages, the courts may prescribe any measures, such as sequestration, seizure and others, which are appropriate to prevent or put an end to an invasion of personal privacy. In case of emergency those measures may be provided for by interim order. This comprehensive protection of the private life was complemented by the introduction of the right to respect of the presumption of innocence into art 9–1 of the *Code Civil* in 1993.[35] Violations of this right entitle the victim to

---

30   *Brüggemeier* (fn 20) 10 ff.

31   Tribunal civil de la Seine, 16 June 1858, Dalloz (D) 1858, 3, 62 (*Félix v O'Connell*). Sketches of the photograph of a famous actress on her deathbed were commercially marketed without the consent of the family.

32   Cour d'appel de Paris, 16 March 1955, D 1955, 295 (*Marlene Dietrich v Société France-Dimanche Subsequent Developments*).

33   Cour de cassation, 12 July 1966, Droit des Sociétés (DS) 1967. 181 (*SARL France Editions et publication v Veuve Gérard Philipe*). For injunctive relief in interlocutory proceedings see also Paris civil court, 8 July 1965, Juris Classeur Périodique (JCP) 1965.ii. 14443 (*Rothschild v Peyrefitte et Editions Flammarion*).

34   Act no 70–643 of 17 July 1970.

35   Act no 93–2 of 4 January 1993.

damages and to rectification at the expense of the tortfeasor (art 9–1 para 2 *Code Civil*).[36]

14 Today French law provides for rather comprehensive protection of personality rights. The right to privacy according to art 9 *Code Civil* is a distinctive personality right and entitles the victim to compensation when he can show that his private life was invaded. Fault need not be shown and damage is presumed.[37] The same applies to the right to respect of the presumption of innocence under art 9–1 *Code Civil*. Both rights also include the protection from unwanted photographs if the taking or the circulation of the picture amounts to a violation of the respective right.[38] Apart from that the right to one's image, like the right to one's name and voice, is protected under the general tort law provision of art 1382 *Code Civil*. Compensation thus requires fault to be established. The same applies to the right to one's honour. Violations by the media are, however, exclusively regulated by the Act on Freedom of the Press 1881,[39] which sanctions – in criminal proceedings – only voluntary infringements of the honour of another person, in concreto defamation and insult, by the award of damages for the incurred immaterial harm and also provides for a right of reply.[40]

15 Attributable damages comprise monetary compensation for material and immaterial damage alike. In cases where the infringement concerns a celebrity the commercial value of the person's name or picture is taken into account for the assessment of the awarded damages, but there is no open skimming off of profits by the courts.[41] The assessment of non-pecuniary damage is left to the discretion of the court. When the plaintiff participated in his own injury, only nominal damages may be awarded. Although courts are sometimes ready to take the profit which the defendant derived from the tortious act into account when assessing damages, punitive damages are not available in French law.[42]

---

36   Act no 2000–516 of 15 June 2000.

37   *K Anterion/O Moréteau*, The Protection of Personality Rights against Invasions by Mass Media in France, in: H Koziol/A Warzilek (eds), Persönlichkeitsschutz gegenüber Massenmedien (2005) no 16.

38   *Anterion/Moréteau* (fn 37) nos 20, 22.

39   Act no 637–125 of 29 July 1881.

40   Art 29 ff of the Freedom of the Press Act; see *A Lucas-Schlötter* in: G Brüggemeier/A Colombi Ciacchi/P O'Callaghan, Personality Rights in European Tort Law (2010) 92 ff.

41   *Anterion/Moréteau* (fn 37) no 32; *Lucas-Schlötter* (fn 40) 389.

42   *Anterion/Moréteau* (fn 37) no 36 ff.

16 In English law the personality rights are protected by several torts.[43] Of special relevance are the tort of defamation and the tort of breach of confidence. English law does not provide for a distinctive tort for the protection of privacy, but courts, under the influence of art 8 ECHR, tend to use the law of breach of confidence to remedy the unauthorised disclosure of private information.[44] The tort of defamation, which was comprehensively reformed by the Defamation Act of 25 April 2013, sanctions harm to another person's reputation by publications in written or other permanent form (libel) or in transient form (slander). In order to be defamatory, a statement must cause or be likely to cause serious harm to the claimant's reputation or, if the claimant is an enterprise, serious financial loss (sec 1 Defamation Act 2013). This requirement aims to strike a balance between the right to freedom of expression, according to art 10 ECHR, and respect for private life under art 8 ECHR.[45] With respect to an action in defamation a number of special defences apply. The defendant may justify a defamatory statement by proving that it is substantially true or that it expresses an honest opinion[46] or the defendant may invoke a privilege as a defence, such as a statement in Parliament or in the course of judicial proceedings, or the defence of publication on a matter of public interest.[47] Another defence is the defence of innocent dissemination developed by common law and also provided by section 1 Defamation Act 1996, which can be pleaded by a non-culpable defendant who shows that he was not the author, editor or publisher of the defamatory statement.

17 Liability in defamation is strict, but a defendant may stop litigation by an offer of amends, which comprises the offer to make and publish a suitable correction and sufficient apology and to pay appropriate compensation either agreed by the parties or determined by the court (secs 2–4 Defamation Act 1996). The offer serves as a defence to defamation proceedings if the plaintiff cannot prove that the defendant had known or had reason to know that the statement referred to the plaintiff and that it was both false and defamatory of the plaintiff.[48]

---

43   Further applicable torts are malicious falsehood, trespass to the person and passing off. The following summary is based on *Brüggemeier* (fn 20) 25 ff; *WVH Rogers*, The Protection of Personality Rights against Invasions by Mass Media in England, in: H Koziol/A Warzilek (eds), Persönlichkeitsschutz gegenüber Massenmedien (2005) 59; *M Lunney/K Oliphant*, Tort Law: Text & Materials (5th edn 2013) 686 ff.

44   See *Rogers* (fn 43) no 62 ff; *Lunney/Oliphant* (fn 43) 771 ff.

45   *Lunney/Oliphant* (fn 43) 699.

46   Secs 2 and 3 Defamation Act 2013.

47   *Lunney/Oliphant* (fn 43) 729 ff.

48   Sec 4 (3) Defamation Act 1996.

18 The tort of defamation has been traditionally tried by a jury under the guidance of the court, a procedure unknown in the civil law systems, but sec 11 of
the Defamation Act 2013 now provides that trial shall be without a jury unless
the court orders otherwise. If there is a jury trial, the assessment of damages is
a matter for the jury, but can be reviewed by the Court of Appeal.

19 The successful plaintiff in a defamation action based on libel is entitled to recover compensatory damages. The attributed sum shall compensate him for
the damage to his reputation and hurt feelings and, if the defamatory statement relates to the plaintiff's business activities, also for general loss of business profits or specific economic loss. Compensation for libel thus covers both
the plaintiff's economic and non-economic loss without the need of further
specification. A claim in slander, however, requires proof of actual economic
loss, except where the defendant imputes to the claimant criminal conduct
punishable with imprisonment or unfitness in business.[49] The tort of defamation does not allow the skimming off of the profits from the tortfeasor,[50] but
exemplary (punitive) damages are commonly awarded. Punitive damages shall
punish the tortfeasor and deter him and others from wrongful behaviour.[51] In
cases where the defendant commits defamation in order to gain profits punitive damages serve a comparable purpose as the amount of damages can be
assessed on the basis of such profits.[52] Punitive damages can also be awarded
in case of breach of confidence. Like in defamation available damages cover
pecuniary and non-pecuniary loss as well.[53]

C *Other Remedies*

1   Injunction and Removal of Interference (Reparative Injunction)

20 German law allows for injunctive relief for the infringement of the personality
right. This is not explicitly provided in the BGB, but was gained by the courts
by way of analogy to specific rules providing for injunctive relief in case of the
violation of the right to one's name in § 12 BGB and in case of interference with

---

49   The other two cases, imputation of certain contagious diseases and imputation of un-
chastity against a woman, were abolished by sec 14 Defamation Act 2013.

50   *G Howells/P Rott* in: G Brüggemeier/A Colombi Ciacchi/P O'Callaghan (eds), Personality
Rights in European Tort Law (2010) 385 f.

51   For a comprehensive review see *Law Commission*, Aggravated, Exemplary and Restitutionary Damages (Law Com No 247, 1997). See further sec 34 ff Crime and Courts Act 2013,
note in *Lunney/Oliphant* (fn 43) 752, 851.

52   See *Rogers* (fn 43) no 54.

53   *Rogers* (fn 43) no 82.

possession (§ 862 BGB) or ownership (§ 1004 BGB).[54] Injunctive relief requires unlawfulness of the interference, but fault need not be established.

21 An injunction is available if the infringement has already occurred and there is danger of repetition of the infringement which is presumed. This presumption can be rebutted, but usually courts will require the defendant to deliver a declaration of discontinuance supported by a penalty clause (*strafbewehrte Unterlassungserklärung*). Injunctive relief is further awarded if the infringement has not yet occurred, but if there is immediate danger that the personality right will be infringed (preventive injunction).[55] An interim injunction may also be available.

22 Moreover, the claimant may also seek a reparative injunction in order to eliminate the violation of the personality right.[56] Dependent on the type of infringement the claimant may require the correction of a defamatory statement (*Widerruf*), the destruction of pictures unlawfully taken or published, or the removal of a false signature on an artwork or the deletion of a tape recording or of electronic data.[57] The legal basis for a reparative injunction is the same as for a standard injunction. It requires unlawfulness of the interference but not the establishment of fault.

23 French law is also very open in this respect. Article 9 (2) *Code Civil* entitles the court to 'prescribe any measures, such as sequestration, seizure and others, which are appropriate to prevent or put an end to an invasion of personal privacy.' This includes the right to an injunction and the right of removal, eg the destruction of an illegally obtained photograph. In case of emergency those measures may be provided for by interim order (art 9 Civil Code, art 809 Code of Civil Procedure).

24 English law provides for the legal devices of interim injunction to prevent the tortfeasor from going ahead until full trial of the case and of permanent injunction. For breach of confidence which evolved from the law of equity it is in the discretion of the court whether an injunction is awarded and the court will refuse it if damages are adequate.[58] For interim injunctive relief in civil proceedings to restrain the publication of information the Master of the Rolls issued Practice Guidance for Interim Non-Disclosure Orders[59] which sets out

---

54 MünchKomm/*Rixecker* (fn 24) Anhang § 12 no 214.

55 MünchKomm/*Rixecker* (fn 24) Anhang § 12 no 215 f.

56 MünchKomm/*Rixecker* (fn 24) Anhang § 12 no 219 ff.

57 MünchKomm/*Rixecker* (fn 24) Anhang § 12 no 220 f.

58 *Rogers* (fn 43) no 83.

59 [2012] 1 Weekly Law Reports (WLR) 1003. This guidance came into effect on 1 August 2011.

the process recommended to be followed in the conduct of such cases by applicants and courts. In defamation cases an interim injunction is only granted if the case is clear.[60] Although the defendant is given some procedural incentive by the law to make a correction or an apology in order to avoid or mitigate impending sanctions, he cannot be forced by way of court order to do so.[61]

2   Reimbursement of Unjustified Enrichment

25 German law allows for a claim in restitution if somebody exploits the legally protected interest of another (§ 812 BGB). The claim, which is irrespective of fault, requires that the protected interest has an economic value and that the plaintiff was entitled to dispose of the interest in a legal way. The infringement of a personality right that is not marketable, because it would be illegal or against *bonos mores* to do so, can only entitle the victim to immaterial damages.[62] Case law, however, requires for the award of restitutionary damages that the plaintiff would have consented to the contested interference if he had been asked. This ruling, which goes back to the *Herrenreiter* case,[63] is criticised in legal doctrine with the convincing argument that the right to restitution should not remunerate the holder of the personality right for the fictitious disposition of the right but compensate the plaintiff for the illegal infringement of the right[64] and was revised by the BGH in one of its recent decisions.[65]

26 An action in restitution entitles the plaintiff to claim that the defendant returns the benefits he gained from the interference. This usually amounts to a hypothetical licence fee, which consists of the amount of money the defendant would have been obliged to pay if he had sought the plaintiff's consent beforehand.[66] A claim in unjust enrichment does not comprise the right to claim the defendant's profits. Such a claim, however, can be based on the rules on *negotiorum gestio* according to § 687 (2) BGB. In German law restitution under the law of unjust enrichment or *negotiorum gestio* and compensatory damages under tort law are not exclusive remedies. It is thus up to the claimant to choose the most appropriate remedy for the infringement of his personality right.[67]

---

60   *Lunney/Oliphant* (fn 43) 762 with reference to *Coulson v Coulson* (1887) 3 Times Law Reports (TLR) 846 and *Kaye v Robertson* [1991] Fleet Street Reports (FSR) 62.
61   *Rogers* (fn 43) no 47.
62   See MünchKomm/*Rixecker* (fn 24) Anhang § 12 no 250.
63   BGH 14 February 1958, BGHZ 26, 349.
64   See MünchKomm/*Rixecker* (fn 24) Anhang § 12 no 250.
65   BGH 26 October 2006, BGHZ 169, 340 (*Lafontaine*).
66   MünchKomm/*Rixecker* (fn 24) Anhang § 12 no 250.
67   *Wagner* (fn 20) no 113 ff.

27 This is different in French law. French law allows for claims for the restitution of gains achieved by the violation of a personality right under art 1371 *Code Civil*, but this is a subsidiary device which can only be employed if no other cause of action is available.[68]

28 English law does not have a general rule on restitution for unjust enrichment. Stripping away the gains made by a wrongdoer is well recognised for proprietary torts, such as conversion, nuisance, trespass to goods and trespass to land as well as for violations of intellectual property rights. The applicable remedies comprise an action for 'money had and received,' an 'account of profits' and restitutionary damages.[69] With respect to non-proprietary torts, the availability of such remedies varies. While not available under the tort of defamation, the right to restitution is generally applicable to cases of breach of confidence.[70] *Rogers*,[71] however, rightly indicates that this distinction cannot be upheld in cases where breach of confidence concerns the violation of privacy rather than the breach of trade secrets, which are the traditional cases tried under breach of confidence.

IV   Conclusions

29 In Europe the personality rights of the individual are well protected. Although the national private law systems have always granted some protection of the non-bodily aspects of the personality, especially the protection of one's name or honour, it was under the influence of the diverse catalogues for the protection of human rights, first and foremost the European Convention on Human Rights and Fundamental Freedoms of the Council of Europe, that the national private law systems developed the comprehensive protection we now enjoy. Private law remedies for the protection of personality rights comprise (1) the attribution of damages under tort law, (2) injunctive relief in order to prevent an imminent infringement of a personality right or to stop the tortfeasor from committing further infringements and (3) various methods to skim off the profits which the tortfeasor gained from the infringement. The particulars of these remedies, however, vary to a large extent. Examples for such differences are the

---

68   *Anterion/Moréteau* (fn 37) no 39. Art 1371 Code Civil was replaced by art 1300 Code Civil (in force since 1 October 2016).

69   *Law Commission*, Aggravated, Exemplary and Restitutionary Damages (Law Com No 247, 1997) Part III 1.3.

70   *Law Commission*, Aggravated, Exemplary and Restitutionary Damages (Law Com No 247, 1997) Part III 1.30 ff.

71   *Rogers* (fn 43) no 82.

requirement of fault for an action in tort which is the tradition in German, but not in French and English law, the restrictive stance on the award of damages for immaterial loss in German law which is probably incomprehensible for a French or English lawyer, the award of punitive damages and the trial by a jury in English law which is totally alien to the civil law, or the sophisticated system and interplay between tort law and the law of unjust enrichment in German law which is not known in French and English law.

CHAPTER 4

Human Rights and the Protection of Personality Rights in Europe: Comparative Reflections

Ernst Karner

I Comparative Survey

1 Today, the protection of personality rights is by a common European principle, which is, however, put into effect in quite different ways. For more than 200 years – since 1811 – the Austrian provision of § 16 of the General Civil Code (*Allgemeines Bürgerliches Gesetzbuch*, ABGB) states: '*Every person has inherent rights, which are evident by nature.*' This very provision is anything but a pure declaration as some and even famous Austrian scholars in the 19th century had taught.[1] Quite the contrary – § 16 ABGB is a legal rule of paramount importance for Austrian law.[2] Nonetheless, the Austrian Supreme Court recognized the *general personality right* enshrined in § 16 ABGB for the first time as late as 1978.[3] Astonishingly enough, it took almost 170 years to bring § 16 ABGB to life and to awake this crucial provision from a deep sleep.

2 Another path was taken by the French *Code civil* from 1804, which is the second codification from the age of the so-called natural law still in force today. Contrary to the Austrian Civil Code (ABGB), the French *Code civil* does not include a general rule for the protection of personality rights. However, relatively quickly, French doctrine managed to deduce from art 1382 *Code civil* – a provision according to which every culpable action resulting in harm leads to damages – a comprehensive protection of *single personality rights* including compensation for non-pecuniary loss.[4] On this basis a right to one's image was

---

1 *J Unger*, System des österreichischen allgemeinen Privatrechts I (1856) 71 fn 16.

2 *J Aicher* in: P Rummel (ed), ABGB (3rd edn 2000) § 16 no 3 with further references.

3 Austrian Supreme Court (Oberster Gerichtshof, OGH) 4 Ob 91/78 = SZ 51/146 = Recht der Arbeit (RdA) 1979/24 with cmt by *R Reischauer* = Zeitschrift für Arbeitsrecht und Sozialrecht (ZAS) 1979/24 with cmt by *F Marhold*.

4 See *K Martin*, Das allgemeine Persönlichkeitsrecht in seiner historischen Entwicklung (2007) 122 ff; *G Brüggemeier*, Haftungsrecht: Struktur, Prinzipien, Schutzbereich. Ein Beitrag zur Europäisierung des Privatrechts (2006) 272 ff, 298.

recognized in the famous *Rachel* case as early as 1858: the proliferation of the picture of the once famous actress *Rachel* lying on her deathbed, which was undertaken without prior agreement, was thus forbidden and the surviving dependants were granted damages;[5] also, an early example of a post-mortal protection of personality rights.

3 In the quite similar *Bismarck* case, the German Court of the Reich (*Reichsgericht*) had, by contrast, to refer to *trespass*, specifically to an invasion of one's home. This was the only way to justify the destruction of illegally taken photographs of the deceased Chancellor of the Reich.[6] Likewise, the protection of personality rights was left untackled in the deliberations over the German Civil Code (*Bürgerliches Gesetzbuch*, BGB). As a consequence, the German *Reichsgericht* stated as late as 1908: '*The civil law in force today does not recognize a general subjective personality right.*'[7] It was not until the midst of the 20th century that a remarkable change of court practice took place: referring to arts 1 and 2 of the German Constitution (*Grundgesetz*), which enshrines human dignity and free development of the personality, the German Federal Supreme Court (*Bundesgerichtshof*, BGH) developed a *general personality right* (*allgemeines Persönlichkeitsrecht*).[8] Since the famous *Herrenreiter* decision from 1958, damages include compensation for non-pecuniary loss if the infringement of personality is severe.[9]

4 With this change of court practice German law achieved the level of protection provided for by Swiss law. Like the modern German law, Swiss law recognizes a general personality right. Furthermore, damages for non-pecuniary loss, which are called *Genugtuung für die erlittene Unbill,* are granted according to art 49 of the Swiss Law of Obligations (*Obligationenrecht*, OR) in case of a severe infringement of one's personality. The solution provided by Swiss law was adopted by the Greek Civil Code.[10] German jurisprudence in turn influenced the Portuguese *Código civil* and Italian court practice.[11] All in all these transnational interactions serve as a beautiful example of a *spontaneous*

---

5   Tribunal Civil Seine, 16 June 1858, Dalloz 1858, 3, 62.

6   Court of the Reich (Reichsgericht, RG) in RGZ (Decisions of the RG in Civil Matters) 45, 170; *Brüggemeier* (fn 4) 297 f.

7   RG in RGZ 69, 401, 403 (*Nietzsche*-letters).

8   Federal Supreme Court (Bundesgerichtshof, BGH) in BGHZ (Decisions of the BGH in Civil Matters) 13, 334, 338.

9   BGH in BGHZ 26, 349.

10   *PJ Zepos*, Der Schutz der Persönlichkeit nach dem griechischen Zivilgesetzbuch, FS von Caemmerer (1978) 1139 ff.

11   See *C von Bar*, Gemeineuropäisches Deliktsrecht I (1996) no 23, 586 f and II (1999) no 81.

harmonization of law which is based on the power of arguments only and is thus so convincing.[12]

5   As we have seen, the continental European jurisdictions take their starting point either – like Germany or Switzerland – from a *general personality right* or – like France or the Scandinavian countries[13] – from different *single personality rights*. The legal situation in England is – as may be expected of an island – totally different.

6   Contrary to continental European jurisdictions English law does not concentrate on the protected interests – a general or a single personality right – but on the *act of violation* itself.[14] Therefore, it is decisive if a specific *tort*, i.e. an individual tortious case scenario, is applicable, for example *libel* and *slander* or *breach of confidence*. However, such a concept of individual case scenarios, which focuses on the act of violation, leads, at least to some extent, to a patchwork system and easily creates inconsistencies and legal loopholes. It is therefore not astonishing that an English court still stated in 1991 quite laconically in *Kaye v Robertson*: '*It is well known that in English law there is no right to privacy.*'[15]

7   Not until the Human Rights Act 1998, which implemented the European Convention on Human Rights (ECHR) in English law, did a fundamental change take place also in England.[16] The famous *Mosley v News Group Newspapers* case may illustrate this.[17] As is well known, the former president of the International Automobile Federation (*Fédération Internationale de l'Automobile*, FIA)

---

12   For the difference between a 'spontaneous' and 'planned' harmonization of law see *H Dölle*, Gezielte und gewachsene Rechtsvereinheitlichung, Zeitschrift für Rechtsvergleichung, Internationales Privatrecht und Europarecht (ZfRV) 1963, 133 ff.

13   *Von Bar*, Gemeineuropäisches Deliktsrecht II no 81 fn 508 with further references.

14   See *Hans Stoll*, Haftungsfolgen im bürgerlichen Recht (1993) 364 f; *von Bar* (fn 11) Deliktsrecht I no 271 ff. Specifically on the protection of privacy *U Amelung*, Der Schutz der Privatheit im Zivilrecht (2002) 104 ff.

15   *Kaye v Robertson* [1991] Fleet Street Reports (FSR) 62 (CA). Quite different the development in the US-American law, where *S Warren* and *L Brandeis* announced a '*right to be left alone*' in their most influential paper, The Right of Privacy (1890) 4 Harvard Law Review 193 as early as 1890. On this *Amelung* (fn 14) 47 ff.

16   See *Amelung* (fn 14) 129 ff; *W Berger*, Die Bedeutung der Europäischen Menschenrechtskonvention für die Europäisierung des Privatrechts – Am Beispiel des Persönlichkeitsschutzes vor der Veröffentlichung privater Tatsachen, ZfRV 2006, 107 ff; *M Lunney/K Oliphant*, Tort Law (5th edn 2013) 28 ff.

17   *Mosley v News Group Newspapers* [2008] England & Wales High Court (EWHC) 1777 (Queen's Bench, QB).

Max Mosley was surreptitiously filmed in a very compromising situation. The film was then passed on to the media and circulated globally. With reference to art 8 ECHR (*Right to respect for private and family life*) Mosley was awarded £ 60,000, at that time the highest amount of damages ever for an '*invasion of privacy*.'

II   Protection of Personality Rights in Systematic Perspective

A   *General Personality Right or Single Personality Rights?*

8 As the comparative survey has shown, the civil protection of personality rights in Europe features *three quite distinctive lines of development*.[18] Whereas the continental European jurisdictions focus partly on a general personality right, partly on a number of different single personality rights, English law pays greater attention to the act of violation itself and hence concentrates on individual case scenarios.

9 As an example for the continental European discussion, one might refer to § 16 ABGB[19] as it was always controversial if this provision enshrines a general personality right,[20] or rather serves as a basis for the development of several single personality rights.[21]

10 A couple of reasons can be given for the acknowledgement of a general personality right:[22] the need for a comprehensive protection of the personality is highlighted, the danger of loopholes and inconsistencies is diminished and such a general right is open for further development. Then again, one has to be aware that the different aspects of personality deserve a different level of protection, which is easily demonstrated by a comparison between the right to life on the one hand and the right to one's own image on the other. Furthermore some areas enjoy no protection at all: for example, the mere infliction of annoyance can neither be averted legally nor result in damages. Finally, it has to be taken into consideration that a whole set of specific and sharply defined

---

18   See *Brüggemeier* (fn 4) 264 ff.

19   For a comparative survey see *G Lazarakos*, Gemeinsame europäische Prinzipien zum Schutz des allgemeinen Persönlichkeitsrechts am Beispiel Deutschlands, Österreichs, Griechenlands und Großbritanniens, ZfRV 2002, 1 ff and *E Ondreasova*, Personality Rights in Different European Legal Systems: Privacy, Dignity, Honour and Reputation, in this volume.

20   See eg Rummel/*Aicher* (fn 2) § 16 no 14 with further references.

21   See eg *H Koziol*, Österreichisches Haftpflichtrecht II (2nd edn 1984) 6.

22   On the following *E Karner/H Koziol*, Der Ersatz ideellen Schadens im österreichischen Recht und seine Reform, Gutachten für den 15. ÖJT (2003) II/1, 33 ff.

personality rights has already been developed, particularly the right to life, to health, to freedom or to one's own name. These rights enjoy a comparatively comprehensive protection; an infringement of such legal positions thus indicates the wrongfulness of the violation.

11 The debate over the legal nature of personality rights cannot be carried further in the given context and it is not even necessary to do so, because it is commonly acknowledged that the difference between the various starting points is of quite limited practical impact.[23] The doctrine of a general personality right highlights the comprehensive protection of the personality, nevertheless it is always necessary to consider if, and under which conditions, the single aspects of personality enjoy protection. The doctrine of single personality rights, on the other hand, has always to consider if a protected right was violated and to which extent the given right is worth protection. The doctrine of single personality rights hence rightly stresses the fact that personality interests are manifold and diverse and can therefore all not be treated in the same way and tarred with the same brush.

12 The best way to solve the debate therefore seems to follow the approach of *Canaris*:[24] the crucial point is to work out and formulate the quite *different areas of protection*.

B   *Different Areas of Protection*

13 According to the general rules, the scope of protection depends – as *Koziol* has convincingly pointed out – on several criteria: of particular importance is whether a legal position is sharply defined as well as evident and which rank a lawful position is bestowed by the legal system.[25] Those legal positions which concern the core area of personality – such as life, physical integrity and liberty – are sharply defined, evident and take the top positions in the legal hierarchy. Consequently, these rights enjoy a very extensive legal protection and belong to the absolute rights. Due to the comprehensive protection of these legal positions, any infringement might generally be considered illegal: the violation of the right indicates the wrongfulness of the act.

14 The right to one's own image and to one's own word, the right to privacy as well as the right to one's honour are, by way of contrast, considerably less sharply

---

23   Cf Rummel/*Aicher* (fn 2) § 16 no 14; *W Posch* in M Schwimann (ed), ABGB (4th edn 2011) § 16 no 13 f; *BC Steininger*, The Protection of Personality Rights in Comparative Perspective: Basic Questions no 4 ff, in this volume.

24   *C-W Canaris*, Grundprobleme des privatrechtlichen Persönlichkeitsschutzes, Juristische Blätter (JBl) 1991, 210.

25   See in detail *H Koziol*, Österreichisches Haftpflichtrecht I (3rd edn 1997) no 4/24 ff.

defined, to a lesser extent evident and of lesser rank and value than the core personality rights. Consequently, the protection of such rights is distinctly weaker: such rights do not enjoy comprehensive protection, and hence mere interference does not indicate the illegality of the act. On the contrary, such legal positions are only protected against *rather specific conduct and behaviour.* To find out if a violation is illegal, a comprehensive weighing of interests is therefore necessary and also conflicting personality rights have to be taken into consideration: for example, the right to one's honour or privacy has to be balanced with the freedom of speech.

15 As we have seen, one has to differentiate between areas of personality which are protected with reference to a specific legal right and such areas which are merely protected with reference to a rather specific behaviour.[26] Despite these differences, a general provision like § 16 ABGB seems very useful: due to the inclusion of all personality spheres, such a comprehensive clause helps to prevent legal loopholes and supports a thorough level of protection even in regard of newly emerging personality interests.

16 Only the dogmatic analysis brings light to the comparative report: one should not follow one of the different solutions found in the surveyed countries – Germany, France or England – exclusively. Instead the appropriate content of each of the diverging concepts should be combined. Only in this way will the harmonization of law not result in a loss, but in a rise in the legal standard.

III   The Influence of Human Rights

A   *Basics*

17 If one turns the focus to the influence of human rights on the protection of the personality, it seems useful to cast a glance once again at § 16 ABGB. Much less attention is paid to the second sentence of this provision: *'Slavery and serfdom are not permitted in these countries'*[27] than to the first sentence regarding *'inherent rights.'* At first glance the Austrian Civil Code confounds two quite different issues: on the one hand *personality rights*, which have to be observed by everybody and which belong to the civil law; on the other hand *constitutional rights*, which are designed to protect citizens against the State.[28] The

---

26   See *Koziol* (fn 25) no 4/23.

27   Cf *G Wielinger*, Spezifika des Menschenrechtsschutzes, Öffentliche Sicherheit (ÖffS) 9–10/2012, 71 f.

28   Cf on this *F-S Meissel*, Verfassungsrechtliche Aspekte des § 16 ABGB, FS Mayer (2011) 371 ff.

preliminary draft of the ABGB, drawn by *Martini*, contained a whole set of such fundamental rights.

18 This mixture was certainly the reason why *Martini's* concept met with such opposition at the final stage of the codification – due to the Napoleonic Wars a time of great external danger. Some therefore fiercely argued that '*all such stuff like human rights and inherent civil liberty*' should be eliminated thoroughly from the Code. Consequently, *Martini's* concept was only partly accepted by *Zeiller*, the main editor of the ABGB. The crucial core, however, § 16 ABGB remained and is even today an important gateway for the implementation of significant fundamental rights positions in private law. Also in this respect – the *interdependence of constitutional and personality rights* – is the Austrian ABGB surprisingly up to date.

19 As is commonly acknowledged, constitutional rights have no direct, but an *indirect effect* (*mittelbare Drittwirkung*) on private law: such fundamental rights have to be taken into consideration while interpreting rather vague general clauses like § 16 ABGB. The same is true in regard of the human rights enshrined in the European Convention on Human Rights. Quite rightly, as early as 1978 the Austrian Supreme Court referred to art 8 of the European Convention to develop a *right to secrecy* enshrined in § 16 ABGB.[29] With this reference the Supreme Court also recognized the indirect effect of fundamental rights on private law.

20 In respect of the Convention, one has to bear in mind that also *positive obligations* (*obligations positive*) of the State are deduced from the human rights.[30] The State is therefore under an obligation to protect citizens against assaults by other citizens.[31]

B *The Influence of the European Convention on Human Rights*

1 Starting Point

21 What are the substantial influences of the European Convention on Human Rights on the civil protection of personality rights? To organize the topic, influences on Austrian law and influences which are relevant for the harmonization of law as such can be distinguished. To start with, let us turn now to Austrian law.

---

29 OGH 4 Ob 91/78 = SZ 51/146 = RdA 1979/24 with cmt by *R Reischauer* = ZAS 1979/24 with cmt by *F Marhold*.

30 See *M Hinteregger*, The Protection of Personality Rights in Private Law: Remedies, in this volume.

31 *C Grabenwarter/K Pabel*, Europäische Menschenrechtskonvention (5th edn 2012) § 19 no 1 ff.

2   Influence on Austrian Law

22 From all the provisions of the European Convention on Human Rights, art 5
ECHR (*Right to liberty and security*) has had the greatest influence on Austrian
civil law. For a long time the Austrian Supreme Court held the very restrictive
opinion that damages for non-pecuniary loss have only to be granted if the law
expressly states so. This restrictive line of argumentation was even confirmed
in cases of *false imprisonment*. After the Second World War, the Austrian Supreme Court consequently rejected damages for non-pecuniary loss even to
victims who were incarcerated in concentration camps or by the Gestapo, i.e.
the German Secret Police: the applicable provision, § 1329 ABGB, would not
allow compensation of non-pecuniary loss because it did not enshrine such
damages expressly.[32] It was not until 1975 that the Supreme Court took art 5
subsec 5 ECHR into account and changed its restrictive standpoint: if a citizen
is falsely imprisoned by the State, this is a case of strict liability and damages
include full compensation of non-pecuniary loss.[33] If the tortfeasor is a citizen,
the victim has a claim at least in case of gross negligence, which is justified by
the Supreme Court with reference to art 5 ECHR, which gives direction to the
interpretation of the Civil Code, namely the applicable § 1329 ABGB.[34]

3   The European Court of Human Rights as a Driving Force behind
           Legal Harmonization

23 If one reflects upon the impact of the European Convention on Human Rights
on the harmonization of law as such, the practice of the European Court of Human Rights (ECtHR) is naturally of key importance. The ECtHR interprets the
Convention in a *dynamic and evolutionary way* and considers the Convention
to be '*a living instrument, which must be interpreted in the light of present day
conditions.*'[35] In the context of autonomous interpretation of the Convention,
the Court conducts an *evaluative comparison of laws* and looks for the common
denominator in all the different jurisdictions, i.e. the '*European standard.*'[36]
Naturally, the rapid increase in member States of the Convention makes it increasingly harder to find such a common European standard. Moreover, the
question arises, is it really necessary that the same rules apply in the whole of

---

32   OGH in Evidenzblatt (EvBl) 1950/414; JBl 1951, 377 with cmt by *H Klang*; JBl 1952, 465 with
      cmt by *H Klang*.
33   OGH in SZ 48/69 = JBl 1975, 645 with cmt by *R Strasser* = EvBl 1976/30.
34   OGH in SZ 52/28 = JBl 1980, 372 with cmt by *H Koziol* = EvBl 1979/100 = Das Recht der Ar-
      beit (DRdA) 1980, 387 with cmt by *P Apathy*.
35   On this *Grabenwarter/Pabel* (fn 31) § 5 no 12 ff.
36   See *Grabenwarter/Pabel* (fn 31) § 5 no 9 ff.

Europe from Reykjavik to Vladivostok?[37] Be that as it may, it is certainly not wrong to acknowledge that the ECtHR sets important precedents.

24 This is exemplified by the fundamental decision *Caroline of Hannover v Germany*, which is a case concerning the conflict between the rights under art 8 ECHR (*right to respect for private and family life*), on the one hand, and art 10 ECHR (*freedom of expression*), on the other.[38] The subject of the trial was photographs of the Monegasque princess *Caroline*, which were taken by *paparazzi* without consent. In the photos one could see *Caroline* riding, shopping and performing other quite ordinary tasks. The German Constitutional Court (*Bundesverfassungsgericht*) considered these pictures lawful because even entertainment should, at least in principle, be protected by the right to freedom of speech.[39] The ECtHR issued a distinctly different opinion and found that the photos constituted a violation of art 8 ECHR.[40]

25 Many lawyers were taken by surprise and the decision aroused a certain amount of criticism:[41] It was pointed out that the Court itself stressed the wide *margin of appreciation* that exists as far as positive obligations of the State are at stake, which was indeed the case in *Caroline*. This argument has some merit as the level of protection accorded to the right to one's own picture ranges quite widely in the various European jurisdictions: in France this protection is very strong, in England quite weak, Germany occupies the middle ground.

26 However, what crucial arguments were the basis for the Court's decision? The European Court differentiates between *information*, which helps to form a public opinion, and pure *entertainment* about people with no official function. Pictures, which are only destined to satisfy the curiosity of the public and to serve the commercial interests of newspapers therefore enjoy only limited protection under freedom of speech. Ultimately, this reasoning seems

---

37   *R Rebhahn*, Zivilrecht und Europäische Menschenrechtskonvention, Archiv für die civilistische Praxis (AcP) 210 (2010) 552.

38   In detail *A Heldrich*, Persönlichkeitsschutz und Pressefreiheit nach der Europäischen Menschenrechtskonvention, in: H Koziol/A Warzilek (eds), Persönlichkeitsschutz gegenüber Massenmedien (2005) 479 ff.

39   Constitutional Court (Bundesverfassungsgericht, BVerfG) in Neue Juristische Wochenschrift (NJW) 2000, 1021 ff.

40   ECtHR *Von Hannover v Deuschland*, 24.6.2004, no 59320/00 = Europäische Grundrechte-Zeitschrift (EuGRZ) 2004, 404.

41   In detail *C Grabenwarter*, Schutz der Privatsphäre versus Pressefreiheit: Europäische Korrektur eines deutschen Sonderweges? Archiv für Presserecht (AfP) 2004, 309 ff; *idem*, Medienfreiheit und Bildnisschutz nach der Menschenrechtskonvention, FS Ress (2005) 979 ff.

quite sensible. The Austrian Supreme Court, by the way, followed this line of argumentation.[42]

27 By contrast, the case law of the European Court regarding insults, especially in a political context, raises some concerns. The Court has held that freedom of expression (art 10 ECHR) even justifies calling a Federal Chancellor '*undignified*' and '*immoral*'[43] or using such a harsh expression as '*idiot*' to refer to a politician.[44] It is certainly true that torts such as libel and slander can be misused to silence critics. For the benefit of the State, such torts should therefore be interpreted narrowly, at least as a rule.[45] However, one also has to take into consideration that freedom of speech only requires the right to express one's own opinion freely and openly, but not the right to do this in the most offensive way possible. Offensive expressions can, therefore, only be justified in this respect if they are really unavoidable in order to express one's own opinion.[46]

IV   Legal Consequences of a Violation of Personality Rights[47]

28 If a personality right is illegally endangered, the person at risk can ask for *injunctive relief,* which does not require faulty behaviour on the part of the defendant. In case of an ongoing infringement, the plaintiff has a *claim for removal,* which aims at the removal of the source of disruption. Like the injunction relief, the claim for removal only requires an illegal action, whereas faulty behaviour of the defendant is not a prerequisite of such a claim. The plaintiff could, for example, ask for a revocation of false allegations or the destruction of photographs which were secretly taken and are an infringement of the right to privacy.

29 Furthermore, all jurisdictions allow damages for *pecuniary loss* if the requirements for a tortious claim are met. However, in case of a violation of personality rights, damages for *non-pecuniary loss* are even more important for two reasons. Firstly, the harm done relates to the very core of personality and is thus

---

42   See OGH 4 Ob 121/08k; 4 Ob 165/08f et al.

43   ECtHR *Lingens v Austria*, 8.7.1986, Serie A 103 (1986) 11, 26 = EuGRZ 1986, 424.

44   ECtHR *Oberschlick v Austria* (*No 2*), 1.7.1997, no 20834/92.

45   See *JA Frowein* in: JA Frowein/W Peukert, EMRK (3rd edn 2009) art 10 no 30.

46   See *Koziol*, Der Schutz der Persönlichkeitsrechte gegenüber Massenmedien: Zusammenfassung und Ausblick, in: H Koziol/A Warzilek (eds), Persönlichkeitsschutz gegenüber Massenmedien (2005) 666 f.

47   See also the detailed report of *Hinteregger* (fn 30) in this volume.

especially damaging. Secondly, one has to bear in mind that the infringement of personality would in many cases remain without any legal consequences if the non-pecuniary damage was not compensable:[48] It is quite often too late for injunctive relief and also the prerequisites for a claim for removal or for damages for pecuniary loss are frequently not met. Consequently, the compensation of non-pecuniary losses is nothing less than a litmus test of whether a jurisdiction is prepared to protect personality rights duly and properly or not.[49]

30 German as well as Swiss law can serve as a model in this respect. In case of a severe violation of personality rights, non-pecuniary loss also has to be compensated. The Austrian ABGB has provided a similar rule since 1811: pursuant to §§ 1323, 1324 ABGB, damages for non-pecuniary loss (*Tilgung der erlittenen Beleidigung*) are due if the tortfeasor has acted with gross negligence.[50]

31 In this context it is important to bear in mind that tort law primarily has the function of compensating the victim for their harm and not of punishing the tortfeasor, which is true also in respect of non-pecuniary losses. Consequently, and with good reason, most European jurisdictions do not grant punitive damages.[51] As *Franz Bydlinski* has convincingly pointed out, punishment contravenes the fundamental principle that, under private law, legal consequences need mutual justification (*Prinzip der zweiseitigen Rechtfertigung*).[52] Hence, there should not only be justification as to why one person is awarded a favourable legal position while a disadvantageous legal consequence is imposed on another person, but also a further justification must be given to explain why this arrangement affects exactly these two persons. In other words, there must be good reason why one person obtains rights against precisely this one particular other person and, vice versa, why the other person is under an obligation to precisely this obligee. Applying this principle to the issue of punitive

---

48   *Canaris*, JBl 1991, 220; *F Bydlinski*, Der immaterielle Schaden in der österreichischen Rechtsentwicklung, FS von Caemmerer (1978) 785; *F Bydlinski*, System und Prinzipien des Privatrechts (1996) 223.

49   *F Bydlinski* (fn 48) FS von Caemmerer 785.

50   See *F Bydlinski*, Der Ersatz ideellen Schadens als sachliches und methodisches Problem, JBl 1965, 179 f, 182, 240, 247; following *Koziol* (fn 25) no 11/6; *E Karner*, Der Ersatz ideeller Schäden bei Körperverletzung (1999) 76 ff; *Karner/Koziol* (fn 22) 17 ff; *H Mayrhofer*, Schuldrecht I: Allgemeiner Teil (1986) 323; *T Schobel*, Der Ersatz frustrierter Aufwendungen (2003) 23.

51   See in depth *H Koziol*, Punitive Damages: Admission into the Seventh Legal Heaven or Eternal Damnation? in: H Koziol/V Wilcox (eds), Punitive Damages: Common Law and Civil Law Perspectives (2009) 275 ff.

52   *F Bydlinski* (fn 48) 92 ff.

damages, the following conclusion can be drawn: even if there are very strong arguments for imposing a sanction on the defendant, these arguments alone cannot justify awarding the plaintiff an advantage despite the fact that he has suffered no corresponding damage. Such a payment would be an unjustified windfall for the claimant and leads to further problems if there is more than one victim: should the victim who claims first really be granted all the damages whereas the second victim gets nothing? The bottom line is this: if there are only arguments for punishing or deterring one party but not for a claim by the other party, criminal and not private law is the appropriate answer.

32 Although damages for non-pecuniary loss only serve a compensatory function according to continental European law, the German Federal Supreme Court held quite a different view in the famous and widely discussed *Caroline* decision.[53] This case was about an infringement of the right to privacy by mass media, which published paparazzi photos of *Caroline* and her children. The Federal Supreme Court held the view that in such a case damages for non-pecuniary loss should be assessed with regard to the profits the media made through their unlawful publications. The Federal Supreme Court hence expressly stated: 'The imposition of pecuniary damages can only serve the function of prevention, which is required by the personality right, if the amount awarded reflects the fact that the purpose of the infringement of the personality right was the aim to make a profit.' Thus, the German courts granted *Caroline* damages ranging from € 75,000 to € 100,000. As a result, *punitive damages* were imported to Germany.

33 The main arguments against such punitive damages have already been emphasized. However, an in-depth analysis of the *Caroline* case highlights another important point. In actual fact, the *Caroline* case is not primarily about non-pecuniary losses – *Caroline* later sold the same photos in France to the media herself – but about unlawfully gained profits. Accordingly, the case should not have been solved with the means of tort law but by the rules of *unjust enrichment*.[54] Consequently, such unlawful profits should not be taken into regard when assessing damages but should in their entirety be skimmed off and

---

53   BGH in BGHZ 128, 1 = NJW 1995, 861 = Juristenzeitung (JZ) 1995, 360 with cmt by *P Schlechtriem* = Lindenmaier-Möhring, Kommentierte BGH Rechtsprechung (LM) § 823 (Ah) BGB Nr 119 with cmt by *H Ehmann* = European Review of Private Law (ERPL) 1997, 237 with cmt by *HP Westermann* (Caroline von Monaco I).

54   *C-W Canaris*, Gewinnabschöpfung bei Verletzung des allgemeinen Persönlichkeitsrechts, FS Deutsch (1999) 85 ff, 105 ff. For a comparative view see *M Hinteregger* (fn 30) in this volume.

transferred to the person who has suffered the infringement of their personality rights. In the end, the German Federal Supreme Court went too far by granting punitive damages, and did not go far enough by rejecting a claim for the full profits based on unjust enrichment. This is regrettable, because the *disgorgement of illegal profits* based on unjust enrichment is of paramount importance especially in mass media cases, as it is the only means to *effective prevention* and the protection of personality rights.

PART 2

On the Legal Protection of Personality Rights in General: China

∵

Codifying Personality Rights in China: Legislative Innovation or Scaremongering?

Chen Lei

I   Introduction: Working Definition

1   In the last few years, the most controversial issue in Chinese civil law is that of how to legislate personality rights. Several questions arise as to how to protect personality rights, how to deal with the interplay between legislated personality rights and the Tort Liability Law (TLL), and whether there should be a separate book on personality rights in the future Chinese Civil Code. The concept of personality rights is not new. In classical natural law, a variety of human rights which are inalienable form the basis of the modern concept of personality rights. While these rights are protected constitutionally in one way or another, they are of private law in the sense that they are non-patrimonial, non-transferable and uninheritable. In other words, they are innate and inextricably linked with personhood. In view of their private law nature, a working definition of personality rights is required in order to better understand the concept of personality rights.

2   The Quebec Civil Code provides that 'every person is the holder of personality rights, such as the right to life, the right to the inviolability and integrity of his person, and the right to the respect of his name, reputation and privacy. These rights are inalienable.'[1] *Christian von Bar* offers a more comprehensive definition by listing the right to life, protection against physical injury and against deprivation of liberty, the right to name, image, honour and self-esteem, and protection against unlawful disclosure of personal information and interference with family life.[2] *Johann Neethling* provides a very comprehensive list of personality rights from an uncodified mixed jurisdiction's perspective, namely, the right to life, the rights to bodily integrity and to personal security, the right to physical liberty, the right to honour and reputation, the right to dignity in the narrow sense (self-esteem, honour, and freedom from insult), the right to

---

1   Art 3 of the Quebec Civil Code.

2   *C von Bar*, The Common European Law of Torts II (2000) 61.

privacy, the right to informational privacy (non-disclosure of private information), the right to identity or image, the right to publicity (appropriation of
image and reification of right to privacy and image), the moral right to copyright, the right to autonomy, personality rights in family relationships, and personality rights after death.[3]

3 In China, at the jurisprudential level, personality rights entail a bundle of
rights which protect the innate attributes of the human being. At the positive
level, according to the revised provision on the causes of action in civil cases
issued by the Supreme People's Court, personality rights refer to the right of
name, the right of portrait, the right of reputation, the right of honour, the
right of privacy, the right to marriage, personal liberty, and the right to personal data.[4] The Judicial Interpretations of the Supreme People's Court on the
Issues regarding Determining the Tort Liability for Compensation for Mental
Suffering provides protection for some other rights such as the right of body
and the right of personal dignity.[5] It is worth noting that the above list of protected personality rights is not closed but open-ended, thus leaving room for
recognizing new types of personality rights.

4 It seems that no one doubts the necessity for legal protection of personality
rights, particularly in view of the rapid development of the internet and new
media technology.[6] However, the way in which personality rights are (and
should be) legislated has been heatedly debated. Against this background, this
paper explores the protection of personality rights in China by first examin-
ing the extent to which personality rights are currently protected in China.
Subsequently, it discusses the interplay between concepts of general personality rights and specific personality rights, including the extent that Chinese
law approaches personality rights from the TLL perspective as compared to
the recognized rights perspective. This paper also evaluates the legislative proposal on the inclusion of a separate book on personality rights in a future Chinese Civil Code. PRC statutes, court judgments, and surrounding literature are
referred to and conflicting views about whether personality rights should be
included in a future Chinese Civil Code are analyzed.

---

3   *J Neethling/JM Potgieter /PJ Visser*, Neethling's Law of Personality (2nd edn 2005).
4   Notice of the Supreme People's Court on Issuing the Revised Provisions on Causes of Action
    in Civil Cases (2011).
5   Arts 1, 3 and 4 of the Judicial Interpretation.
6   *G Resta*, The New Frontiers of Personality Rights and the Problem of Commodification: Euro-
    pean and Comparative Perspectives (2011) 26 Tulane European & Civil Law Forum 32.

II   Current Statutory Framework Regarding Personality Rights Protection

5 While it is necessary to further improve the legal protection of personality rights in China, insufficiencies in their current protection should not be exaggerated. As elsewhere, personality rights in China are protected by a range of legal mechanisms, spread out amongst inter alia the Tort Liability Law, criminal law and constitutional law. Specifically, personality rights are regulated awkwardly by a plethora of statutory instruments, such as the PRC Constitution, the General Principle of Civil Law, the TLL, the Consumer Protection Law, State Council regulations, ministerial and departmental circulars and the Supreme People's Court's judicial interpretations (see Table 5.1 below).

6 The current Chinese legal and statutory framework on personality rights is fragmented and unsystematic. Differences can be seen from the legal recourse triggered by the infringement of different personality rights. Legal remedies can be obtained from civil, administrative,[7] or criminal (the crime of insult or defamation) avenues or a combination of remedies.

7 It is interesting to note that there is an overlap in classifying certain personality rights into different spheres of laws, i.e. civil, criminal and constitutional. The right of reputation, for example, is a fundamental right guaranteed by the

TABLE 5.1   *Current PRC legal and statutory framework relating to the protection of personality rights*

Type of personality rights	Protection conferred by
personal freedom	art 37 Constitution; art 2 LL (covered by the non-exhaustive list of personality rights);
personal dignity	art 38 Constitution;
residences not to be violated	art 39 Constitution
freedom and privacy of personal correspondence	art 40 Constitution
right of life	art 98 GPCL; art 2 TLL; art 1 Judicial Interpretations of the Supreme People's Court on the Issues regarding Determining the Tort Liability for Compensation for Mental Suffering (the 'Judicial Interpretation on Mental Suffering')

7   Art 62 Law of the People's Republic of China on the Protection of Disabled Persons.

TABLE 5.1   *Current PRC legal and statutory framework relating to the protection of personality rights* (cont.)

Type of personality rights	Protection conferred by
right of health	art 98 GPCL; art 2 TLL; art 1 Judicial Interpretation on Mental Suffering
right of body	art 1 Judicial Interpretation on Mental Suffering
right of name (natural person and legal person)	art 99 GPCL; art 2 TLL; art 1 Judicial Interpretation on Mental Suffering
right of portrait	art 100 GPCL; art 2 TLL; art 1 Judicial Interpretation on Mental Suffering
right of reputation	art 101 GPCL; art 2 TLL; art 1 Judicial Interpretation on Mental Suffering
right of honour	art 102 GPCL; art 2 TLL; art 1 Judicial Interpretation on Mental Suffering
right of marital autonomy	art 103 GPCL; art 2 TLL; art 1 Judicial Interpretation on Mental Suffering
right to privacy	art 2 TLL; art 1 Judicial Interpretation on Mental Suffering
personality interest of the dead	art 3 Judicial Interpretation on Mental Suffering; art 2 TLL (covered by the non-exhaustive list of personality rights)
a special memento of personal significance	art 4 Judicial Interpretation on Mental Suffering

Remedies

cessation of infringement	art 134 GPCL; art 15 TLL
removal of obstruction and elimination of danger	art 134 GPCL; art 15 TLL
elimination of adverse impact and restoration of reputation	art 134 GPCL; art 15 TLL
compensation for losses	art 134 GPCL; art 15 TLL
apology	art 134 GPCL; art 15 TLL
compensation for mental distress	art 1, 3 and 4 Judicial Interpretation on Mental Suffering; art 22 TLL

Constitution.[8] The violation of the right of reputation can also be a criminal offence.[9] The General Principles of Civil Law (the 'GPCL') enumerate a number of personal rights, including the right of reputation.[10] Certain personality rights are also protected under procedural laws. For example, the right of privacy was protected in both the Criminal Procedure Law[11] and the Civil Procedure Law.[12]

8   In addition, most personality rights are protected by the TLL. According to art 2 of the TLL, the right to life, the right to health, the right to name, the right to reputation, the right to honour, the right to self-image, the right of privacy and the right of marital autonomy are specifically protected. The compensation for infliction of mental distress in case of infringement of personal rights is also admitted.[13] A special judicial interpretation is devoted to the right of reputation, namely the Judicial Interpretation of the Supreme People's Court on Several Issues about the Trial of Cases Concerning the Right of Reputation.[14] The Supreme People's Court has also recently published eight guiding cases concerning internet infringement upon personality rights.[15]

9   Finally, it is worth noting that some provisions concerning personality rights are provided to protect some vulnerable groups. For example, the Consumer Protection Law provides for the right of human dignity,[16] and the protection of individual information.[17] Other examples can be seen in the Law on the Protection of Women's Rights and the Law on Minor Protection and the Law on the Protection of Disabled Persons. Some professional duties are specifically promulgated, for example, the Advertisement Law protects the respect of

---

8   Art 37 of the PRC Constitution.

9   Art 246 of the Criminal Law: crime of insult and defamation.

10   Art 101 of the General Principles of Civil Law.

11   Arts 52, 150, 183 of the Criminal Procedure Law of the PRC.

12   Arts 68, 156 of the Civil Procedure Law of the PRC.

13   Art 22 of the Tort Liability Law of the PRC.

14   The Judicial Interpretation of the Supreme People's Court on Several Issues about the Trial of Cases Concerning the Right of Reputation was issued by the Supreme People's Court in 1993.

15   The Notice of publication of the 10th Batch of guiding cases by the Supreme People's Court, Fa [2015] no 85, 最高人民法院关于发布第十批指导性案例的通知, 法【2015】85号, see <http://www.court.gov.cn/shenpan-xiangqing-14240.html>.

16   Art 14 of the Consumer Protection Law of the PRC.

17   Art 50 of the Consumer Protection Law.

the right of portrait;[18] the Lawyer's Law protects clients' privacy;[19] and the TLL mandates the protection of patients' private data by medical institutions.[20]

III   General Personality Rights v Specific Personality Rights

10 Most personality rights, being fundamental rights, enjoy constitutional protection. Therefore, they are primary rights but their infringement is a tort, which demands a secondary obligation on the tortfeasors to remedy. Worldwide, there are a few models of protection mechanisms regarding personality rights depending upon whether the emphasis is on the concept of right or remedy. In order to make an informed decision for China's law-making, it is instructive to refer to some experienced jurisdictions for a comparative survey. At the risk of over-simplification, a brief comparative summary is set out below.

11 The first legislative approach is more right-based than remedy-based, namely, a general personality rights approach. Some civil law jurisdictions such as Germany recognize a concept of general personality rights as a foundation to provide comprehensive personality protection, although such a concept was not included in the BGB (the German Civil Code).[21] It was the German courts that developed a 'general right of personality' (*allgemeines Persönlichkeitsrecht*).[22] This right guarantees the protection of human dignity as well as the right to freely develop one's personality. This generalist approach covers all aspects of personality and can be regarded as the foundation from which all specific personality rights arise and develop. Hence, the general right is essentially a source on which expansion of personality protection can be based.

12 The second approach is more remedy-based than right-based in the sense that the focus is on the tortious action and its conditions and limits. French law, for example, has sidestepped the general right approach. Instead, French courts have developed an extensive protection of personality interests based on the overarching tortious liability provisions in the French Civil Code by extending these to personality rights infringements. Gradually, the French courts

---

18   Art 25 of the Advertisement Law.

19   Art 35 of the Lawyer's Law.

20   Art 66 of the Tort Liability Law.

21   *K Larenz/C-W Canaris*, Lehrbuch des Schuldrechts I/2 (1994) 491; *W van Gerven et al*, Tort Law (2000) 142.

22   See *E Ondreasova*, Personality Rights in Different European Legal Systems: Privacy, Dignity, Honour and Reputation no 20 ff, and *E Karner*, Human Rights and the Protection of Personality Rights in Europe: Comparative Reflections, both in this volume.

developed a body of specific personality rights such as the rights to physical integrity, dignity, good name, privacy and identity. Some of these rights have eventually been embodied in legislation, in addition to judicial recognition.[23] Consequently, there is no need for the recognition of a general right of personality as in German law.

13 The third approach is a hybrid approach with elements of both the first and second approaches. Dutch law, similar to the French model, with a general tortious liability clause of the *Burgerlijk Wetboek* (BW, Dutch Civil Code), allows the award of damages for non-pecuniary loss where there is an infringement of dignity, reputation, psychiatric injury and/or invasion of privacy. Moreover, the *Hoge Raad* (Dutch Supreme Court) recognized the existence of the general right to personality in 1994.[24] This right is claimed to underpin other fundamental rights such as the right to privacy, although its meaning remains vague. It is worth noting that although Dutch law recognizes rights of personality via its courts, it seems that the Dutch legislature has been slow to embrace new personality rights.[25]

14 The fourth approach is the polar opposite to the first approach. This is the approach adopted by English law, which remains 'mistrustful of generalized rights.'[26] Under English law, recognition of systematic personality rights is virtually non-existent and protection of personality is based on the English law of torts. English tort liability law is fragmented in the sense that there is a collection of autonomous torts and 'torticles'[27] to address individual rights' infringements. A wide range of torts to the person include, *inter alia*, assault, battery, false imprisonment, defamation (libel, slander), malicious falsehood, mental suffering, and breach of confidence. None of these torts alone is sufficient to serve as the basis for a comprehensive protection of personality rights. It might be argued that the English law is conservative because it prefers to adapt existing institutions rather than creating new ones.[28]

---

23   See further *Ondreasova* (fn 22) no 13 ff, in this volume.

24   *R Nehmelman*, Het algemeenpersoonlijkheidsrecht. Een rechtsvergelijkendestudie naarbet algemeen persoonhjkheidsrecbtin Duitsland en Nederland (2002) 268.

25   *K Lemmens* The protection of privacy between a rights-based and a freedom-based approach: what the Swiss example can teach us (2003) 10 Maastricht Journal of European and Comparative Law 381, 385–387.

26   *H Carty*, Personality Rights and English Law, in: N Whitty/R Zimmermann (eds), Rights of Personality in Scots Law (2009) 384.

27   *B Rudden*, Torticles (1991–1992) 6/7 Tulane Civil Law Forum 105, 109.

28   *B Markesinis*, The Familiarity of the Unknown, in: W Swadling/G Jones (eds), The Search for Principle (1999) 65. See further *Ondreasova* (fn 22) no 23 ff, in this volume.

Comparative Evaluation

15 (a) In spite of the divergent approaches to the recognition of a general right of personality, in all of the above systems, specific personality rights are recognized either by statutes or the courts.

16 (b) It appears that the concept of a general personality right is too abstract to be practically useful.[29] A concretization of specific rights of personality is therefore still necessary when courts decide particular cases. Even in Germany, the 'general right of personality' is in practice treated as a bundle of rights that protects different aspects of an individual's personality. German courts have built a system of individualizing the 'general right of personality.'[30]

17 (c) With a specific personality rights regime, it is easy to conduct the demarcation of these rights with a precise description. This would promote certainty and predictability by rendering them dogmatically and practically manageable with (somewhat) objective standards. This is particularly important because, when it comes to remedies, the courts will be able to consistently articulate, develop and award appropriate legal protections.

18 (d) Having said the above, it does not necessarily mean that a general personality rights regime is not beneficial, but that it is only beneficial in regimes where there is no general tort liability clause covering personality rights protection and where the courts are skilled enough to recognize new types of personality rights. Otherwise, the introduction of a general personality right regime is at best window-dressing, and at worst may result in abuse by unsophisticated Chinese judges wrongly creating new types of personality rights.

19 (e) In German law, although a general personality right is recognized, there is the possibility of constitutional review when the civil courts decide to introduce new personality rights based on the weighing up of the competing interests in question.[31] In other words, a control mechanism is put in place when a big issue such as recognizing a new personality right is triggered. However, in

---

29 *Yin Tian*, The Legislative Model of Personality Right Protection: the Abolition of the Concept of a General Personality Right, 尹田:《论人格权概况保护的立法模式——'一般人格权'概念的废除》.

30 *G Brüggemeier/AC Ciacchi/P O'Callaghan*, Personality Rights in European Tort Law (2010) 13–15.

31 For example, on 17 September 2012, the Federal Constitutional Court ruled that describing a lawyer as being 'radically right wing' was protected by freedom of speech (1 BvR 2979/10). Prior to the proceedings, an internet debate had taken place in which the claimant lawyer made various comments including, 'the super-wealthy families in England, France and Holland – mostly Khazarian, so non-Semitic Jews – determine the world economic events.' The Federal Constitutional Court ruled that to describe this person as being 'radically right wing' was a statement of opinion rather than fact and was not an

China, as there is no constitutional review in the German fashion, it appears that there would not be any safeguards should some Chinese judges boldly (but wrongly) introduce new personality rights.

20 (f) To summarize, since there is no consensus in the Chinese legal community on what personality rights should be protected, it is proposed that China should develop a pragmatic approach, halfway between the general tort liability protection under French law and the casuistic approach of English law. It is suggested that the Dutch approach should be seriously considered when the Chinese legislature ponders on this statutory choice. In order to facilitate the practical handling of personality rights protection, the approach should include a specific rights regime in addition to the general rights located in the general principles section of a future Chinese Civil Code vindicating recognised rights.

IV   Whether to Codify Personality Rights as an Independent Book in a Future Chinese Civil Code

21 Whether personality rights should be codified into an independent book in a future Chinese civil code is open to debate. Many civil law scholars have expressed their views by road-mapping the complex personality rights regime. It has been argued by some that the protection of personality rights should be dealt with in the General Part of the future Chinese Civil Code[32] as any attempts to enact a special book on personality rights may be futile and awkward.[33] Moreover, it has been argued that the rationale for enacting personality rights law is not convincing. The Civil Code should not be structured by ranking the importance of different rights, but should have its own inherent logic.[34] The focus of debate about the Civil Code should be on its protection of personal dignity, personality rights and human rights, instead of on the arrangement of the different laws or chapters. If personality rights deserve special protection,

---

infringement of the general personality right insofar as the opinion was supported by a factual reference.

32   *Tian Yin*, The Theoretical Defects in Making a Separate Book on Personality Rights (2007) 5 Law Science Magazine 7–11.

33   *Liang Huixing*, Observations on Drafting a Civil Code China (2001) 2 Modern Law Science 5 /梁慧星. 制定民法典的设想 [J]. 现代法学 (2001), 2:5.

34   *Liang Huixing*, On Several Issues of the Complication of China's Civil Code (2003) 26 Journal of Shanxi University (Philosophy & Social Science) 18 /梁慧星. 中国民法典编纂的几个问题 [J]. 山西大学学报(哲学社会科学版), 2003 26:18.

one could argue that equally important environmental rights should also be encompassed by another special book in a future Chinese Civil Code.[35]

22 On the other hand, several reasons warrant the inclusion of personality rights as a separate book in the proposed 'Twenty-first Century Civil Code.'[36] First, the PRC Constitution only provides somewhat sketchy and symbolic provisions on protecting personality rights. Such skeletal Constitutional provisions cannot be directly applied when Chinese courts decide cases. Codifying personality rights in a stand-alone book in the future Chinese Civil Code will improve such a situation.[37] It has been further maintained that vulnerable groups such as the old, minors or women deserve better protection listed in an independent book in the Civil Code.[38] Moreover, China does not have a human rights law, or a constitutional court. Therefore, there is an urgent need to grant protection to personality rights by entrenching them in the private law sphere through their inclusion in the future Chinese Civil Code.

23 Second, from a remedial perspective, the TLL cannot by itself adequately protect personality rights.[39] It is still necessary for an independent book on personality rights to set out certain basic issues, such as the definition or the scope of personality rights.[40] In addition, the TLL only provides for insufficient and limited protections.[41] Other remedies, such as restitution for unjust enrichment, should also have a part to play.

24 Third, some personality rights are currently regulated under the GPCL. However, some scholars have pointed out that personality rights cannot be

---

35 *Lei Chen*, Introduction, in: Lei Chen/CH Van Rhee (eds), Towards a Chinese Civil Code, Historical and Comparative Perspectives (2012) 8.

36 *Yang Lixin,* Three Urgent Issues concerning the Legislation of the Personal Right Law (2008) 3 Journal of National Prosecutions College 113 /杨立新. 制定我国人格权法应当着重解决的三个问题, 国家检察官学院学报, 2008 (6): 113.

37 *Wang Liming*, The Dignitary Values and their Realization in a Future Chinese Personality Rights Law 人格权法中的人格尊严价值及其实现 (2013)7 Tsinghua Law Journal 19.

38 *Wang Liming*, The Zeitgeist and Codifying Pace of a Civil Code 民法典的时代特征和编纂步骤 (2014) 8 Tsinghua Law Journal 12 /王利明, 清华法学.

39 *Wang Liming*, Several Issues in Making Personality Rights Law 人格权法制定中的几个问题 (2012) 3 Jinan Journal (Philosophy and Social Sciences) 3 / 王利明, 暨南学报 (哲学社会科学版).

40 *Wang Liming*, The Position of Personality Rights in the Future Chinese Civil Code, Chinese Journal of Law 2 (2003) 35 f.

41 *Ma Junju/Cao Zhiguo*, Conservation and Creation – Some Ideas of the Formulation of the Civil Code of PRC (2003) 5 Law Science (Journal of Northwest University of Politics and Law) 45 /马俊驹,曹治国. 守成与创新— 对制定我国民法典的几点看法 [J]. 法律科学(西北政法学院学报) 2003 (5) 45.

protected sufficiently under the GPCL given their increasing significance.[42] Furthermore, personality rights as currently regulated refer only to natural persons' personality rights and do not include legal persons' rights, so there is a statutory lacuna.[43] This is a defect of the proposed structure. Having a separate book will be clearer and provide more comprehensive rules on personality rights, which will be more helpful to judges.[44]

25 Fourth, it will be a legislative innovation to frame personality rights as an independent book in a proposed Civil Code. This is because even in the French and German Civil Codes, there are no separate books on personality rights. Most European civil codes were drafted long ago and understandably they did not anticipate so many practical problems concerning personality rights arising in this era of mass media and digital.[45] In China's case, drafters should seize this opportunity to prepare a modern civil code which meets the current social and economic conditions. Otherwise personality rights, being extremely significant rights in civil law, will not be paid sufficient attention if the Chinese drafters adopt old-fashioned European structures. As such, this innovation is claimed to be inevitable for the future Chinese Civil Code.[46]

26 For a while, the view supporting the inclusion of personality rights gained ground and such a proposal was even put on the legislative agenda. However, at the time of the writing of this paper, the National People's Congress has called upon the Chinese civil law community to work on the revision of other areas of law (the Law of Succession and the Consumer Protection Law.) So, whether these proposals (which will include a special personality rights law) will finally be adopted, remains to be seen.

Evaluation

27 (a) At the constitutional level, arguments for an independent book of personality rights in the new Chinese Civil Code sound very humanist in character, but these arguments may be quite simplistic. The real question is, therefore, whether private law can take over public law's function? For constitutional reviews, the complex balancing process involves not only the level of fault and

---

42 *Liming*, Chinese Journal of Law 2 (2003) 35 f.

43 *Liming*, Chinese Journal of Law 2 (2003) 35 f.

44 *Huang Zhong*, Personality Right Designed as Separate Title in Civil Code: From the Perspective of System Theory (2013) 35 Modern Law Science 55 / 黄忠. 人格权法独立成编的体系效应之辨识 [J]. 现代法学, (2013) 35:55.

45 *Yang Lixin*, The Legislative Report on the Personality Rights Law in China (2005). 杨立新:《中国人格权法立法报告》, 知识产权出版社 2005年版.

46 *Lixin* (fn 45).

degree of harm suffered, but also the persuasiveness of the countervailing interests held by the other party, to reach a compromise between lawful but contradictory interests/values. Civil law judges at the local level may not properly manage such a balancing exercise between constitutionally recognized values.

28 (b) Those opposing the creation of an independent book of personality rights have not provided convincing justifications. The mainstream views for an independent book have political leverage as the leading figure, *Wang Liming*, is president of the Chinese Civil Law Association and has been delegated to draft the Chinese Civil Code by the National People's Congress, the top Chinese legislative body.

29 In this author's view, whether to have an independent book on personality rights is more a political judgment call than an academic issue. Given the dynamic nature of personality rights, one needs to focus on the substance instead of the form.[47] Viewed from the functionalist perspective, what is required, as analysed in the above comparative study, is a combination of the recognition of personality rights in the Civil Code and a cluster of detailed provisions regarding remedies. So long as there is a declarative provision recognizing protection of personality rights in the GPCL, coupled with concrete remedial provisions in the TLL and restitution for unjust enrichment, that would be sufficient.[48] In present-day China, the focus of personality rights protection should be placed primarily on natural persons. Nevertheless, the rights protection provisions can be amended should this concept be introduced. Therefore, this is just a minor technical issue and does not affect the proposed structural changes.

v   The Chinese Courts' Stance on the Extent of Protection

30 It is widely acknowledged that the TLL is based on the concept of compensation instead of punishment. Therefore, there is no justification for punitive damages. Moreover, compensation for non-pecuniary losses must not be determined by the enrichment that the tortfeasor gained. This is because the purpose of TLL is to compensate for damage, not to recover profits made by others. However, very often, the limitations in the compensation payable for infringement of personality rights cannot prevent or deter future infringements. For example, under Chinese law, name and image rights are protected

---

47   *Zhang Xinbao*, The Internal System of Law of Personality Rights, 2003 (4) Legal Forum, 6. 张新宝:《人格权法的内部体系》, 载《法学论坛》2003 第4期, 第6页.

48   钟瑞栋:《人格权法不能独立成编的五点理由》, 载《太平洋学报》2008 第2期.

in the sense that the image of a person cannot be used commercially without that person's permission. However, as the basis of damages with regard to portrait rights is psychological harm caused to the subject, the tortfeasor shall at most bear civil liability for offering a public apology, remedying any negative effects and paying compensation for mental anguish. The compensation for image rights, by contrast, includes actual loss, infringement gain, attorneys' fees and mental anguish. In most circumstances, it is not possible to protect image rights as such under the TLL regime. The case of *Liu Xiang v. Life Style Newspaper*[49] concerned Liu Xiang, a famous Chinese athlete who won a gold medal in the 110 metre hurdle race at the 2004 Olympic Games. Liu Xiang sued Life Style Newspaper for infringing his portrait rights after it used a picture of him, without his permission, as a cover page to advertise the opening of a new department store. Liu Xiang claimed for RMB 1.25 million in compensation. The court at the first instance held that Life Style Newspaper's use of Liu's image constituted a news report rather than advertising and did not infringe his portrait rights. The court therefore rejected his claims. Liu appealed and the appellate court ruled that Life Style Newspaper's use of Liu's image without permission had infringed his portrait rights, and that the newspaper should make a public apology and pay compensation of RMB 20,000 for mental anguish – considerably less than the RMB 1.25 million that Liu had requested.[50] It seems that the profit gained by omitting to verify the information or to obtain the permission ex ante is often higher than the damages to be paid ex post. This would not prevent similar violations of personality rights from occurring.

31 How should courts address these deficiencies in the protection of Liu's image rights? On what basis or according to which formula has the RMB 20,000 in damages been calculated? These questions all point to one issue: should Chinese law adopt punitive damages in protecting personality rights? In this author's view, as stated above, the TLL lacks a preventive function and there is no need to apply the law of tort to recover profits gained. Rather, as proposed in the *Marlene Dietrich* case by the German Supreme Court (BGH), the law of unjust enrichment could be invoked because personality rights may have commercial value.[51] According to the German BGH, 'the general right of personality and its special forms also protect those interests of the person which

---

49   *Liu Xiang v Life Style Newspaper* [2005] (2005)Beijing No 1 Immediate Court Civil Appeal case No 8144 (一中民中字第8144号民事判决书).

50   *Meryl Wang*, Filling the gaps in protection, World Trademark Review, October/November 2010, available at <http://www.worldtrademarkreview.com/Magazine/Issue/27/Country-correspondents/China-Kangxin-Partners-PC> (accessed 10 April 2015).

51   BGH 1 December 1999 Neue Juristische Wochenschrift (NJW) 2000, 2195; G Wagner, The Protection of Personality Rights against Invasions by the Mass Media in Germany, in:

are of financial value.'[52] In the past, the focus of remedies was on the recovery of non-pecuniary losses arising from the infringement of personality rights. The emphasis now, however, is on the exploitation of the commercial value of personality and the restitution of profits arising from unjust enrichment as a result of non-consensual use of personality rights. Chinese law-makers should be heedful of this development when framing China's own legislation.

VI   Concluding Observations

32 Many issues regarding the legislative model of personality rights in China depend on whether Chinese law looks at personality rights through tort law lenses or through recognised rights lenses. If a general personality rights clause is introduced in the General Principle part of the Civil Code, it will still be necessary to refer to specific rights in ascertaining the conditions of infringement and the extent of the remedy. Whether there is a need to have a separate book on personality rights in a future Chinese Civil Code is a matter of legislative policy. For those who disagree with this legislative innovation, a separate personality rights book seems superfluous and one would ask 'why fix what is not broken.' Some scholars recommend amending the provisions embracing the protection of personality rights rather than creating something structurally new.

33 A comparison with other jurisdictions shows that the development of protection on particular types of infringement usually evolves through a body of judicial decisions rather than legislation or academic literature. In English law and French law, it is the courts that took the lead in directing the protection of personality rights. Similarly, the German courts not only recognized the general personality right complementing the protected interests specifically listed in § 823 (1) BGB, but also extended the remedies to include recovery of losses even where the loss is entirely non-pecuniary, by making available damages as a remedy for the serious infringement of personality rights.

H Koziol/A Warzilek (eds), Persönlichkeitsschutz gegenüber Massenmedien (2005) 137–179 no 110.

52   BGH 1 December 1999 NJW 2000, 2195.

Type of personality rights	Protection offered by
Personal Freedom	**Constitution, art 37:** Freedom of the person of citizens of the People's Republic of China is inviolable. No citizen may be arrested except with the approval or by decision of a people's procuratorate or by decision of a people's court, and arrests must be made by a public security organ. Unlawful detention or deprivation or restriction of citizens' freedom of the person by other means is prohibited, and unlawful search of the person of citizens is prohibited.[a] **TLL, art 2** *(covered by the non-exhaustive list of personality rights)*: Those who infringe upon civil rights and interests shall be subject to the tort liability according to this Law. 'Civil rights and interests' used in this Law shall include the right to life, the right to health, the right to name, the right to reputation, the right to honor, right to self image, right of privacy, marital autonomy, guardianship, ownership, usufruct, security interest, copyright, patent right, exclusive right to use a trademark, right to discovery, equities, right of succession, and other personal and property rights and interests.[b]
Personal Dignity	**Constitution, art 38:** The personal dignity of citizens of the People's Republic of China is inviolable. Insult, libel, false accusation or false incrimination directed against citizens by any means is prohibited.[c]

a   The English version of the Constitution of the People's Republic of China on the website of NPC http://www.npc.gov.cn/englishnpc/Law/2007-12/05/content_1381903.htm accessed 30 November 2015.

b   The English version of the Tort Liability Law of the People's Republic of China on the website of PKU Law http://en.pkulaw.cn/display.aspx?cgid=125300&lib=law, accessed 30 November 2015.

c   The English version of the Constitution of the People's Republic of China on the website of NPC http://www.npc.gov.cn/englishnpc/Law/2007-12/05/content_1381903.htm accessed 30 November 2015.

Type of personality rights	Protection offered by
Residences not to be Violated	**Constitution, art 39:** The residences of citizens of the People's Republic of China are inviolable. Unlawful search of, or intrusion into, a citizen's residence is prohibited.[d]
Freedom and Privacy of Personal Correspondence	**Constitution, art 40:** Freedom and privacy of correspondence of citizens of the People's Republic of China are protected by law. No organization or individual may, on any ground, infringe upon citizens' freedom and privacy of correspondence, except in cases where, to meet the needs of State security or of criminal investigation, public security or procuratorial organs are permitted to censor correspondence in accordance with the procedures prescribed by law.[e]
Right of Life	GPCL, **art 98:** Citizens shall enjoy the rights of life and health.[f] TLL, **art 2** (*covered by the non-exhaustive list of personality rights*): Those who infringe upon civil rights and interests shall be subject to the tort liability according to this Law. 'Civil rights and interests' used in this Law shall include the right to life, the right to health, the right to name, the right to reputation, the right to honor, right to self image, right of privacy, marital autonomy, guardianship, ownership, usufruct, security interest, copyright, patent right, exclusive right to use a trademark, right to discovery, equities, right of succession, and other personal and property rights and interests.[g]

d   The English version of the Constitution of the People's Republic of China on the website of NPC http://www.npc.gov.cn/englishnpc/Law/2007-12/05/content_1381903.htm, accessed 30 November 2015.

e   The English version of the Constitution of the People's Republic of China on the website of NPC http://www.npc.gov.cn/englishnpc/Law/2007-12/05/content_1381903.htm, accessed 30 November 2015.

f   The English version of the General Principles of the Civil Law of the People's Republic of China on the website of NPC http://www.npc.gov.cn/englishnpc/Law/2007-12/12/content _1383941.htm, accessed 30 November 2015.

g   The English version of the Tort Liability Law of the People's Republic of China on the website of PKU Law http://en.pkulaw.cn/display.aspx?cgid=125300&lib=law, accessed 30 November 2015.

Type of personality rights	Protection offered by
	Interpretation of the Supreme People's Court on Problems regarding the Ascertainment of Compensation Liability for Emotional Damages in Civil Torts (the 'Judicial Interpretation on Mental Suffering'),[h] **art 1:** The people's court shall accept according to law cases brought forth claiming emotional damages for illegal infringement of any of the following rights of personality: (1) Right of life, right of health, right of body; (2) Right of personal name, right of portrait, right of reputation, right of honor; (3) Right of personal dignity; right of personal freedom. The people's court shall accept according to law cases arising from the violation of societal public interests or societal morality by infringing upon a person's privacy or other interests of personality, and brought to the court by the victim as a civil tort for claiming emotional damages.[i]
Right of Health	**GPCL, art 98:** Citizens shall enjoy the rights of life and health.[j]
	TLL, art 2 (*covered by the non-exhaustive list of personality rights*):

h　最高人民法院关于确定民事侵权精神损害赔偿责任若干问题的解释(2001) is interpreted by PKU Law as Interpretation of the Supreme People's Court on Problems regarding the Ascertainment of Compensation Liability for Emotional Damages in Civil Torts, see http://www.pkulaw.cn/fulltext_form.aspx?Db=chl&Gid=34937&keyword=最高人民法院关于确定民事侵权精神损害赔偿&EncodingName=&Search_Mode=like accessed 30 November 2015.

i　The English version of the Interpretation of the Supreme People's Court on Problems regarding the Ascertainment of Compensation Liability for Emotional Damages in Civil Torts on the website of PKU Law http://en.pkulaw.cn/display.aspx?cgid=34937&lib=law, accessed 30 November 2015.

j　The English version of the General Principles of the Civil Law of the People's Republic of China on the website of NPC http://www.npc.gov.cn/englishnpc/Law/2007-12/12/content_1383941.htm accessed 30 November 2015.

Type of personality rights	Protection offered by
	Those who infringe upon civil rights and interests shall be subject to the tort liability according to this Law. 'Civil rights and interests' used in this Law shall include the right to life, the right to health, the right to name, the right to reputation, the right to honor, right to self image, right of privacy, marital autonomy, guardianship, ownership, usufruct, security interest, copyright, patent right, exclusive right to use a trademark, right to discovery, equities, right of succession, and other personal and property rights and interests.[k]
	Judicial Interpretation on Mental Suffering, art 1: The people's court shall accept according to law cases brought forth claiming emotional damages for illegal infringement of any of the following rights of personality: (1) Right of life, right of health, right of body; (2) Right of personal name, right of portrait, right of reputation, right of honor; (3) Right of personal dignity; right of personal freedom. The people's court shall accept according to law cases arising from the violation of societal public interests or societal morality by infringing upon a person's privacy or other interests of personality, and brought to the court by the victim as a civil tort for claiming emotional damages.[l]
Right of Body	**Judicial Interpretation on Mental Suffering, art 1:** The people's court shall accept according to law cases brought forth claiming emotional damages for illegal infringement of any of the following rights of personality:

---

k   The English version of the Tort Liability Law of the People's Republic of China on the website of PKU Law http://en.pkulaw.cn/display.aspx?cgid=125300&lib=law, accessed 30 November 2015.

l   The English version of the Interpretation of the Supreme People's Court on Problems regarding the Ascertainment of Compensation Liability for Emotional Damages in Civil Torts on the website of PKU Law http://en.pkulaw.cn/display.aspx?cgid=34937&lib=law, accessed 30 November 2015.

Type of personality rights	Protection offered by
	(1) Right of life, right of health, right of body; (2) Right of personal name, right of portrait, right of reputation, right of honor; (3) Right of personal dignity; right of personal freedom. The people's court shall accept according to law cases arising from the violation of societal public interests or societal morality by infringing upon a person's privacy or other interests of personality, and brought to the court by the victim as a civil tort for claiming emotional damages.[m]
Right of Name (natural person and legal person)	GPCL, art 99: Citizens shall enjoy the right of personal name and shall be entitled to determine, use or change their personal names in accordance with relevant provisions. Interference with, usurpation of and false representation of personal names shall be prohibited. Legal persons, individual businesses and individual partnerships shall enjoy the right of name. Enterprises as legal persons, individual businesses and individual partnerships shall have the right to use and lawfully assign their own names.[n] TLL, art 2 (*covered by the non-exhaustive list of personality rights*): Those who infringe upon civil rights and interests shall be subject to the tort liability according to this Law. 'Civil rights and interests' used in this Law shall include the right to life, the right to health, the right to name, the right to reputation, the right to honor, right to self image,

m   The English version of the Interpretation of the Supreme People's Court on Problems regarding the Ascertainment of Compensation Liability for Emotional Damages in Civil Torts on the website of PKU Law http://en.pkulaw.cn/display.aspx?cgid=34937&lib=law, accessed 30 November 2015.

n   The English version of the General Principles of the Civil Law of the People's Republic of China on the website of NPC http://www.npc.gov.cn/englishnpc/Law/2007-12/12/content _1383941.htm, accessed 30 November 2015.

Type of personality rights	Protection offered by
	right of privacy, marital autonomy, guardianship, ownership, usufruct, security interest, copyright, patent right, exclusive right to use a trademark, right to discovery, equities, right of succession, and other personal and property rights and interests.[o] **Judicial Interpretation on Mental Suffering, art 1:** The people's court shall accept according to law cases brought forth claiming emotional damages for illegal infringement of any of the following rights of personality: (1) Right of life, right of health, right of body; (2) Right of personal name, right of portrait, right of reputation, right of honor; (3) Right of personal dignity; right of personal freedom. The people's court shall accept according to law cases arising from the violation of societal public interests or societal morality by infringing upon a person's privacy or other interests of personality, and brought to the court by the victim as a civil tort for claiming emotional damages.[p]
Right of Portrait	**GPCL, art 100:** Citizens shall enjoy the right of portrait. The use of a citizen's portrait for profits without his consent shall be prohibited.[q] **TLL, art 2** (*covered by the non-exhaustive list of personality rights*):

o The English version of the Tort Liability Law of the People's Republic of China on the website of PKU Law http://en.pkulaw.cn/display.aspx?cgid=125300&lib=law, accessed 30 November 2015.

p The English version of the Interpretation of the Supreme People's Court on Problems regarding the Ascertainment of Compensation Liability for Emotional Damages in Civil Torts on the website of PKU Law http://en.pkulaw.cn/display.aspx?cgid=34937&lib=law, accessed 30 November 2015.

q The English version of the General Principles of the Civil Law of the People's Republic of China on the website of NPC http://www.npc.gov.cn/englishnpc/Law/2007-12/12/content_1383941.htm accessed 30 November 2015.

Type of personality rights	Protection offered by
	Those who infringe upon civil rights and interests shall be subject to the tort liability according to this Law. 'Civil rights and interests' used in this Law shall include the right to life, the right to health, the right to name, the right to reputation, the right to honor, right to self image, right of privacy, marital autonomy, guardianship, ownership, usufruct, security interest, copyright, patent right, exclusive right to use a trademark, right to discovery, equities, right of succession, and other personal and property rights and interests.[r]
	Judicial Interpretation on Mental Suffering, art 1: The people's court shall accept according to law cases brought forth claiming emotional damages for illegal infringement of any of the following rights of personality: (1) Right of life, right of health, right of body; (2) Right of personal name, right of portrait, right of reputation, right of honor; (3) Right of personal dignity; right of personal freedom. The people's court shall accept according to law cases arising from the violation of societal public interests or societal morality by infringing upon a person's privacy or other interests of personality, and brought to the court by the victim as a civil tort for claiming emotional damages.[s]

r   The English version of the Tort Liability Law of the People's Republic of China on the website of PKU Law http://en.pkulaw.cn/display.aspx?cgid=125300&lib=law, accessed 30 November 2015.
s   The English version of the Interpretation of the Supreme People's Court on Problems regarding the Ascertainment of Compensation Liability for Emotional Damages in Civil Torts on the website of PKU Law http://en.pkulaw.cn/display.aspx?cgid=34937&lib=law, accessed 30 November 2015.

Type of personality rights	Protection offered by
Right of Reputation	**GPCL, art 101:** Citizens and legal persons shall enjoy the right of reputation. The personality of citizens shall be protected by law, and the use of insults, libel or other means to damage the reputation of citizens or legal persons shall be prohibited.[t] **TLL, art 2** (*covered by the non-exhaustive list of personality rights*): Those who infringe upon civil rights and interests shall be subject to the tort liability according to this Law. 'Civil rights and interests' used in this Law shall include the right to life, the right to health, the right to name, the right to reputation, the right to honor, right to self image, right of privacy, marital autonomy, guardianship, ownership, usufruct, security interest, copyright, patent right, exclusive right to use a trademark, right to discovery, equities, right of succession, and other personal and property rights and interests.[u] **Judicial Interpretation on Mental Suffering, art 1:** The people's court shall accept according to law cases brought forth claiming emotional damages for illegal infringement of any of the following rights of personality: (1) Right of life, right of health, right of body; (2) Right of personal name, right of portrait, right of reputation, right of honor; (3) Right of personal dignity; right of personal freedom.

---

t   The English version of the General Principles of the Civil Law of the People's Republic of China on the website of NPC http://www.npc.gov.cn/englishnpc/Law/2007-12/12/content _1383941.htm, accessed 30 November 2015.

u   The English version of the Tort Liability Law of the People's Republic of China on the website of PKU Law http://en.pkulaw.cn/display.aspx?cgid=125300&lib=law, accessed 30 November 2015.

Type of personality rights	Protection offered by
	The people's court shall accept according to law cases arising from the violation of societal public interests or societal morality by infringing upon a person's privacy or other interests of personality, and brought to the court by the victim as a civil tort for claiming emotional damages.[v]
Right of Honour	**GPCL, art 102:** Citizens and legal persons shall enjoy the right of honour. It shall [be] prohibited to unlawfully divest citizens and legal persons of their honorary titles.[w] **TLL, art 2** (*covered by the non-exhaustive list of personality rights*): Those who infringe upon civil rights and interests shall be subject to the tort liability according to this Law. 'Civil rights and interests' used in this Law shall include the right to life, the right to health, the right to name, the right to reputation, the right to honor, right to self image, right of privacy, marital autonomy, guardianship, ownership, usufruct, security interest, copyright, patent right, exclusive right to use a trademark, right to discovery, equities, right of succession, and other personal and property rights and interests.[x] **Judicial Interpretation on Mental Suffering, art 1:** The people's court shall accept according to law cases brought forth claiming emotional damages for illegal infringement of any of the following rights of personality:

v   The English version of the Interpretation of the Supreme People's Court on Problems regarding the Ascertainment of Compensation Liability for Emotional Damages in Civil Torts on the website of PKU Law http://en.pkulaw.cn/display.aspx?cgid=34937&lib=law, accessed 30 November 2015.

w   The English version of the General Principles of the Civil Law of the People's Republic of China on the website of NPC http://www.npc.gov.cn/englishnpc/Law/2007-12/12/content _1383941.htm, accessed 30 November 2015.

x   The English version of the Tort Liability Law of the People's Republic of China on the website of PKU Law http://en.pkulaw.cn/display.aspx?cgid=125300&lib=law, accessed 30 November 2015.

Type of personality rights	Protection offered by
	(1) Right of life, right of health, right of body;
	(2) Right of personal name, right of portrait, right of reputation, right of honor;
	(3) Right of personal dignity; right of personal freedom. The people's court shall accept according to law cases arising from the violation of societal public interests or societal morality by infringing upon a person's privacy or other interests of personality, and brought to the court by the victim as a civil tort for claiming emotional damages.[y]
Right of Marital Autonomy	GPCL, art 103: Citizens shall enjoy the right of marriage by choice. Mercenary marriages, marriages upon arbitrary decision by any third party and any other acts of interference in the freedom of marriage shall be prohibited.[z]
	TLL, art 2 (*covered by the non-exhaustive list of personality rights*): Those who infringe upon civil rights and interests shall be subject to the tort liability according to this Law. 'Civil rights and interests' used in this Law shall include the right to life, the right to health, the right to name, the right to reputation, the right to honor, right to self image, right of privacy, marital autonomy, guardianship, owner-ship, usufruct, security interest, copyright, patent right, exclusive right to use a trademark, right to discovery, equities, right of succession, and other personal and property rights and interests.[aa]

y   The English version of the Interpretation of the Supreme People's Court on Problems re-
    garding the Ascertainment of Compensation Liability for Emotional Damages in Civil Torts
    on the website of PKU Law http://en.pkulaw.cn/display.aspx?cgid=34937&lib=law, accessed
    30 November 2015.
z   The English version of the General Principles of the Civil Law of the People's Republic of
    China on the website of NPC http://www.npc.gov.cn/englishnpc/Law/2007-12/12/content
    _1383941.htm, accessed 30 November 2015.
aa The English version of the Tort Liability Law of the People's Republic of China on the
    website of PKU Law http://en.pkulaw.cn/display.aspx?cgid=125300&lib=law, accessed 30
    November 2015.

Type of personality rights	Protection offered by
	Judicial Interpretation on Mental Suffering, art 1: The people's court shall accept according to law cases brought forth claiming emotional damages for illegal infringement of any of the following rights of personality: (1) Right of life, right of health, right of body; (2) Right of personal name, right of portrait, right of reputation, right of honor; (3) Right of personal dignity; right of personal freedom. The people's court shall accept according to law cases arising from the violation of societal public interests or societal morality by infringing upon a person's privacy or other interests of personality, and brought to the court by the victim as a civil tort for claiming emotional damages.[bb]
Right to Privacy	TLL, art 2 (*covered by the non-exhaustive list of personality rights*): Those who infringe upon civil rights and interests shall be subject to the tort liability according to this Law. 'Civil rights and interests' used in this Law shall include the right to life, the right to health, the right to name, the right to reputation, the right to honor, right to self image, right of privacy, marital autonomy, guardianship, ownership, usufruct, security interest, copyright, patent right, exclusive right to use a trademark, right to discovery, equities, right of succession, and other personal and property rights and interests.[cc]

bb The English version of the Interpretation of the Supreme People's Court on Problems regarding the Ascertainment of Compensation Liability for Emotional Damages in Civil Torts on the website of PKU Law http://en.pkulaw.cn/display.aspx?cgid=34937&lib=law, accessed 30 November 2015.

cc The English version of the Tort Liability Law of the People's Republic of China on the website of PKU Law http://en.pkulaw.cn/display.aspx?cgid=125300&lib=law, accessed 30 November 2015.

Type of personality rights	Protection offered by
	Judicial Interpretation on Mental Suffering, art 1: The people's court shall accept according to law cases brought forth claiming emotional damages for illegal infringement of any of the following rights of personality: (1) Right of life, right of health, right of body; (2) Right of personal name, right of portrait, right of reputation, right of honor; (3) Right of personal dignity; right of personal freedom. The people's court shall accept according to law cases arising from the violation of societal public interests or societal morality by infringing upon a person's privacy or other interests of personality, and brought to the court by the victim as a civil tort for claiming emotional damages.[dd]
Personality Interest of the Dead	**Judicial Interpretation on Mental Suffering, art 3:** The people's court shall accept according to law cases arising from any of the following infringements related to the death of a person that caused mental suffering to the close relative of the deceased, and brought to the court by the relative for claiming emotional damages: (1) Infringement upon the name, portrait, reputation or honor of a deceased person by insulting, libeling, disparaging, vilifying or by other means contrary to the societal public interests or societal morality; (2) Illegal disclosure or use of the privacy of a deceased person or infringement upon the privacy by other means contrary to the societal public interests or societal morality;

dd   The English version of the Interpretation of the Supreme People's Court on Problems
      regarding the Ascertainment of Compensation Liability for Emotional Damages in Civil
      Torts on the website of PKU Law http://en.pkulaw.cn/display.aspx?cgid=34937&lib=law,
      accessed 30 November 2015.

Type of personality rights	Protection offered by
	(3) Illegal use of or damage to the remains of a deceased person or infringement upon the remains by other means contrary to the societal public interests or societal morality.[ee]

TLL, art 2 (*covered by the non-exhaustive list of personality rights*):
Those who infringe upon civil rights and interests shall be subject to the tort liability according to this Law. 'Civil rights and interests' used in this Law shall include the right to life, the right to health, the right to name, the right to reputation, the right to honor, right to self image, right of privacy, marital autonomy, guardianship, ownership, usufruct, security interest, copyright, patent right, exclusive right to use a trademark, right to discovery, equities, right of succession, and other personal and property rights and interests.[ff] |
| A Special Memento of Personal Significance | **Judicial Interpretation on Mental Suffering, art 4:**
The people's court shall accept according to law cases arising from any tortious act that causes permanent destruction or damage to a special memento of personal significance, and brought to the court by the owner of the memento for claiming emotional damages.[gg] |

ee   The English version of the Interpretation of the Supreme People's Court on Problems regarding the Ascertainment of Compensation Liability for Emotional Damages in Civil Torts on the website of PKU Law http://en.pkulaw.cn/display.aspx?cgid=34937&lib=law, accessed 30 November 2015.

ff   The English version of the Tort Liability Law of the People's Republic of China on the website of PKU Law http://en.pkulaw.cn/display.aspx?cgid=125300&lib=law, accessed 30 November 2015.

gg   The English version of the Interpretation of the Supreme People's Court on Problems regarding the Ascertainment of Compensation Liability for Emotional Damages in Civil Torts on the website of PKU Law http://en.pkulaw.cn/display.aspx?cgid=34937&lib=law, accessed 30 November 2015.

Type of personality rights	Protection offered by

Remedies

Cessation of	GPCL, art 134:
Infringement	The main methods of bearing civil liability shall be:

     (1)   Cessation of infringements;

     (2)   Removal of obstacles;

     (3)   Elimination of dangers;

     (4)   Return of property;

     (5)   Restoration of original condition;

     (6)   Repair, reworking or replacement;

     (7)   Compensation for losses;

     (8)   Payment of breach of contract damages;

     (9)   Elimination of ill effects and rehabilitation of reputation; and

     (10) Extension of apology.

The above methods of bearing civil liability may be applied exclusively or concurrently.

When hearing civil cases, a people's court, in addition to applying the above stipulations, may serve admonitions, order the offender to sign a pledge of repentance, and confiscate the property used in carrying out illegal activities and the illegal income obtained therefrom. It may also impose fines or detentions as stipulated by law.[hh]

TLL, art 15:

The methods of assuming tort liabilities shall include:

1.   Cessation of infringement;

2.   Removal of obstruction;

3.   Elimination of danger;

4.   Return of property;

5.   Restoration to the original status;

---

hh   The English version of the General Principles of the Civil Law of the People's Republic of China on the website of NPC http://www.npc.gov.cn/englishnpc/Law/2007-12/12/content_1383941.htm, accessed 30 November 2015.

Type of personality rights	Protection offered by
	6. Compensation for losses;
	7. Apology; and
	8. Elimination of consequences and restoration of reputation.
	The above methods of assuming the tort liability may be adopted individually or jointly.ii
Removal of Obstruction and Elimination of Danger	GPCL, art 134: The main methods of bearing civil liability shall be:
	(1) Cessation of infringements;
	(2) Removal of obstacles;
	(3) Elimination of dangers;
	(4) Return of property;
	(5) Restoration of original condition;
	(6) Repair, reworking or replacement;
	(7) Compensation for losses;
	(8) Payment of breach of contract damages;
	(9) Elimination of ill effects and rehabilitation of reputation; and
	(10) Extension of apology.
	The above methods of bearing civil liability may be applied exclusively or concurrently.
	When hearing civil cases, a people's court, in addition to applying the above stipulations, may serve admonitions, order the offender to sign a pledge of repentance, and confiscate the property used in carrying out illegal activities and the illegal income obtained therefrom. It may also impose fines or detentions as stipulated by law.jj

ii   The English version of the Tort Liability Law of the People's Republic of China on the website of PKU Law http://en.pkulaw.cn/display.aspx?cgid=125300&lib=law, accessed 30 November 2015.

jj   The English version of the General Principles of the Civil Law of the People's Republic of China on the website of NPC http://www.npc.gov.cn/englishnpc/Law/2007-12/12/content _1383941.htm, accessed 30 November 2015.

Type of personality rights	Protection offered by
	TLL, art 15: The methods of assuming tort liabilities shall include: 1. Cessation of infringement; 2. Removal of obstruction; 3. Elimination of danger; 4. Return of property; 5. Restoration to the original status; 6. Compensation for losses; 7. Apology; and 8. Elimination of consequences and restoration of reputation. The above methods of assuming the tort liability may be adopted individually or jointly.[kk]
Elimination of Adverse Impact and Restoration of Reputation	**GPCL, art 134:** The main methods of bearing civil liability shall be: (1) Cessation of infringements; (2) Removal of obstacles; (3) Elimination of dangers; (4) Return of property; (5) Restoration of original condition; (6) Repair, reworking or replacement; (7) Compensation for losses; (8) Payment of breach of contract damages; (9) Elimination of ill effects and rehabilitation of reputation; and (10) Extension of apology. The above methods of bearing civil liability may be applied exclusively or concurrently.

kk   The English version of the Tort Liability Law of the People's Republic of China on the website of PKU Law http://en.pkulaw.cn/display.aspx?cgid=125300&lib=law, accessed 30 November 2015.

Type of personality rights	Protection offered by
	When hearing civil cases, a people's court, in addition to applying the above stipulations, may serve admonitions, order the offender to sign a pledge of repentance, and confiscate the property used in carrying out illegal activities and the illegal income obtained therefrom. It may also impose fines or detentions as stipulated by law.[ll]
	TLL, art 15: The methods of assuming tort liabilities shall include: 1. Cessation of infringement; 2. Removal of obstruction; 3. Elimination of danger; 4. Return of property; 5. Restoration to the original status; 6. Compensation for losses; 7. Apology; and 8. Elimination of consequences and restoration of reputation. The above methods of assuming the tort liability may be adopted individually or jointly.[mm]
Compensation for Losses	GPCL, art 134: The main methods of bearing civil liability shall be: (1) Cessation of infringements; (2) Removal of obstacles; (3) Elimination of dangers; (4) Return of property; (5) Restoration of original condition;

ll   The English version of the General Principles of the Civil Law of the People's Republic of China on the website of NPC http://www.npc.gov.cn/englishnpc/Law/2007-12/12/content _1383941.htm accessed 30 November 2015.

mm   The English version of the Tort Liability Law of the People's Republic of China on the website of PKU Law http://en.pkulaw.cn/display.aspx?cgid=125300&lib=law, accessed 30 November 2015.

Type of personality rights	Protection offered by

(6) Repair, reworking or replacement;

(7) Compensation for losses;

(8) Payment of breach of contract damages;

(9) Elimination of ill effects and rehabilitation of reputation; and

(10) Extension of apology.

The above methods of bearing civil liability may be applied exclusively or concurrently.

When hearing civil cases, a people's court, in addition to applying the above stipulations, may serve admonitions, order the offender to sign a pledge of repentance, and confiscate the property used in carrying out illegal activities and the illegal income obtained therefrom. It may also impose fines or detentions as stipulated by law.[nn]

TLL, art 15:

The methods of assuming tort liabilities shall include:

1. Cessation of infringement;

2. Removal of obstruction;

3. Elimination of danger;

4. Return of property;

5. Restoration to the original status;

6. Compensation for losses;

7. Apology; and

8. Elimination of consequences and restoration of reputation.

The above methods of assuming the tort liability may be adopted individually or jointly.[oo]

---

nn   The English version of the General Principles of the Civil Law of the People's Republic of China on the website of NPC http://www.npc.gov.cn/englishnpc/Law/2007-12/12/content _1383941.htm, accessed 30 November 2015.

oo   The English version of the Tort Liability Law of the People's Republic of China on the website of PKU Law http://en.pkulaw.cn/display.aspx?cgid=125300&lib=law, accessed 30 November 2015.

Type of personality rights	Protection offered by
Apology	GPCL, art 134: The main methods of bearing civil liability shall be: (1) Cessation of infringements; (2) Removal of obstacles; (3) Elimination of dangers; (4) Return of property; (5) Restoration of original condition; (6) Repair, reworking or replacement; (7) Compensation for losses; (8) Payment of breach of contract damages; (9) Elimination of ill effects and rehabilitation of reputation; and (10) Extension of apology. The above methods of bearing civil liability may be applied exclusively or concurrently. When hearing civil cases, a people's court, in addition to applying the above stipulations, may serve admonitions, order the offender to sign a pledge of repentance, and confiscate the property used in carrying out illegal activities and the illegal income obtained therefrom. It may also impose fines or detentions as stipulated by law.[pp] TLL, art 15: The methods of assuming tort liabilities shall include: 1. Cessation of infringement; 2. Removal of obstruction; 3. Elimination of danger; 4. Return of property; 5. Restoration to the original status;

pp The English version of the General Principles of the Civil Law of the People's Republic of China on the website of NPC http://www.npc.gov.cn/englishnpc/Law/2007-12/12/content _1383941.htm accessed 30 November 2015.

Type of personality rights	Protection offered by
	6. Compensation for losses; 7. Apology; and 8. Elimination of consequences and restoration of reputation. The above methods of assuming the tort liability may be adopted individually or jointly.qq
Compensation for Mental Distress	**Judicial Interpretation on Mental Suffering, art 1:** The people's court shall accept according to law cases brought forth claiming emotional damages for illegal infringement of any of the following rights of personality: (1) Right of life, right of health, right of body; (2) Right of personal name, right of portrait, right of reputation, right of honor; (3) Right of personal dignity; right of personal freedom. The people's court shall accept according to law cases arising from the violation of societal public interests or societal morality by infringing upon a person's privacy or other interests of personality, and brought to the court by the victim as a civil tort for claiming emotional damages.rr **Judicial Interpretation on Mental Suffering, art 3:** The people's court shall accept according to law cases arising from any of the following infringements related to the death of a person that caused mental suffering to the close relative of the deceased, and brought to the court by the relative for claiming emotional damages: (1) Infringement upon the name, portrait, reputation or honor of a deceased person by insulting, libeling, disparaging, vilifying or by other means contrary to the societal public interests or societal morality;

---

qq   The English version of the Tort Liability Law of the People's Republic of China on the website of PKU Law http://en.pkulaw.cn/display.aspx?cgid=125300&lib=law, accessed 30 November 2015.

rr   The English version of the Interpretation of the Supreme People's Court on Problems regarding the Ascertainment of Compensation Liability for Emotional Damages in Civil Torts on the website of PKU Law http://en.pkulaw.cn/display.aspx?cgid=34937&lib=law, accessed 30 November 2015.

Type of personality rights	Protection offered by

(2) Illegal disclosure or use of the privacy of a deceased person or infringement upon the privacy by other means contrary to the societal public interests or societal morality;

(3) Illegal use of or damage to the remains of a deceased person or infringement upon the remains by other means contrary to the societal public interests or societal morality.[ss]

Judicial Interpretation on Mental Suffering, art 4:
The people's court shall accept according to law cases arising from any tortious act that causes permanent destruction or damage to a special memento of personal significance, and brought to the court by the owner of the memento for claiming emotional damages.[tt]

TLL, art 22:
Where any harm caused by a tort to a personal right or interest of another person inflicts a serious mental distress on the victim of the tort, the victim of the tort may require compensation for the infliction of mental distress.[uu]

---

ss   The English version of the Interpretation of the Supreme People's Court on Problems regarding the Ascertainment of Compensation Liability for Emotional Damages in Civil Torts on the website of PKU Law http://en.pkulaw.cn/display.aspx?cgid=34937&lib=law, accessed 30 November 2015.

tt   The English version of the Interpretation of the Supreme People's Court on Problems regarding the Ascertainment of Compensation Liability for Emotional Damages in Civil Torts on the website of PKU Law http://en.pkulaw.cn/display.aspx?cgid=34937&lib=law, accessed 30 November 2015.

uu   The English version of the Tort Liability Law of the People's Republic of China on the website of PKU Law http://en.pkulaw.cn/display.aspx?cgid=125300&lib=law, accessed 30 November 2015.

CHAPTER 6

The Structure of the Interest in Personality and the Introduction of a Statutory Right of Personality

Zhang Pinghua

I   The Multi-Dimensional Nature of the Interest in Personality

1   The structure of the interest in personality is multi-dimensional. The internal aspect of the interest refers to its inherent nature, that is, the interest that every person has in the satisfaction of the essential requirements of human personality. The external aspect of the interest refers to the derivative interests that are derived from the inherent interest. The inherent interest is an essential part of what makes humans human, and should not be restricted or taken away. It is natural and self-evident, and its justification is to be found in the subject possessing the right of personality rather than its instrumental value. The inherent interest not only reflects the basic purpose of private law, but also determines the semantic range of the rules applicable to the right of personality, demonstrating its *socially typical and manifest nature* (in German: *sozialtypische Offenkundigkeit*). The subject possessing the right of personality is intangible, although it is placed in a body controlled by that subject. It is something that exists as a whole. However, the targets of the right of personality can be both tangible and intangible,[1] and have a partial nature; they demonstrate the range of specific interests associated with different elements of the right of personality. Only if they are determined according to function can the right of personality be made whole and its various incidents distinguished. Otherwise, we may find ourselves in a situation where the right of personality is absorbed by a variety of more specific rights (the right to health, right to name, etc) and we have only a diversity of such rights.

2   Derivative interests in personality generally come into existence and cease to exist alongside the inherent interest. By way of exception to this general congruence, the inherent interest does not exist before birth and is extinguished after death, but derivative interests may survive death, which highlights the

---

1   As to rights in 'tangible' personality, see *CM Jordan Jr/CJ Price*, First Moore, then Hecht, Isn't it Time We Recognize a Property Right in Tissues, Cells and Gametes? (2002) 37 Real Property, Probate and Trust Journal 151.

need for discussion of the extent of the protection to be given to the right of personality.[2] Derivative interests, which are not a necessary condition of 'what makes humans human,' differ from person to person in type and extent, but commonly include the so-called 'implicated interest,' 'carrier interest,' 'trust interest' and public interest. The implicated interest refers to an interest which does not belong to the inherent interest but is in an implicated relationship with it. Such relationships include relationships of method and purpose and of cause and effect. An example would be the relationship of the right to education with the right to name: infringement of the former may be by means of infringing the latter. In one case, where the plaintiff had been unable to join the army because the defendant had used his identity for school enrollment and the relocation of his *hukou* (official household registration: rural/urban), the plaintiff needed only to claim in respect of his right of name and his right of *hukou* and consequently his right to join the army would without more be protected.[3] The plaintiff is thus given a 'free ride.'

3   Because of its characteristic intangibility, the inherent interest can be 'carried' by or contained within other rights and interests, which is what the term 'carrier interest' refers to.[4] Carrier interests demonstrate the full useful range of the right of personality. There is seldom a carrier interest in concrete personality rights but carrier interests are common in intangible personality rights, for example the right of identity. A typical example is the trademark in the design of a celebrity portrait. Although the inherent interest is natural, it also exists in social relationships and this social character contributes to the generation of the reliance interest and public interest.[5] In order to protect the bona fide third party, it is necessary to allow reliance upon the state of the subject as projected by his appearance, especially in relation to the recognition and protection of the right of identity. The public interest refers to the interests of unspecific members of society and is based on the needs of public administration or the maintenance of public order. The character of personality is both social and natural, and the public interest should reflect the inherent content and basic nature of the right of personality. The reason why the public interest is defined as a derivative interest rather than an inherent interest is so as to emphasise

2   *Yang Lixin*, Extensive Protection of Personality Right (1995) 2 Legal Research in China.

3   *The Guo Shuai Chuang v Guo Xue Chuang for Infringing Name, the Right to Education*, Typical Cases in People's Court 2004 (People's Court Press, 2005) 345.

4   *The Guo Shuai Chuang v Guo Xue Chuang for Infringing Name, the Right to Education*, Typical Cases in People's Court 2004 (People's Court Press, 2005) 345.

5   *K Larenz/M Wolf*, Allgemeiner Teil des Bürgerlichen Rechts (9th edn 2004) 886 – translated by Wang Xiaoye, Law Publishing House 2004.

the private characteristic of the inherent interest and to distinguish it from the objects of public law. The public interest may require the limitation of the right of personality; public figures in particular may have to accept a high level of such limitations.[6]

4 Derivative interests are external to the subject and their justification derives from the value flowing from the right of personality and the material advantages associated with it, rather than from the elements of personality itself. Consequently, new types of derivative interest may emerge with developments in the economy, society and culture. Despite this external characteristic, derivative interests cannot entirely avoid limitations applicable to the inherent interest and cannot completely escape to free space or become personality interests of an entirely new type. In principle, derivative interests do not possess the characteristic of a socially typical and manifest nature (*sozialtypische Offenkundigkeit*), and their type and extent cannot be concisely clarified according to function. On the whole, derivative interests have not been completely accepted by the public, though there are variations in individual cases, and frequently exceed the reasonable expectations of the parties concerned and the scope of intended legal regulation. Therefore, where such interests are infringed, it is not easy to find a basis for liability.

II   The Boundaries of the Right to Personality

5 The boundary of the interest in personality is vague from both static and dynamic perspectives. From the static perspective, this vague character refers to the uncertain state of personality when we observe such right without regard to its enforcement or the countervailing rights of others. The concrete personality rights should not be precisely delimited because of the difficulty of identifying the relevant boundaries. However, owing to the uncertainty relating to the existence and scope of derivative interests, the concrete personality rights nevertheless have to be delimited, leading to a situation in which the right of name, right of reputation and right of privacy perform the role of the general right of personality in many cases.[7] However, whenever the concrete rights are delimited, it becomes hard to weigh them against each other, which leads to

---

6   *Yofi Tirosh*, A Name of One's Own: Gender and Symbolic Legal Personhood in the European Court of Human Rights (2010) 33 Harvard Journal of Law & Gender 247.

7   *Wang Liming*, Re-Definition of Right to Privacy (2012) 1 The Jurist 108.

a failure to establish a hierarchy of rights.[8] That inevitably frustrates efforts to resolve conflicts of rights or to establish appropriate remedies.

6 In order to maintain the static stability of the structure of the right of personality, it is necessary to keep the balance of 'centripetal' and 'centrifugal' forces. The former is a force directed towards the inherent interest which can clarify the boundaries of the right of personality; the latter refers to a force which is driven by derivative interests and which can easily obscure the boundaries of the right of personality. Among the concrete personality rights, the substantial right of personality has the strongest stability while the stability of the right to identity is weak.

7 The vagueness of the boundary of the right of personality in dynamic perspective refers to uncertainties in the enforcement of the right, which mainly occurs in two situations: first, where there is a conflict of personality rights (one person's enforcement of his right of personality infringes the right of personality of another and it is hard to determine which has legal precedence); second, where there exist concurrent bases of liability for infringement of one person's right of personality.[9]

8 The problems associated with the vague boundaries of the right of personality cannot be resolved by interpretative legal analysis. The analysis of the inherent interest might be more objective and more accurate because it is a legal concept and is restrained by its literal scope and the legislative purpose. The analysis of derivative interests tends to be more subjective because it does not involve purely legal concepts and so has to take account of the real-world demands. Judges have to balance different interests claimed by rival parties and make difficult and subjective judgments.[10] Ideally, these conflicts would be resolved by reference to an established legal hierarchy, but interpretations of derivative interests may not be based on different hierarchies and produce different results. For example, if there is a conflict between the right of portrait and copyright, we may decide not to protect the former on the basis that it is outweighed by a higher ranking right. The existence of concurrent bases of liability may also lead to uncertain outcomes, as where there is an infringement of the plaintiff's right of name and his right of reputation by way of the publication of his article under another author's name without his consent, and it is uncertain on which basis judgment in his favour should be made.

---

8   *Zhang Pinghua*, The Definition of Conflict of Rights (2006) 6 Science of Law 60.

9   See *Zhang Yinfeng v Chen Huaiyou for Infringement of Right of Name Dispute*, Nanjing Intermediate People's Court (2000) Civil Judgment No 964.

10   *PM Schwartz/K-N Peifer*, Prosser's Privacy and the German Right of Personality: Are Four Privacy Torts Better than One Unitary Concept? (2010) 98 California Law Review 1925.

III   Legal Recognition of the Right to Personality

9   Having a statutory right of personality means that the types and contents of the right of personality are fixed by law. The right cannot be sold or otherwise transferred. We believe that the right should be given statutory for a number of reasons. Specifying its different aspects would help to prevent category errors and could ensure that the right is kept distinct from the right to identity and intellectual property rights. Having regard to its intangible character, the functions of the inherent interest should be clarified by law in order to fix its various forms, determine its content and ensure its primacy. Putting the right of personality on a statutory basis ensures the public promulgation of its aspects and contents, so that others can identify its scope and order their affairs accordingly.[11] From this perspective, the greater the degree of intangibility of the inherent interest, the more desirable it is that it should be statutory. But a statutory right of personality amongst the fundamental rights recognised in the Constitution is not a substitute for a right of personality in civil law.[12] The regulation of personality rights should be in accordance with the overall system of law, ensuring coherence in the treatment of general rules and sub rules, concrete personality rights and general personality rights. It is for the judges to restrain the application of the latter.[13]

10   The derivative interests give a heterogenous content to the right of personality, which can cause confusion as to its true nature. Therefore, fixing the types of personality right is conducive to clarification of the nature of concrete personality rights and reducing the vagueness of their boundaries. By this means, with reference to the phenomenon of the commercialisation of personality rights, the so-called 'commercialisation right' could be identified as a new property right rather than derivative from the right of personality. This would not only avoid category error and ensure coherence, but would also enable the conveyance and inheritance of commercialisation rights to be allowed.[14] Nevertheless, for the avoidance of doubt and in the interests of convenience, new types of property right of this nature could be regulated in legislation relating to personality rights.

---

11   *H Koziol*, Unification of Tort Law: Wrongfulness (2007) 20.

12   *Igarashi Kiyoshi*, The Law on Personality Right (2009) 11 – translated by Gemin, Peking University Press 2009.

13   *WV Horton Rogers* (ed), Damages for Non-Pecuniary Loss in a Comparative Perspective (2001) 120–123.

14   *G Resta*, The New Frontiers of Personality Rights and the Problem of Commodification: European and Comparative Perspectives (2011) 26 Tulane European & Civil Law Forum 33.

11 Fixing the types of personality right will also help to guarantee minimum ethical standards in social interaction, to avoid the alienation of personality that is
generated by the derivative interests, and to prevent the abuse of administrative rights and the unreasonable limitation of personality rights. Additionally,
personality rights legislation should contain principles relating to the types
of public interest that should be recognised and their content. This provides
a mechanism for the coordination of the right of personality with other rights
and the effective resolution of conflicts between countervailing rights.

12 Putting the right of personality on a statutory basis is also conducive to the
rationalisation of relief mechanisms. If the existence of a personality right cannot be determined independently, the only mechanism that offers relief for its
infringement is the law of tort. Because this is an indirect means of protection
involving high cost, many countries have sought in recent years to introduce
new procedures which allow the personality right to be identified first, before
relief is pursued in tort law. The law of tort has long been divided between 'general' and 'special' torts, which does not leave sufficient space for the remedy
for infringing concrete personality rights. Tort's customary structure bases the
imposition of liability on such abstract factors as damage, illegality and fault,
which provide an inadequate basis for the protection of personality rights.
Therefore, it is necessary to give the right of personality a statutory basis so as
to help improve that protection. Specifically, it would provide better protection
in the following ways:

(1)   by defining the scope of the inherent interest and its derivative interests;[15]
(2)   by clarifying the boundaries of specific personality rights;[16]
(3)   by clarifying the obligation to respect the right of personality;
(4)   by clarifying the reasons for imposing liability in respect of interference
      with the various concrete personality rights, and distinguishing the fault
      giving rise to liability for interference with the inherent interest in per-
      sonality from that giving rise to liability for interference with the deriva-
      tive interest; and
(5)   by determining whether the violation of a concrete personality right can
      give rise to liability to compensate for immaterial damage or to pay puni-
      tive damages.

---

15   *Zhang Jian Gang v Kunming Peace Intellectual Property Agency co, LTD for Name Dispute
     Cases*, Kunming Intermediate People's Court Civil Judgments (2008) No 691; The Supreme
     Court' Interpretation on some Issues of Reputation Case, art 10.
16   *Wang Liming*, The Draft Civil Code of China: Recommendations and Instructions (China
     Legal Publishing House, 2004) 45.

13 Personality right legislation should not strive to be exhaustive. However, it
should at least define the types of personality right that accord with the demands of logic or social needs. The rights would be subject to judicial interpretation and the analogical judicial recognition of new types of personality right
so as to provide effective protection of the inherent interest in personality. Because the right of personality cannot be transferred and is heterogenous in
character, it is impossible to specify all its functions and all its content. Therefore, it should not be classified as a property right but regarded as sui generis.
The best approach would be to provide illustrative legislative examples of
different types of inherent interests and typical infringements of them, while
leaving enough room for judicial interpretation of the types of derivative interests that should be recognised and of *untypical* forms of infringement.

PART 3

Special Topics Relating to the Protection of Personality Rights by Private Law

∴

CHAPTER 7

Personality Rights and the Internet in Europe

Laura Emilia Weissel

I   Introduction

1 The protection of personality rights generally faces many challenges: the fact
that the concept of personality rights is defined differently in many European jurisdictions,[1] the different remedies in the various jurisdictions,[2] and the
problem that the infringement of personality rights can often hardly be assessed in money or sometimes even be assessed at all.[3]

2 All these issues related to personality rights become even more evident
on the Internet. The possibility to almost anonymously state, post, repost,
tweet, retweet, comment, or upload any information with a quick click surely
increases the risk of thoughtlessly or even deliberately infringing upon other
people's personality rights. Additionally, in contrast to conventional publications predating the Internet era,[4] one automatically reaches a broad – typically
worldwide – audience.[5] It comes as no surprise that the Internet is even referred
to as a *'powerful instrument for the bully and the abuser.'*[6] Even more so as such
comments, information or content usually remain available on the Internet

---

1 For details on the development of personality rights see *E Ondreasova*, Personality Rights in
Different European Legal Systems: Privacy, Dignity, Honour and Reputation in this volume
no 3 ff.

2 For details regarding the various remedies for personality rights infringements see
M Hinteregger, Protection of Personality Rights in Private Law, in this volume.

3 *H Koziol*, Basic Questions of Tort Law from a Germanic Perspective (2012) no 5/11 ff;
E Karner/H Koziol, Der Ersatz ideellen Schadens im österreichischen Recht und seine Reform
(2003) 119 ff.

4 Regarding the issues arising out of personality rights in the mass media see *T Thiede*, Personality Rights and the Mass Media, in this volume.

5 The manifold aspects and problems regarding the conflict of laws of the infringement of
personality rights are not considered here due to the confines of this article. For details see
eg *T Thiede*, Internationale Persönlichkeitsrechtsverletzungen durch Massenmedien – Eine
kollisionsrechtliche Interessenanalyse unter Berücksichtigung des deutschen, englischen,
französischen und europäischen Rechts (2010), with extensive references.

6 *M Schultz*, The Responsible Web: How Tort Law Can Save the Internet (2014) Journal of
European Tort Law (JETL) 184.

for a long period of time (*the Internet never forgets*)[7] and may be interlinked with other pages – thus multiplying its effect. However, the balance between the protection of personality rights on the one hand and the right to freedom of expression, freedom of information and the freedom to conduct business on the other hand has to be carefully assessed.[8]

3 The present paper aims at illustrating the European perspective on some issues related to personality rights and the Internet: first, it will give an overview on the subjects of liability, their obligations, and the remedies, including damages and injunctions that may be awarded, and, second, it will analyse recent European cases in order to illustrate some of the issues at hand relating to search engines.

II   Challenges of Personality Rights and the Internet

A   *Subjects of Tortious Liability*

4 The central question that arises when personality rights are infringed via the Internet is: who shall be held tortiously liable? The Internet user, the service provider, or maybe the search engine?[9]

1   The Internet User

5 It is fairly clear that the Internet user infringing other people's personality rights shall be held liable, whether he acted on facebook, twitter, on a blog etc; the liability for Internet users does not differ from the general principles of liability and follows the respective national provisions. Under Austrian law for example, art 1330 *Allgemeines Bürgerliches Gesetzbuch* (Austrian Civil Code, ABGB)[10] is a crucial provision for personality rights protection on the Internet,

---

7   *Schultz* (2014) JETL 188.

8   See the Opinion of Advocate General *Jääaskinen*, Case C-131/12, delivered on 25 June 2013, no 2 and the Judgment of the Court (Grand Chamber), Case C-131/12, decided upon on 13 May 2014, no 99.

9   For many potential addressees of related claims see *BA Koch*, Cyber Torts: Something Virtually New? (2014) JETL 152 ff. See also *R Perry/TZ Zarsky*, Liability for Online Anonymous Speech (2014) JETL 205 ff for a comparative perspective on the US-American, Israeli, EU and English approaches.

10   § 1330 ABGB: '(1) If a person has suffered actual loss or loss of profit through defamation, he is entitled to claim compensation. (2) This also applies if someone divulges facts which endanger the credit, earning or prospects of another when he knows or ought to have known of their untruthfulness. In such case revocation and its publication may also be demanded. For communications made in private, when the person making the

protecting the right to honour. Whoever causes actual damage or loss of profit through defamation by his fault – whether via the Internet or not – may be held liable to compensate for material damage; the compensation of non-pecuniary losses is excluded under art 1330 ABGB.[11] Also other personality rights such as the right to privacy or the right to one's name and image may come into play,[12] in which cases also immaterial damage may be awarded under certain circumstances.[13] Similarly, also other European jurisdictions protect personality rights: a central provision for the infringements of such rights can for example be found in art 9 of the French *Code Civil*, which protects the right to respect for private life (which includes the right to privacy, the sanctity of home and the confidentiality of correspondence).[14] Under German law, constitutional provisions guarantee the protection of personality rights: arts 1 and 2 of the *Grundgesetz* (Basic Law) protect the respect of human dignity and the right to free development of the *persona*. However, under civil law, damages for the infringement of personality rights are rather limited and only severe infringements of said rights may be compensated in money.[15] The English approach to personality rights was – since it is a common law country – developed case by case and includes for example defamation ('libel' and 'slander'), protecting the right to reputation and honour.[16]

6 The national provisions must, however, be read in light of fundamental European rights, which *inter alia* protect the right to respect for private and family

---

communication does not know of its untruthfulness, he is not liable provided that the recipient of the communication had a legitimate interest in it.' For translations of tort legislation also of other European countries see *K Oliphant/BC Steininger* (eds), European Tort Law – Basic Texts (2011).

11 See *KH Danzl* in: H Koziol/P Bydlinski/R Bollenberger, Kommentar zum ABGB (2014) § 1330 no 11 with further extensive references; *Karner/Koziol* (fn 3) 98 f. Regarding the scope of protected personality rights in Europe see e.g. *G Brüggemeier/A Colombi Ciacchi/P O'Callaghan*, Personality Rights in European Tort Law (2010) and the national reports in *H Koziol/A Warzilek*, The Protection of Personality Rights against Invasions by Mass Media (2005).

12 For details see *H Koziol/A Warzilek*, Der Schutz der Persönlichkeitsrechte gegenüber Massenmedien in Österreich, in: H Koziol/A Warzilek (eds), The Protection of Personality Rights against Invasions by Mass Media (2005) no 12 ff.

13 For example for the infringement of the right to privacy or the right to one's name where the tortfeasor acted with gross negligence (see §§ 1323, 1324 ABGB), for details see *H Koziol*, Österreichisches Haftpflichtrecht (3rd edn 1997) nos 11/2 ff, 11/24 with further extensive references.

14 For details see *Thiede* (fn 5) no 4/1 ff; *Ondreasova* (fn 1) 62 with further references.

15 *Ondreasova* (fn 1) no 20 f with further references.

16 For details see *M Lunney/K Oliphant*, Tort Law: Text & Materials (5th edn 2013) 686 ff.

life, home and communications, the right to the protection of personal data, the right to freedom of expression and information and the freedom to conduct a business.[17] Accordingly, one must follow the national legal provisions in order to assess the liability of a potential tortfeasor when personality rights – interpreted in accordance with European law – are infringed via the Internet.

7 But what liability regime applies to the various forms of 'providers' and search engines? For which kind of services shall they be held liable – instead of or in addition to the Internet user?[18] As Internet users who infringe upon personality rights can often hardly be identified or may not be worth pursuing, it may therefore be tempting to try to establish a liability of service providers.[19] Yet one must bear in mind the sensitive balance between the opposite rights – namely the personality right of the victim and the rights to freedom of expression, information and to conduct business of the service provider.[20] Furthermore, the technical feasibility of obligations to monitor information has to be taken into account.

8 The starting point for analysing the various obligations and the resulting (exemptions from) liabilities of potential tortfeasors from a European perspective is the E-Commerce Directive (ECD).[21] This Directive was adopted in 2000 with the aim to *'create a legal framework to ensure the free movement of information society services between Member states,'*[22] which *'in many cases [can] be a specific reflection ... of a more general principle, namely freedom of expression.'*[23] To this end, the ECD clearly states that the liability of service providers in every Member State shall be excluded for certain services (see in particular arts 12 to 15 ECD). One main reason for clearly stating that a service provider shall not

---

17   Arts 7, 8, 11 and 16 of the Charter of Fundamental Rights of the European Union.

18   For an analysis of the various combination of these liabilities from a legal and economic perspective see *Perry/Zarsky* (2014) JETL 205 ff.

19   See *BA Koch* (2014) JETL 152, 153 f and *Perry/Zarksy* (2014) JETL 205, 229 ff. Regarding the various reasons for holding service providers liable see also *P Frech*, Zivilrechtliche Haftung von Internet-Providern bei Rechtsverletzungen durch ihre Kunden (2009) 16 ff.

20   Similarly, also *Spindler* holds that '[t]he overall issue of liability, however, seems to be too hot a topic [and thus refraining the Commission to modify the ECD], as different interest of lobbying groups such as rightholders on the one side and the Internet industry on the other, are clashing,' see *G Spindler*, EU Internet Policy, in: A Savin/J Trzaskowki (eds), Research Handbook on EU Internet Law (2014) 9.

21   Directive 2000/31/EC of the European Parliament and of the Council of 8 June 2000 on certain legal aspects of information society services, in particular electronic commerce, in the Internal Market (Directive on electronic commerce) Official Journal (OJ) L 178, 17.7.2000, 1–16. See also *Perry/Zarsky* (2014) JETL 205, 219 ff.

22   Recital 8 ECD.

23   Recital 9 ECD.

be liable for these – usually merely technical and automated services – lies in
the *'purpose of making the transmissions [of information] more efficient.'*[24] The
Directive addresses the Member States and therefore had to be transposed into
national law.[25] Accordingly, when assessing the liability of service providers,
one has to first verify whether or not the service provider would be liable under
the general principles of liability applicable under national law, and – in case
that the service provider would be held liable – in a second step see if such a liability is excluded because of the national legislation based on the Directive.[26]

2   The Internet Service Providers (ISPs)
9   The ECD defines 'service providers' in art 2 (b) as *'any natural or legal person
providing an information society service.'* This shall not only include online sell-
ing of goods, but also offering online information, providing tools allowing for
online searching, providing access to a communication network or hosting information provided by the recipient of the service.[27]
10   ISPs usually offer different services, which result in different obligations and
corresponding liabilities. It is therefore necessary to distinguish between the
numerous kinds of providers according to their services,[28] a task that is nowadays hard to undertake.[29]

---

24   Recital 42 ECD.
25   Austria for example implemented the ECD with the adoption of the *E-Commerce
      Gesetz* (ECG), Bundesgesetz, mit dem bestimmte rechtliche Aspekte des elektronischen
      Geschäfts- und Rechtsverkehrs geregelt werden, Bundesgesetzblatt (BGBl 152/2001).
      A German-English version is available at: <http://www.ris.bka.gv.at/Dokumente/Erv/
      ERV_2001_1_152/ERV_2001_1_152.pdf> (last accessed 13 December 2015). Germany trans-
      posed the ECD in the *Telemediengesetz* (TMG) of 26 February 2007 (BGBl I S 179), and Italy
      enacted the Directive via legislative decree, see *Decreto Legislativo 9 Aprile 2003 no 70*. For
      details on the implementation of the Directive and the respective legislation and case
      law see *T Verbiest/G Spindler/GM Riccio/A Van der Perre*, Study on the Liability of Internet
      Intermediaries. Available at <http://ec.europa.eu/internal_market/e-commerce/docs/
      study/liability/final_report_en.pdf> (last accessed 13 December 2015).
26   See *H Koziol*, Providerhaftung nach ECG und MedienG, in: W Berka/C Grabenwarter/
      M Holoubek (eds), Persönlichkeitsschutz in elektronischen Massenmedien (2012) 43, 48.
27   Recital 18 ECD. For details see *Koziol* (fn 26) 41 ff with further references.
28   The following categorisation of providers follows *Koziol* (fn 26) 41 ff. Similar also *P Baist-
      rocchi*, Liability of Intermediary Service Providers in the EU Directive on Electronic Com-
      merce (2003) Santa Clara Computer & High Technology Law Journal (Santa Clara Comp
      & High Tech LJ) 116 f.
29   For details see e.g. *Frech* (fn 19) 7 ff, 26 f; *C Reed*, Internet Law (2004) 32 ff. The categorisa-
      tion of the providers in the ECD is also referred to as 'no longer comprehensive,' *Perry/
      Zarsky* (2014) JETL 205, 221.

a)   *Content Provider*

11 Generally speaking, a 'content provider' is an ISP that makes its *own* information available on the Internet.[30] The ECD does not have specific provisions for
the content provider, since it is its own information that it shares on the Internet, which it can therefore easily control.[31] Accordingly, its obligations to
not infringe other people's personality rights do not differ from the general
principles; the same applies for its liability.[32]

b)   *Intermediary Service Provider (Host and Access Provider)*

12 The ECD only regulates activities of intermediary service providers and determines that intermediary service providers shall – inasmuch as they are *'bridge
builders between content providers and Internet users'* [33] – not be liable for certain activities.[34] Usually, their activity is merely passive and the intermediary
ISP has no knowledge of the stored or transmitted information.[35] Simplified,
intermediary service providers may be categorised as host and access providers: 'Access providers' offer the user mere access to the Internet by enabling
them to connect to their network; 'host providers' as a second category are
ISPs that – unlike content providers – make information of *third parties* available on the Internet. As the name indicates, host providers *host* information,
which can be accessed by the users, potentially including a forum or bulletin
boards.[36] Even a facebook page of an individual or a company falls into this
category.[37]

13 According to art 12 ECD, an intermediary service provider is – in accordance
with the general principles for the imputation of liability – not liable for the
mere transmission of third party information or the provision of access to a
communication network, as long as it does not initiate the transmission, does
not select the receiver and does not select or modify the information. Likewise,

---

30   For more details on the difficulty to differentiate between *own* and *third-party* informa-
      tion see e.g. *Frech* (fn 19) 109 f with further references.

31   See also *T Hoeren*, Unterlassungsansprüche gegen Host Provider – die Rechtslage nach
      dem Ricardo-/Rolex-Urteil des BGH, in: U Wackerbarth/T Vormbaum/HP Marutschke
      (eds), Festschrift für Ulrich Eisenhardt zum 70. Geburtstag (2007) 244.

32   *Koziol* (fn 26) 43. See below for details.

33   Opinion of Advocate General *Jääaskinen*, Case C-131/12, no 36.

34   The ECD does not provide a liability regime itself, but rather establishes that certain
      ISPs – intermediaries – shall not be held liable. Regarding the historical background and
      the dogmatic issues see *Frech* (fn 19) 100 ff with further extensive references.

35   Recital 42 ECD.

36   *Baistrocchi* (2003) Santa Clara Comp & High Tech LJ 116, 122.

37   *C Benes*, Shitstorm auf Facebook-Seiten: Wer haftet? (2013) ecolex 399, 400.

mere (short term) 'caching' of information shall also not lead to the liability of the intermediary service provider (cf art 13 ECD).[38]

14 Somewhat peculiar is the provision regarding hosting third party information. According to art 14 ECD, *'the service provider is not liable for the information stored at the request of a recipient of the service.'* This applies only if the provider does not know of illegal activity or information (art 14 (a)); or if the provider expeditiously removes or disables the access to information after obtaining knowledge or awareness of an apparently illegal activity or information. Especially the terms 'knowledge' and 'awareness' give rise to manifold issues,[39] including the problem that an ISP itself must judge whether or not information or an activity is *apparently illegal* and it therefore has to disable the access to this information.[40]

3   Search Engines

15 Since the ECD does not contain any special provisions for search engines, the liability and exemptions from liability can vary under the different legal systems.[41] Under Austrian law, search engines[42] and their liability follow the same principles as the liability of intermediary service providers.[43] According to art 14 ECG, a search engine *'shall not be responsible for the information retrieved, provided the service provider 1. does not initiate the transmission of the retrieved information; 2. does not select the receiver of the retrieved information; and 3. does not select or modify the retrieved information.'* Recently, many cases have brought up issues regarding the liability of search engines, since it is difficult to define if the activities of search engines may be defined as *'mere conduit,'* 'caching' or 'hosting' in the sense of the ECD.[44]

---

38   For details see e.g. *Baistrocchi* (2003) Santa Clara Comp & High Tech LJ 116, 119 ff.

39   For a detailed analysis see *Koziol* (fn 26) 48 ff; *Verbiest et al.* (fn 25) 36 ff.

40   *Baistrocchi* (2003) Santa Clara Comp & High Tech LJ 116, 124 ff. See also *T Hoeren*, Internetrecht (2012) 451 ff.

41   This loophole was criticised by *Baistrocchi* (2003) Santa Clara Comp & High Tech LJ 116, 127 ff. Also the German TMG does not contain any provision regarding search engines. For details on the liability and duties of search engines in German law see e.g. *Hoeren* (fn 40) 460 ff with further extensive references. For English law see *Lunney/Oliphant* (fn 16) 716 f. For a European overview see *Verbiest et al.* (fn 25) 85 ff.

42   According to § 14 ECG, a search engine is 'a service provider which provides users with a search engine or other electronic aids to search for third-party information.'

43   The Austrian proposal by the government intended to expand the scope of application of the Directive and applied the same principles to search engines and links in §§ 14 and 17, see 'proposal from the government' (Regierungsvorlage) 817 XXI GP 32 ff.

44   See below no 22 ff.

B   *Obligation to Monitor?*

16 The cardinal question regarding the liability of host providers in particular is the extent of their obligation to monitor stored information. Generally speaking, only where there is a duty to preserve another from damage by positive act, a liability by omission – not blocking or taking down information – may lead to liability.[45] The ECD clearly states in art 15 para 1 that *'Member States shall not impose a general obligation on [access and host] providers ... to monitor the information which they transmit or store, nor a general obligation actively to seek facts or circumstances indicating illegal activity.'* Yet a specific obligation to monitor arises where the ISP has knowledge or awareness of illegal activities.[46] Such monitoring obligations shall be feasible and may be *'reasonably expected'* from an ISP.[47] Accordingly, an ISP may be held liable for damages if it fails to fulfil its obligation where a specific obligation to monitor is established and the ISP is at fault.[48]

17 However, contrary to the 'notice and take down' system established in the US,[49] the ECD gives no specification of a similar 'notice and take down' system, but leaves the option of establishing such a procedure to the Member States (art 15 para 2 ECD).[50]

C   *Damages*

18 Where the requirements of tortious liability are fulfilled – namely damage, causation, wrongfulness and fault[51] – the person whose personality rights were infringed may claim pecuniary compensation from the tortfeasor, since

---

45   *P Widmer,* Duty to Protect Others from Damage, in: Principles of European Tort Law – Text and Commentary (2005) no 1; *Koziol* (fn 3) 191 f.

46   Such a specific monitoring obligation is in accordance with the ECD, see recital 47 ECD. For details under Austrian law see *C Pichler*, Besondere Kontrollpflicht für Host-Provider (2007) ecolex 189 ff.

47   Recital 48 ECD.

48   That such a specific obligation to monitor shall arise only under certain circumstances also follows the general approach of art 4:103 Principles of European Tort Law (PETL), which suggests that a duty to protect others from damage may arise 'when the seriousness of the harm on the one side and the ease of avoiding the damage on the other side point towards such a duty' see <http://www.egtl.org/> for various translations of the PETL.

49   For details see e.g. *Frech* (fn 19) 76 ff with further extensive references.

50   For details on the different implementation of such a 'notice and take down' system in the European jurisdictions see *Verbiest et al.* (fn 25) 106 ff. See also *Perry/Zarsky* (2014) JETL 205, 241 ff for an analysis from an economic perspective.

51   For details see *Koziol* (fn 3) 109 ff with further extensive references and *Frech* (fn 19) 27 ff.

restoration in kind will hardly be possible.[52] According to general principles inherent in continental European law, damages shall not exceed the loss suffered. The victim may seek compensation from the Internet user or the ISP – if the ISP's liability is established:[53] in such case, the Internet user and the ISP are solidarily liable.[54] It is important to note in this context that the exemptions from liability set out in the ECD are only applicable for liability in damages (and not injunctions),[55] also including immaterial damages.

D   *Injunctions*

19 Injunctions – whether they are preventive or reparative – play a crucial role in cases of personality rights infringement via the Internet.[56] In this context, 'injunction' may be delineated as an order *'to block or remove illicit content and prevent future infringements.'*[57] The ECD clearly states that the exemptions from liability do not *'affect the possibility for a court or administrative authority ... of requiring the service provider to terminate or prevent an infringement'* (art 12 para 3, art 13 para 2 and art 14 para 3 ECD).[58] Where often an ISP cannot be held liable under tort, it still may have to take other measures such as disconnecting an Internet user or blocking specific web pages. Since the legal consequences of injunctions are not as far-reaching as the remedies of tort law, the requirements for injunctions differ from the requirements for tortious liability.[59] Usually, no damage has to have occurred (yet), the unlawful endangerment of personality rights suffices.[60] Preventive as well as reparative injunctions are non-fault based and – in addition to the requirement of knowing (or having

---

52   See *Koziol/Warzilek* (fn 12) no 148 ff.

53   Critical as regards the vast exemptions for ISPs see e.g. *V Zeno-Zencovich*, Media Liability in the Information Society, in: H Koziol/A Warzilek (eds), The Protection of Personality Rights against Invasions by Mass Media (2005) no 13.

54   *Koziol* (fn 26) 53. For details on damages in the US, Germany and Switzerland see *Frech* (fn 19) 285 ff.

55   See e.g. *Baistrocchi* (2003) Santa Clara Comp & High Tech LJ 116, 117 f; *Koziol* (fn 26) 53. Hoeren argues that the exemption of liability shall also be applicable for (reparative) injunctions, see *Hoeren* (fn 31) 250 ff. For a detailed analysis see also *Frech* (fn 19) 250 ff.

56   See *Verbiest et al.* (fn 25) 19, 28. For details on injunctions see ibid 48 ff.

57   *Verbiest et al.* (fn 25) 48.

58   Critical as regards to German law *Hoeren* (fn 31) 250 ff with further references. § 19 of the Austrian ECG states that injunctions are not prejudiced by the exemption for liability, see *W Zankl*, E-Commerce-Gesetz, Kommentar und Handbuch (2002) no 296 ff.

59   See e.g. *Koziol* (fn 3) no 2/7.

60   For details see *Koziol* (fn 3) nos 2/7 ff, 2/15 ff; *Koziol/Warzilek* (fn 12) no 174 ff.

the possibility to know) of the potential infringement – merely require *'the
unauthorised infringement upon a third-party right or interest.'* [61]

20 Having fewer requirements for injunctions is justifiable because the action required by the injunction does not burden the ISP heavily – especially if compared to compensation for damage as required under tort law.[62]

E   *Hot Issues of Personality Rights Infringement via the Internet*

21 Many issues arise when it comes to the infringement of personality rights via
the Internet.[63] Examples include the liability of search engines, the liability
of a 'source' of defamation if an untrue statement is reproduced via social
networks,[64] liability for 'flame wars,'[65] liability of online archives[66] or liability
for unauthorised dissemination of information (for example the 'Wikileaks' in-
cident[67]). In the following, I will discuss the legal implications relating to some
cases concerning the liability of search engines, as many European courts currently have to deal with related questions.

III   Cases

22 Google – being the world's most popular search engine[68] – has to fight several
legal battles regarding its potential liability for personality rights infringement.
Since search engines are not explicitly covered by the ECD, the liability may

---

61   *Koziol* (fn 3) no 2/16 ff with further references and details on the various approaches.

62   *Koziol* (fn 3) no 2/7.

63   See especially JETL 2014, volume 5 no 2, Special Issue: Cyber Torts.

64   For an example of often retweeted libel see The Guardian, 23 November 2012 'McAlpine
libel: 20 tweeters including Sally Bercow pursued for damages,' available at <http://www
.guardian.co.uk/tv-and-radio/2012/nov/23/mcalpine-libel-bercow-monbiot-davies>
(accessed 13 December 2015). See also The New York Times, 25 November 2012 'Libel Case
That Snared BBC Widens To Twitter,' available at <http://www.nytimes.com/2012/11/26/
technology/26iht-twitter26.html?_r=1&> (accessed 13 December 2015). See also *Lunney/
Oliphant* (fn 16) 715 f.

65   See e.g. *Benes* (2013) ecolex 399 ff.

66   See e.g. *I Griss*, Persönlichkeitsschutz in Online-Medien, in: W Berka/C Grabenwarter/
M Holoubek (eds), Persönlichkeitsschutz in elektronischen Massenmedien (2012) 64 ff.

67   See *C Kurz*, WikiLeaks, in: H Koziol/J Seethaler/T Thiede, Medienpolitik und Recht II
(2013) for a historical overview.

68   For recent figures regarding the market share of Google see e.g. <http://searchengineland
.com/google-worlds-most-popular-search-engine-148089>and<http://www.statista.com/
statistics/216573/worldwide-market-share-of-search-engines/> (accessed 13 December
2015).

differ according to national law. The Austrian ECG in its art 14 clearly provides
that search engines shall not be held liable as long as the search engine did not
interfere with the search or its results,[69] yet other countries do not necessarily
have similar provisions.[70] Accordingly, there is a vast range of legal questions
that have to be clarified – again, balancing the rights and interests involved is
at the core of the issues at hand, a question evaluated differently in the various
jurisdictions.[71]

A   *Google vs Defamatory 'auto complete' Suggestions and 'snippets'*

23   Since April 2009, Google automatically completes the search request of a user
by suggesting potential word combinations, which follow an algorithm of previous queries of other users and indexed web pages. Problems arise when the
auto complete function suggests word combinations that interfere with personality rights, for example the right to honour.[72]

24   The German *Bundesgerichtshof* (Federal Court of Justice, BGH) recently had
to deal with an auto complete case, in which Google suggested the words 'Sci-
entology' and 'fraud' (*Betrug*) when the plaintiff's name was typed in.[73] The
plaintiff requested Google to cease the publication of these auto complete suggestions and demanded damages. The BGH decided that Google has no general obligation to monitor the auto complete results, yet it has to impede such
suggestions once Google has knowledge of an infringement of a personality
right. The BGH only ruled on the admissibility of injunctions, and the question
of – limited – damages and compensation of legal fees was not addressed in
the decision at hand.[74]

25   Recently, an Italian court also had to deal with a similar case, in which the
auto complete function of Google suggested 'sect' (*setta*), 'plagiarism' (*plagio*)
and 'fraud' (*truffa*) in addition to the queries regarding the plaintiffs' names.[75]

---

69   See above no 15.

70   For example Italy and Germany. For details on European legislation see *T Verbiest et al.*
(fn 25) 88 ff.

71   For details and further extensive references see e.g. *A Warzilek*, Comparative Report, in:
H Koziol/A Warzilek (eds), The Protection of Personality Rights against Invasions by Mass
Media (2005) no 1 ff.

72   An instructive overview on recent European judicial decisions is given by Eady J in *Metropolitan International Schools Ltd v Designtechnica Corp* [2009] England & Wales High
Court (EWHC) 1765 Queen's Bench (QB) no 97 ff.

73   BGH 14 May 2013, VI ZR 269/12.

74   The BGH only stated that the court of appeal will have to reconsider these questions, see
BGH 14 May 2013, VI ZR 269/12 no 31.

75   Tribunale di Milano N RG 68306/2012, translations by the author.

The Court of Milan held and explicitly stated that 'the provider is not responsible for automatic memorisation.'[76] Furthermore, Google as a 'neutral player' did not have the obligation to remove content or automatic search predictions, unless it was ordered to do so by a court or administrative authority.[77]

26 The Google auto complete implications were also subject to a case in England and Wales: Google was not held liable for the publication of automatically produced 'snippets,' since the search engine's auto complete function works without human intervention and merely facilitates search results.[78] Eady J explicitly stressed that *'when a snippet is thrown up on the user's screen in response to his search, it points him in the direction of an entry somewhere on the Web that corresponds, to a greater or lesser extent, to the search terms he has typed in. It is for him to access or not, as he chooses. It is fundamentally important to have in mind that the Third Defendant [Google Inc] has no role to play in formulating the search terms.'*[79] The extent and effectiveness of blocking defamatory 'snippets' may well leave room for debate.[80]

27 In my opinion, in such auto complete and snippet cases one has to clearly differentiate between tortious liability on the one hand, which could ultimately lead to the obligation of the search engine to provide compensation, and on the other hand, the possibility to grant the victim an injunction against the search engine to cease defamatory or illegal auto complete results. The search engine usually has no knowledge of the predictions or 'snippets' that are shown on its own web page and therefore should not be held liable for damages.[81] Only where there is a specific obligation to monitor or where the search engine has knowledge of illegal circumstances and does not act in accordance with its obligations may a search engine also be held liable for damages. However, to attribute a general liability for defamatory or illegal snippets on search engines would over-reach the goal and certainly significantly inhibit their functioning.

28 In cases of injunctions, however, an analogy with the principles established in the ECD may be drawn and accordingly a reasonable 'notice and take down' system may be a feasible solution: where the search engine gains knowledge of apparent defamatory or illegal search 'snippets,' it should take measures

---

76   Tribunale di Milano N RG 68306/2012 p. 6.

77   Tribunale di Milano N RG 68306/2012 p. 9 f.

78   *Metropolitan International Schools Ltd v Designtechnica Corp* [2009] EWHC 1765 QB.

79   Ibid, no 51.

80   Ibid, no 64.

81   Whether for example because of the exemption from liability, as it is provided in § 14 ECG in Austria, or because the search engine cannot be held liable as publisher, either by authorship or by acquiescence, see *Metropolitan International Schools Ltd v Designtechnica Corp* [2009] EWHC 1765 QB no 64.

to prevent such search predictions. While the efforts and expenditure necessary to build a functioning 'notice and take down' system may be a burden on
search engines, they are less burdensome and very likely less expensive than
paying compensation for personality rights infringement via auto complete
suggestions and snippets. Only where the ISP does not react and take down the
relevant information may it be liable for damages. This approach to allow for
injunctions but to exclude a general liability is in line with the ratio of the ECD,
which points out that under certain circumstances ISPs shall not be liable,
yet that these circumstances do not necessarily affect potential injunctions.[82]
Of course a 'notice and take down' system bears the risk that search engines
become the 'judge' of defamation and illegal activities, yet the cases usually
regard 'apparent' illegal or defamatory material and, where the illegality is not
apparent, a court shall decide whether or not an injunction shall be granted.

B   *Google vs 'the right to be forgotten'?*

29 Another case involving Google is the recent case C-131/12 before the Court of
Justice of the EU (CJEU): the CJEU had to decide upon – amongst other requests for preliminary ruling – the question whether or not a search engine
could be obligated to withdraw from its indexes an item of information that
contains personal data legally published by a third party on a web page. In the
case at hand, when typing in the plaintiff's name, a link appeared in the search
results directing to a widely circulated Spanish newspaper article of a real-
estate auction connected with the plaintiff's social security debts. What was
problematic in this context is the time span lying between the lawful and correct newspaper publication and the search query: the original publishing date
was early 1998, and even years after the proceedings against the plaintiff were
concluded, the search results of a search request of the plaintiff's name lead
to said newspaper publication. The plaintiff filed a complaint with the Spanish Data Protection Agency (*Agencia Española de Protección de Datos*, AEPD),
requesting *inter alia* that Google be required to remove or conceal the personal
data relating to him in order for said link not to appear in the search results.
The plaintiff referred to his 'right to be forgotten' (*derecho al olvido*), which
would be breached if no steps could be taken against auto suggest predictions
that interfered with his right to privacy and protection of personal data.[83]

30 While the actual circumstances differed from the cases mentioned above, the
underlying question is related: shall a search engine that via an automated

---

82   See above no 17.

83   For details on the facts and concrete questions of the case see the Opinion of Advocate
      General *Jääskinen*, Case C-131/12, no 18 ff and Case C-131/12 no 14 ff.

system enhances the user queries be held liable for defamatory, illegal or even legal search results, which merely reflect third parties' web pages? Shall injunctions be available against the search engine?

31   The concrete questions referred for a preliminary ruling of the CJEU relating to the 'right to be forgotten' were twofold: first, whether or not a national authority may directly impose on search engines a requirement to withdraw from its indexes an item of information published by third parties, without addressing itself in advance or simultaneously to the owner of the web, and secondly – provided such obligation may be imposed – if such obligation may be excluded in case the item has been lawfully published.

32   The Advocate General in his Opinion stressed that the Data Protection Directive (DPD)[84] did not grant an absolute 'right to be forgotten,' since such right has to be balanced with the rights to freedom of expression and information, and the right to conduct a business.[85] Accordingly, the Advocate General suggested to the CJEU that the data protection rights provided for in the DPD *'do not confer ... a right to address himself to a search engine service provider in order to prevent indexing of the information relating to him personally, published legally on third parties' web pages.'*[86]

33   The Court in its judgment did not follow the Advocates General's line of argument and strengthened the 'right to be forgotten' by ruling that *'the supervisory authority or judicial authority may order the operator of the search engine to remove from the list of results displayed following a search made on the basis of a person's name links to web pages published by third parties containing information relating to that person.'*[87] Said obligation shall not depend on orders to remove the name and information from the web page itself. As a result, the third parties' web page containing the personal information may still remain online, while the search result must not show the link to the respective page. The Court held that such a prerequisite would inhibit the protection of data users, since information published on a web page can easily be reproduced on other pages and often the responsible persons for the publication are not subject to European Union law.[88]

34   The Court clearly stated that the request for deletion of a link does not have to lead to unlawful or inaccurate information on a web page, but that such

---

84   Directive 1995/46/EC of the European Parliament and of the Council of 24 October 1995 on the protection of individuals with regard to the processing of personal data and on the free movement of such data, OJ L 281, 23.11.1995, 31–39.

85   Opinion of Advocate General *Jääskinen*, Case C-131/12, no 104 ff.

86   Opinion of Advocate General *Jääskinen*, Case C-131/12, no 138.

87   CJEU Case C-131/12, no 82.

88   CJEU Case C-131/12, no 84.

request is already justified if the information is *'inadequate, irrelevant or no longer relevant, or excessive in relation to the purposes for which they were processed and in the light of the time that has elapsed.'*[89] Where this is applicable, *'the information and links concerned in the list of results must be erased.'*[90] The CJEU therefore determines that even data legally processed has to be put into a timely perspective.

35 Also with regard to the second question – relating to the scope of the rights guaranteed by the DPD – the Court strengthened the position of the individual's right to the protection of privacy and personal data by confirming that the data subject himself may request that the information may be removed from a list of search results.[91]

36 In its ruling, the Court clearly stated that the protection of the right to privacy and the protection of personal data as a rule override the economic interest of the search engine and the interest of the general public in information on a person upon a search relating to the person's name.[92] This general rule shall not be applicable where the interest of the general public in having access to information outweighs the interests of the data subject:[93] in such case, the search engine may not grant the request for deletion of the respective search result.

37 The reactions to the ruling of the CJEU were – quite naturally – divergent: while search engines, online businesses and advocates for the freedom of speech received it critically, it was well received by others.[94] Google reacted quickly by implementing a system for requests of users to delete links from search results by providing an online form on 29 May 2014.[95] According to Google's transparency report from 29 May 2014 until 13 December 2015, 42.1% of the requests

---

89   CJEU Case C-131/12, no 92 f.

90   CJEU Case C-131/12, no 94.

91   CJEU Case C-131/12, no 99.

92   CJEU Case C-131/12, no 99.

93   CJEU Case C-131/12, no 99.

94   See eg BBC News, 14 May 2014 'Google ruling "astonishing," says Wikipedia founder Wales,' available at <http://www.bbc.com/news/technology-27407017>, and The Drum, 14 May 2014 'Reaction: Brands and agencies question EU court's "right to be forgotten" ruling for Google,' available at <http://www.thedrum.com/news/2014/05/14/reaction-brands-and-agencies-question-eu-courts-right-be-forgotten-ruling-google>. For reactions from an American perspective see The New Yorker, 29 September 2014 <http://www.newyorker.com/magazine/2014/09/29/solace-oblivion> (last accessed 13 December 2015).

95   Available in various languages on the help page of Google, see for example <https://support.google.com/legal/contact/lr_eudpa?product=websearch&hl=en>.

for deletion (in total 356,674 requests concerning 1,263,576 links to web pages) were granted.[96]

38   By ruling in favour of the 'right to be forgotten,' the CJEU strengthened the individual's position and the right to privacy and data protection. Upon request for deletion, the search engine has to assess whether or not a link shall be deleted. Should the request not be granted, the data subject shall have the right to request the supervisory or judicial authority control this decision.[97] Also in these cases, the risk that search engines have to judge the relevant data cannot be denied.[98] However, the individual has the right to appeal to the authorities and – in the cases where the search engine did not fulfil its obligation to take down the information – may also be held liable for damages. While the CJEU confirmed in its ruling that an individual whose rights were infringed by a search engine shall have a right to call upon an authority – yet without mentioning the word 'injunction' and without referring to any liability in damages.

39   The decision of the CJEU was correct: the interest of the (potential) victim of an infringement of personality rights – even to the extent that even accurate information was kept online for too long – shall outweigh the economic interest of search engines. Only where the right to information of the general public is at stake, shall it trump the individual's right and a link may not be deleted. Had the CJEU followed the Opinion of the Advocate General not to grant injunctions, such ruling would have denied a person the chance to 'wipe clean' his name and potential serious implications on his reputation. In times when information and personal data can easily be shared and stored for a long time, adequate measures to set information aright are not too far-reaching. However, the 'right to be forgotten' should not lead to a general liability in damages of a search engine – a question that was not raised in the case at hand – if previously legitimate or even illegal publications are displayed. Only where the search engine did not comply with its specific obligation to monitor, for example if the request for deletion was wrongfully denied, shall a search engine be liable to pay the corresponding compensation.

IV   Conclusion

40   The issues related to the infringement of personality rights via the Internet are manifold. At the centre of attention must lie the peculiar balance of the rights

---

96   Available at <http://www.google.com/transparencyreport/removals/europeprivacy/>.

97   CJEU Case C-131/12, no 77.

98   See already above no 28.

and interests of the involved parties. Where an Internet user must enjoy the right of freedom of expression and where an ISP must be able to freely run its business, the protection of personality rights of the individual must limit the others – and vice versa.

41 The tendency to not hold ISPs liable for merely automated actions is comprehensible, especially when taking into consideration the functioning of the free movement of information society. Yet this aim should not be overstretched and it would be too lax if the services provided by ISPs – and also search engines – were to lead to no legal consequence at all. In my opinion, the possibility to grant injunctions for victims of personality rights infringements is an appropriate measure, since it gives the victim a remedy to stop the infringement. Where an individual wishes to rectify its reputation, it should have the 'right to be forgotten' also in the world wide web. This approach is also reflected in the envisaged General Data Protection Regulation, a draft of which was presented first in 2012 and shall be adopted soon.[99]

42 On the other hand, when it comes to damages for personality rights infringement via the Internet, the victim shall only be entitled to seek compensation from the actual infringer: this might be the Internet user posting illegal information, but this might also be the ISP if a specific obligation to monitor was wrongfully not observed. However, to expand the scope of general liability also to ISPs would overburden their duties and inhibit the functioning of the free movement of information. With the said limitations to the ISPs' liability – which are clearly reflected in the ECD – and the possibility for victims to seek injunctions, the interests at hand seem well balanced, at least from a European perspective.

---

99   See art 17 of the Regulation, entitled 'the right to be forgotten and to erasure,' draft proposal available at <http://ec.europa.eu/justice/data-protection/document/review2012/com_2012_11_en.pdf> (accessed 13 December 2015). For a critical analysis of the divergent approach between the US and the EU see *P Schwartz*, The EU–US Privacy Collision (2014) Harvard Law Review 1994 ff.

CHAPTER 8

The Right to Privacy in the Internet Age: The Chinese Perspective

Wang Jia

I Background

1 In an Internet environment, to submit personal information to corporations and intermediaries has become an essential condition for consumers and Internet users to enjoy the convenience of e-commerce and online social media services. However, the low level of web security and 'big data'[1] technologies that integrate large, diverse and complex datasets at a massive scale and aggregately analyze the data have increasingly rendered consumers and users vulnerable to breaches of privacy in cyberspace.

2 The right to privacy is primarily conceived as a negative right, which protects a person's right to conceal herself from the public.[2] By contrast, other personality rights contain an element of control over personal information that presents the person in a public context and helps develop a unique personality among peers.[3] Privacy rights protect a person against arbitrary interference with personal matters, her private and family life, her body, property and home and the secrecy of her correspondence.[4] In essence, privacy is about retracting personal matters from the public sphere as is shown by the Latin word *privare* which denotes the act of taking something out of the public domain, and is the

---

* Research Fellow, School of Law, South China Institute For International Intellectual Property, Centre for Foreign-related Legal Research with Going Abroad Strategy, Guangdong University of Foreign Studies.

1 *A De Mauro/M Greco/M Grimaldi*, What is Big Data? A Consensual Definition and a Review of Key Research Topics AIP Conference Proceedings, 5–8 September 2014, <http://dx.doi.org/10.1063/1.4907823>.

2 *L Brandeis/S Warren*, The Right to Privacy (1890) 4 Harvard Law Review (Harv L Rev) 193, 193–220.

3 *B van der Sloot*, Privacy as Personality Right: Why the ECtHR's Focus on Ulterior Interests Might Prove Indispensable in the Age of 'Big Data' (2015) 80 Utrecht Journal of International and European Law 25, 26.

4 *AD Moore*, Privacy Rights: Moral and Legal Foundations (2010) 33 f.

© KONINKLIJKE BRILL NV, LEIDEN, 2018 | DOI 10.1163/9789004351714_010

opposite of *publicare* which means to take something from the private to the public domain.[5]

3 The right to privacy and the right to data protection are increasingly intertwined in an Internet environment. On the one hand, as scholars point out, data protection is not only about the protection of liberty and dignity of individuals but has wider implications for the development of Internet users' social identity as citizens as well as consumers.[6] On the other hand, in the context of the omnipresent Internet, privacy is deemed as only one element of modern life that is co-existing with many other important issues such as security, self-development, freedom of speech, accountability, and social productivity.[7] Therefore, the protection of privacy in an online environment is not absolute but needs to be balanced against other goals that the law aspires to achieve in the digital age.

II   An Overview of the Right to Privacy

A   *Privacy and Personality Rights*

4 Privacy is protected in different ways in civil and common law systems. As for the notion of 'personality right,' two types of 'rights' are established in modern civil law: fundamental rights including classic human rights, and social or economic rights requesting public authorities to assist citizens.[8] As an example, art 2 of the German Constitution specifies: 'Everyone has the right to the free development of his personality insofar as he does not violate the rights of others or offend against the constitutional order or the moral code.'[9] This means that comprehensive protection is provided to almost every aspect of one's

5   *P Aries/G Duby*, A History of Private Life: Revelations of the Medieval World (1988) 5.

6   *M Borghi/F Ferrett/S Karapapa*, Online Data Processing Consent under EU Law: A Theoretical Framework and Empirical Evidence from the UK (2013) 21 International Journal of Law and Information Technology (IJLIT) 109, 119.

7   *M Borghi/ML Montagnani*, 'Models for Managing Intellectual Property Rights on the Internet: Online Distribution of Digital Media Content,' Final Report, Counter Project (October 2009), at <http://www.counter2010.org>; *PA Bernal*, Web 2.5: The Symbiotic Web (2010) 24 International Review of Law, Computers & Technology 25, 26.

8   *PM Schwartz/K-N Peifer*, Prosser's Privacy and the German Right of Personality: Are Four Privacy Torts Better than One Unitary Concept? (2010) 98 California Law Review 1925, 1947–1950.

9   Basic Law for the Federal Republic of Germany in the revised version published in the Federal Law Gazette Part III, classification number 100–1, as last amended by the Act of 11 July 2012 (Federal Law Gazette I, 1478).

personal development as long as it does not violate the rights of others. The right to privacy is an essential part of a person's general personality right. At the regional level, the protection of privacy has been incorporated in the 1950 European Convention on the Protection of Human Rights and Fundamental Freedoms (ECHR).[10] Article 8 ECHR provides for protection for privacy in all countries as a common European fundamental right.

5   In contrast, English common law, as Lord Hoffmann indicated, does not know a general right of privacy or any general tort of invasion of privacy.[11] Rather, the protection for privacy is provided by the law of confidence involving unauthorized disclosure of personal information.[12] However, the equitable remedy of 'breach of confidence' serves to protect privacy as envisaged under art 8 ECHR. In the US, the Constitution provides limited scope of protection for privacy while the protection of privacy is a core area in tort law. Since *Warren* and *Brandeis's* article on the tort of privacy published in 1890, privacy has become a synonym in Anglo-American law for many aspects of personality.[13] A common remedy against privacy violation, within the scope of breach of confidence, is damages. In most countries an injunction can be granted under certain conditions.[14]

6   There has been a vast expansion of the right to privacy in Europe.[15] Article 8 of the ECHR was originally adopted as a classic privacy right, but has gradually been interpreted by the European Court of Human Rights (ECtHR) as a personality right.[16] It became something like an umbrella provision that covers a number of personality rights such as the right to dignity and reputation.[17] Moreover, with the development of information networks, the informational aspect of privacy comes into play where a third party is in possession of

---

10   Universal Declaration of Human Rights, 10 December 1948. Council of Europe, Convention on the Protection of Human Rights and Fundamental Freedoms.

11   *Wainwright v Home Office* [2003] United Kingdom House of Lords (UKHL) 53, [2004] 2 Appeal Cases (AC) 406 at [35].

12   The origin of the equitable action for breach of confidence is the case *Prince Albert v Strange* (1849) 64 English Reports (ER) 293.

13   *Warren/Brandeis* (1890) 4 Harv L Rev 193, 193.

14   G *Brueggemeier/AC Ciacchi/Pa O'Callaghan* (eds), Personality Rights in European Tort Law (2010) 576.

15   *Van der Sloot* (2015) 80 Utrecht Journal of International and European Law 25, 44.

16   Ibid, 25, 27. D *Heisenberg*, Negotiating Privacy (2005) Chs 1, 2, 3.

17   *F Boehm*, Information Sharing and Data Protection in the Area of Freedom, Security and Justice: Towards Harmonised Data Protection Principles of Information Exchange at EU Level (2012) 19–22.

personal information.[18] Consequently, the public sphere aspect of personal information is becoming more relevant in contemporary society as the government and businesses process massive amounts of personal data on a daily basis.[19]

7 At least under EU law, privacy and data protection are distinct, yet complementary, fundamental legal rights.[20] The protection of privacy and the protection of data which is of more recent origin[21] are increasingly interrelated with the modern technology that facilitates the collection, storing and processing of personal data.[22] In Europe, the ECtHR has been willing to accept that a number of matters subject to data protection such as transcripts of telephone conversations, photos or hospital records also fall within the scope of the privacy right.[23] Also, the Court clarified that personal data may only be collected for specific and legitimate purposes and has accepted that the States have a positive obligation to provide adequate protection for personal data.[24]

B   *The Digital Challenges*

8 The development of technologies such as web 2.0 and interactive technology greatly facilitated the transmission of personal information. Personal information has been collected and used for commercial communications and direct marketing, which is a key feature of online business models. In Europe, Directive 2002/58/EC[25] ('e-Privacy Directive') is a sector-specific regime with regard to privacy and electronic communications that is applicable to providers of

---

18 *R Gellert/S Gutwirth,* Beyond Accountability, the Return to Privacy? in: D Guagnin/ L Hempel/C Ilten et al. (eds), Managing Privacy Though Accountability (2012) 2.

19 *V Kale,* Guide to Cloud Computing for Business and Technology Managers: From Distributed Computing to Cloudware Applications (2015) 442.

20 *Borghi/Ferrett/Karapapa* (2013) 21 IJLIT 109, 113 f.

21 For a historical review of data protection, see *AC Evans,* European Data Protection Law (1981) 4 American Journal of Comparative Law 571–582.

22 *Organisation for Economic Cooperation and Development,* Guidelines on the Protection of Privacy and Transborder Flows of Personal Data (1981).

23 See for the classic cases: ECtHR *PG and JH v UK,* 25.9.2001, no 44787/98; *Perry v UK,* 17.7.2003, no 63737/00; *Klass and others v Germany,* 6.9.1978, no 5029/71; *Malone v UK,* 2.8.1984,no 8691/79; *Leander v Sweden,* 26.3.1987, no 9248/81.

24 ECtHR *Köpke v Germany,* 5.10.2010, no 420/07. *AR Mowbray,* The Development of Positive Obligations under the European Convention on Human Rights by the European Court of Human Rights (2004) 135–137.

25 Directive 2002/58/EC Official Journal (OJ) L 201, 31.7.2002, 37–47, as amended by Directive 2009/136/EC OJ L 337, 11–36.

publicly available electronic communication services such as telecom and Internet service providers (ISPs) that process personal data. Commentators have indicated that the protection of data has been elevated to the level of fundamental human right in the sense that data protection could not be traded off for economic benefits.[26]

9 Structural changes are evident in privacy protection in an Internet environment where the collection of personal data is instantaneous and at a substantially low cost. The changes are, first, the focus of privacy has shifted from being on private and individual interests to collective and unspecific interests in the context of 'big data.' Individuals are losing control of the collection and utilization of their data, and the data at an aggregated level can inconspicuously influence individuals' behaviour on a large scale.[27] Because the data that has been aggregately gathered and analyzed is unspecific to any individual, it became difficult to prove the causality between harm to a personal interest and the misuse of the data. Consequently, commentators have pointed out that the attention of privacy protection has been diverted from the welfare interests of an individual citizen to the harm to ulterior interests which may lead to a chilling effect in the long term, particularly in the context of State surveillance.[28] Foucault had already proposed in 1975 that the usually overlooked harm arising from the mere knowledge that one was or might be watched can be detrimental to a democratic society.[29] The Snowden case demonstrates citizens' vulnerability to State surveillance which is empowered by interconnected information networks in the 21st century.[30]

10 A second paradigmatic shift in a digital environment is, as pointed out by a Chinese court, that the focus of privacy protection evolves from keeping

---

26   *V Mayer-Schonberger*, Generational Development of Data Protection in Europe, in: PE Agre/M Rotenberg (eds), Technology and Privacy: The New Landscape (1998) 219–241; *S Simitis*, From the Market to the Polis: The EU Directive on the Protection of Personal Data (1995) 80 Iowa Law Review 445, 450.

27   *B Shiller*, First Degree Price Discrimination Using Big Data at <http://benjaminshiller .com/images/First_Degree_PD_Using_Big_Data_Jan_27,_2014.pdf> (accessed 8 October 2015).

28   *NM Richards*, The Dangers of Surveillance (2013) 126 Harv L Rev 1934, 1940.

29   *M Foucault,* Discipline and Punish: The Birth of the Prison, originally published in 1975 (2012).

30   Edward Snowden was a former contractor for the CIA who disclosed to the media details of extensive Internet and phone surveillance by American intelligence in 2013. See BBC report 'Edward Snowden: Leaks that Exposed US Spy Programme' at <http://www.bbc .com/news/world-us-canada-23123964> (accessed 8 October 2015).

personal information confidential to strengthening the control of personal data.[31] Information privacy is based on a notion of the dignity and integrity of the individual.[32] With the development of technology, new genres of personal information such as personal email account and genetic information became the subjects of dispute that have been brought to the court in recent years.[33] In many jurisdictions including China, there are legal restraints applicable to corporations, governmental agencies, and telecommunication and Internet services providers on the processing of information.[34]

11 In Europe, scholars and social activists talk about the 'conceptual reengineering' of traditional conceptions of self, mind and society that have been distorted by citizens' heavy reliance on smartphones, search engines and social media sites. For instance, as the distinction between reality and cyberspace is becoming blurred, the 'Onlife Initiative' formed by a group of social scientists has developed the concept of 'Onlife World'[35] that reflects such a phenomenon. In China, there are similar social movements that engage in the discourse on the presentation and reconstruction of personality in cyberspace, a virtual public sphere.[36]

12 In a word, there is a paradigmatic shift of privacy protection from concealing personal information from the public to the control of personal information that is not confidential but would be kept to a small circle by the rights holder rather than disclosed to the general public. Nowadays the 'born digital' generation would not be necessarily concerned about the possession or even disclosure of their personal information which they see as necessary to use the services offered by social media and corporations in the operation of their

---

31 Shanghai No 1 Intermediary Court in a decision held that the unauthorised disclosure of personal information was damage in itself, regardless of whether the disclosure actually resulted in benefit or loss to the person whose information was disclosed, see (2009) Hu Yi Zhong Min Er Zhong Zi no 4042. *H Wenmin*, On the Legal Protection of Online Privacy, research project report, <http://court.gmw.cn/html/article/201307/03/131503.shtml> (accessed 8 October 2015).

32 Australian Law Reform Commission (1983) Privacy, Report paper no 22, vol 1, p. 22.

33 *Zhang Xinbao*, Legal Protection of the Right to Privacy (2nd edn 2004) 8 f.

34 Art 15 of the Law of the PRC on Statistics 1983 provides that data collected from investigations shall not be disclosed without consent of the data subjects. Art 6 of the Post Law of the PRC 1990 prohibits the disclosure of the information of the users of the post services.

35 <https://ec.europa.eu/digital-agenda/en/onlife-initiative>.

36 *Chen Yue/Shi Kan/Hu Xiaomeng/Li Zhen*, Psychological Influences of Blogging: Blog Use, Personality Trait and Self-concept, Web Society (SWS), 2010 IEEE 2nd Symposium on 16–17 August 2010, DOI: 10.1109/SWS.2010.5607475.

businesses.[37] In turn, the purpose of the disclosure and the utilization of information became the key factor to determine whether the usage is legitimate.

III   The Right to Privacy in China

A   *Privacy, Personal Information and Personality Rights*

13   China has no explicit protection of privacy at the constitutional law level, although privacy and other personal interests have been mentioned in Chapter 2 as fundamental rights of citizens. Article 37 of the Constitution of 1982 protects the freedom of the person,[38] followed by art 38 that protects the personal dignity of citizens and prohibits any 'insult, libel, false accusation or false incrimination.' Article 39 prohibits any unlawful search of, or intrusion into, a citizen's home. Article 40 safeguards 'freedom and privacy of correspondence of citizens.'

14   Provisions relating to privacy are scattered in various legal instruments of different rankings. The General Principles of Civil Law[39] (Civil Law) provides three personality rights: the right to name, the right to portrait and the right to reputation.[40] Two judicial interpretations have been issued by the Supreme People's Court in 1988 and 1993 that clarify the tortious liability for breaching the right of reputation. In the Opinions on Several Questions concerning the Implementation of the General Principles of Civil Law *1988*, the Court stated that defamation shall be determined as an act of infringing the citizen's right of reputation.[41] A more relevant provision can be found in the Reply to Several Questions on Adjudicating the Cases of the Rights of Reputation *1993* that anyone who discloses another person's private information without authorization shall be deemed to have infringed the right of reputation.[42] Moreover, the Interpretation of the Supreme People's Court regarding Issues of Ascertaining the Liability of Compensation for Mental Damage for Tort *2001* clarifies that

---

37   *J Palfrey/U Gasser*, Born Digital: Understanding the First Generation of Digital Natives (2013) 54 f.

38   It provides that '[n]o citizen may be arrested except with the approval or by decision of a People's Procuratorate or by decision of a People's Court, and arrests must be made by a public security organ.' 'Unlawful detention or deprivation or restriction of citizens' freedom of the person by other means is prohibited, and unlawful search of the person of citizens is prohibited.'

39   Promulgated on 12 April 1986 and came into effect on 1 January 1987.

40   Arts 99–101 of the Civil Law.

41   Answer 140 (1) of the Opinion.

42   Answer 7 of the Reply.

the person who infringes upon another citizen's privacy or other personal interests may bear tortious liability.[43]

15 The development of Chinese tort law suggests the possibility to include a privacy right as a personality right in the future Civil Law Code. As mentioned earlier, the Civil Law has provided a series of personality rights[44] without mentioning privacy. However, since the Civil Law pre-dated the Internet age and is very sketchy, other sectors of law can develop the principles established in the Civil Law. The Tort Liability Law which came into effect in 2010 has, for the first time, juxtaposed the right to privacy with other concrete personality rights such as the right to health, the right to name and the right to reputation.[45]

16 As the Tort Liability Law expressly provides remedies for the infringement of privacy, it may be implied that the right to privacy is recognized as a personality right. Chinese scholars have pointed out that the concept of personality right is evolving from being general to being specific.[46] It has been argued that although a general personality right in an open-ended format can afford protection for future unforeseeable forms of infringement of personality rights, it should be aware that a general personality right basically is associated with dignity and freedom of the person, not privacy per se.[47] Moreover, the legislative intention was to make the right to privacy a specific personality right.[48]

17 Although the Tort Liability Law provides remedies for invasions of privacy, scholars argue that such protection only provides an incomplete form of a privacy right which should, in turn, be established by the law of personality rights which is related not only to tort but also to contract and other areas of law.[49] Moreover, the protection of privacy is always in tension with public interests such as security and information transparency.[50]

---

43   Art 1 of the Interpretation.
44   Ch 5 of the Civil Law.
45   Art 2 of the Tort Liability Law.
46   *Guo Mingrui*, The Relationship between Personality, Identity and the Right to Personality and the Personality and Personal Right (2014) 1 Faxue Luntan [Legal Forum] 5, 8 f.
47   *Wang Liming*, The Redefinition of Privacy Right (2012)1 Faxuejia [The Jurist] 108, 113.
48   Art 2 (2) provides 'Civil rights and interests' used in this Law shall include the right to life, the right to health, the right to name, the right to reputation, the right to honour, right to self-image, right of privacy, marital autonomy, guardianship, ownership, usufruct, security interest, copyright, patent right, exclusive right to use a trademark, right to discovery, equities, right of succession, and other personal and property rights and interests'. English translation at <http://www.lawinfochina.com/display.aspx?lib=law&id=7846&CGid=>.
49   *Liming* (2012) 1 Faxuejia 114.
50   *Quzhi*, How much Room is to be Left to Privacy (2003) 32.

18 In Taiwan, the right to privacy is explicitly protected as a personality right in
    the Civil Law Act,[51] while in China there are ambiguities and inconsistences
    in the relevant laws. *Wang Liming*, a leading expert in Chinese civil law, points
    out that the right to privacy should be purely a civil law right,[52] unlike in the US
    where privacy has a constitutional dimension.[53] In contrast, there have been
    scholars arguing in favour of explicit constitutional protection for privacy.[54]
    Even some courts are of the view that China needs to provide constitutional
    protection for privacy which is an essential part of human rights.[55] Admittedly,
    the constitutional protection for dignity provides a ground for protecting pri-
    vacy. The protection of freedom of correspondence also has implications to
    the right to privacy. Nevertheless, in China, since there is no judicial review
    as in the US, the Constitution cannot be directly applied in judicial decisions.
    Given the pressing need to provide protection for privacy while there is no ex-
    press legislation on the right to privacy in the General Principles of Civil Law
    which is foundational, *Wang Liming* argues that it is more practical to make
    the right to privacy a purely civil right to make it immediately available as a
    basis for providing remedies to those who suffer from the breach of privacy.[56]

19 In the context of 'big data,' Chinese scholars, like their European counterparts,
    point out that the protection of personal information and the protection of
    privacy are distinct and should be governed by different laws. The protection
    of data has an emphasis on enhancing citizens' ability to control their per-
    sonal data, while the protection of privacy prohibits unauthorized disclosure
    of information.[57] The scope of each's subject matter is different too. Personal
    information such as name and telephone number which can be publicized

---

51 Art 184 of the Civil Law Act (Taiwan), art 195 of the amendments. *Wang Ze-Jian*, Privacy:
    The Concretion of Personality Right (2009) 2 Journal of Comparative Law 1.

52 *Liming* (2012) 1 Faxuejia 108–111.

53 Arts 4 and 5 of the Bill of Rights of the United States of America. *Griswold v Connecticut*,
    381 United States Supreme Court Reports (US) 479 (1965); *Roe v Wade* 410 US 113 (1973).

54 *Yin Tian*, On the Essence of Personality Right – And on the Provision of Personality Right
    in the Draft of Civil Law (2003) 4 Faxue Yanjiu [Chinese Journal of Law] 1, 5–7.

55 *Hao Wang*, Protecting Privacy in China – A Research on China's Privacy Standards and
    the Possibility of Establishing the Right to Privacy and the Information Privacy Protection
    Legislation in Modern China (2011) 167. Kunming Intermediary Court held that the right
    to privacy is a natural right that a person is entitled to by birth, see (2004) Kun Min Er
    Zhong Zi no 785.

56 *Liming* (2012) 1 Faxuejia 111.

57 *Zhang Xinbao*, From Privacy to Personal Information: Theory and Institutional Arrange-
    ments of the Rebalance of Interests (2015) 3 Zhongguo Faxue [China Legal Science] 38,
    43–45.

may not be subject to privacy protection, depending on the circumstances. Lastly, the remedies for the violation of the protection of personal information and privacy are different. Compensation for mental distress is a remedy for the infringement of privacy, while pecuniary damages are usually available for the breach of personal information which can be commercially exploited. Besides remedies such as injunction and damages afforded by the Civil Law and the Tort Liability Law, art 6 of Amendment Seven to the Criminal Law of the PRC[58] states that the personnel of the sectors of finance, telecommunications, transportation, education, and public health who sell or unlawfully provide citizens' personal information obtained in carrying out their duties or in the course of providing services will be penalized with up to three years' imprisonment. Therefore, the right to personal information should be a separate and different right from the right to privacy.

B   *Legal Framework*

20   Since privacy in an online environment is much related to how intermediaries deal with personal information, no discussion about the protection of privacy can be complete without an examination of the laws and regulations on the protection of electronic personal information. Therefore, particular attention is to be directed to the evolving legal framework governing businesses, governmental agencies, and ISPs involving the processing of personal information.

1   Data Protection Law

21   The Ministry of Industry and Information Technology (MIIT) issued Several Regulations on Standardizing Market Order for Internet Information Services (the 2011 Regulations) in 2011. A year later, the National People's Congress Standing Committee promulgated its Decision on Strengthening Internet Information Protection (the 2012 Decision) which is the highest level law that deals with privacy and data protection. Both the 2011 Regulations and the 2012 Decision include very general obligations on ISPs to strengthen their systems' security to prevent personal information being 'disclosed, damaged or lost.'[59]

22   In the context of privacy protection, three issues are inadequately addressed in the two legal instruments. First, neither the Regulations nor the Decision includes any kind of users' right to access, correct, request blocking, or delete the data. Unfortunately, as scholars point out, the fundamental elements of

---

58   Promulgated and came into effect on 28 February 2009.
59   Art 4.

a data privacy law are missing.[60] Second, although the 2012 Decision clarifies that the 'conduct that infringes a citizen's civil rights and interests shall be subject to civil liability in accordance with law,'[61] and 'person whose rights have been infringed can initiate litigation,'[62] the general language of the provisions does not specify what kind of tortious liability applies. The remedies for the violation of privacy in the data are subject to the governance of the Tort Liability Law.[63] Third, the Regulations restrictively define personal information. Scholars propose that Chinese lawmakers refer to the more comprehensive approach adopted in Directive 95/46/EC on the protection of individuals with regard to the processing of personal data and on the free movement of such data.[64]

23 A soft law, the Information Security Technology–Guidelines for Personal Information Protection within Pubic and Commercial Services Information System (2013 Guidelines), was released by the MIIT Standardization Administration in 2013. These voluntary guidelines may not be as important as the two regulatory instruments issued in 2011 and 2012.[65] However, the 2013 Guidelines apply to a broader scope of businesses, cover key issues and provide more details for application. It is considered to provide an indication of the future codification of those standards into various sectors of law, including the Tort Liability Law.[66]

24 The MIIT issued the Telecommunications and Internet Personal User Data Protection Regulations (User Data Protection Regulations) on 28 June 2013.[67] The User Data Protection Regulations cover both ISPs and telecommunications business operators. They added a significant number of new or stronger forms of regulation: the definition of 'personal user data' may be broader than the previous conventional definitions based on capacity for identification, because it also includes 'other information, as well as the time, and place of the user using the service and other information, collected in the process

---

60   *G Greenleaf,* China's NPC Standing Committee Privacy Decision: A Small Step, Not a Great Leap Forward 2013 (121) Privacy Laws & Business International Report 1, 3. Of note is that the 2011 Regulation has a provision that a user should be able to modify or delete data provided by him/her.

61   Art 10.

62   Art 9.

63   *Greenleaf* (fn 60) 4.

64   *Xinbao* (fn 57) 48.

65   *Xinbao* (fn 57) 46.

66   *Tian George/G Greenleaf,* China Expands Data Protection through 2013 Guidelines: A 'Third line' for Personal Information Protection, with a Translation of the Guidelines (2013) 122 Privacy Law & Business International Report 1, 2.

67   Came into effect on 1 September 2013.

of providing services';[68] and a blunt requirement that prohibits the collection or use of personal user data without user permission.[69] Intermediaries are required to supervise and manage data protection when they utilize third party processing facilities, and 'may not entrust agents who do not conform to personal user data protection requirements.'[70] This appears to impose a strict liability on data controllers for the actions of their processors.

25 China's data protection law is evolving in an incremental way. Although this and the earlier Regulations and Guidelines focus on the Internet and telecommunications sectors, they may be building up a template for data privacy legislation to be extended to the whole of China's private sector.[71]

2   Civil and Tort Liability Law

26 The scope of civil rights has seen a significant expansion since the promulgation of the Civil Law in 1986. However, the existing personality rights like the right of reputation cannot afford adequate protection for privacy. Reputation and privacy have distinct subject matter which should not be protected under the same right of reputation.[72] Consequently, the interests in privacy and reputation are different, and consequently trigger differing tortious liability.[73] Chapter 6 of the Civil Law sets forth the rules regarding torts of intentional and negligent action and strict liability rules applicable to actions subject to no fault requirement. Tortious liability is applicable to harm to reputation or the unauthorized use of a natural person's portrait for commercial purpose.[74] Neither of the torts affords adequate protection for privacy.

27 The Tort Liability Law is, to some extent, built upon the rules established in the Civil Law.[75] As mentioned earlier, the scope of civil rights has been broadened

---

68   Art 4.

69   Art 9.

70   Art 11.

71   *G Greenleaf*, China's Incremental Data Privacy Law: MIIT 'User Data Protection' Regulations (2013) 125 Privacy Laws & Business International Report 18, 19.

72   *Wang Liming*, Legal Protection of Personal Information: Centered on the Line between Personal Information and Privacy (2013) 4 Xiandai Faxue [Modern Law Science] 62, 64–68.

73   *Cao Jingchun*, Protecting the Right to Privacy in China (2005) 36 Victoria University of Wellington Law Review (VUWLR) 645, 658.

74   *Hao Wan*, (fn 55) 55.

75   *Wei Zhang*, The Evolution of the Law of Torts in China: The Growth of a Liability System, conference paper presented on 10th annual conference of Asian Law and Economics Association, National University of Taiwan, Taiwan, June 2014; Singapore Management University School of Law Research Paper no 41/2014, 2.

ever since the promulgation of the Civil Law which provides protection for an exhaustive list of rights. Since the Civil Law was promulgated almost three decades ago, the lawmakers could not foresee fast social changes thereafter and the disputable rights and interests which are not mentioned in the legislative text. According to empirical research, a wide range of personality-related rights which are not listed in the Civil Law have been claimed and litigated with a considerable percentage finding support in the courtroom.[76] Later on, the Supreme People's Court issued its Interpretation on the Determination of Damages for Pain and Suffering Arising from Torts 2001 stating that the law protects the right of dignity and personal freedom,[77] which are not found in the text of the Civil Law.

28 With the expanding scope of rights, new liabilities have been created by a series of legal instruments.[78] The Interpretation on Several Issues Concerning the Application of Law in Adjudicating the Civil Disputes regarding Copyright in Information Networks 2000 and the Regulation on the Protection of the Right on the Information Network 2006 (amended in 2013) (Information Network Regulation) cater for the need to protect rights in an Internet environment. The Provisions of the Supreme People's Court on Several Issues concerning the Application of Law in the Trial of Cases involving Civil Disputes over Infringements upon Personal Rights and Interests through Information Networks 2014 (Supreme People's Court Provisions 2014) provide further protection for personality rights in cyberspace and regulation on ISPs' liability for the breach of personal rights and interests.

29 At the national level, particularly relevant is the Tort Liability Law that regulates individual Internet users as well as ISPs.[79] Article 6 of the Tort Liability Law establishes the principle of fault liability developed from art 106 of the Civil Law. According to the Tort Liability Law, a person shall be subject to tort liability in two circumstances: (1) a person who is at fault for an infringement upon a civil right or interest of another; (2) a person who is presumed to be at fault by law and cannot prove otherwise.[80] The Information Network Regulation imposes tort liability that applies to not only copyright infringement but

---

76 *Wei Zhang* (fn 75) 4.

77 Art 1.

78 *Wei Zhenying*, The Status of Tort Liability Law in Civil Law and Its Relation to other Parts (2010) 2 Zhongguo Faxue [China Legal Science] 27, 38.

79 Art 36.

80 Art 6.

also personal and property rights in general.[81] The Information Network Regulation follows the US Digital Millennium Copyright Act (DMCA) and includes a notice-and-take-down procedure that is akin to the DMCA safe harbour rule to exempt both search and linking service providers and information storage service providers from tort liability if they remove infringing material quickly after they receive a copyright-holder's notification. If a file hosting service provider or a search and linking service provider knew or should have known that linked material is illegal and still continued to assist a user to upload and distribute the material, it cannot be exempted from contributory liability.[82]

30   The Supreme People's Court Provisions 2014 for the first time clarify that genetic information, medical records, criminal records, home addresses and personal activities fall within the scope of privacy.[83] It establishes a harsher liability regime for ISPs. First, if an Internet user is being sued for breach of privacy, the user can request the court to add the ISP involved as a co-defendant or as a third party. This increases the chance for an ISP to be put on trial before a court. Second, in the Information Network Regulation 2006,[84] a valid notification for an ISP to take down certain content must contain preliminary evidence of the claimed infringement. A notable change made by the Provisions 2014 is to replace the 'preliminary evidence' with the 'reasons for the requested deletion.'[85] Therefore, it removes the burden of proof from the right-owner at the initial stage and shifts the responsibility to the ISP to take a piece of content down upon receipt of the notification.

C   *Protection of Online Privacy in Practice*

31   Both the Internet user and the ISP can be liable for a breach of privacy. In most circumstances it is the Internet user who uploads infringing content or discloses someone else's personal information online for a defamatory purpose, or to insult or annoy the person whose information is being disclosed. In principle, the individual Internet user's liability follows the general principles of liability established in the Civil Law and the Tort Liability Law. Nevertheless, as Internet users who infringe privacy may be either difficult to identify or not worth

---

81   *Wang Shengming* (ed), Explanations of the Tort Liability Law of the People's Republic of China (2010) 188 f.

82   Art 22. *JJ Hua*, Toward A More Balanced Approach: Rethinking and Readjusting Copyright Systems in the Digital Network Era (2014) 105. *Wang Weiguo*, The Fault Liability – The Third Wave (2000) 225.

83   Art 12.

84   Art 14.

85   Art 12.

pursuing, the victim prefers to pursue the ISP who acts as a gatekeeper and has deep pockets. Therefore, to demarcate the liability for ISPs is the key issue in maintaining a vibrant and healthy Internet environment. Here, a delicate balance is needed between the personality rights of the victim, particularly the right to privacy, and the right to freedom of speech and other social values.

32 Since the existing laws are scattered and somewhat inconsistent, many important issues are left silent. The judges have to interpret, and sometimes even to stretch the law to fill the gaps. In developing the protection of privacy without an express privacy right as a personality right in the Civil Law, courts at both district and intermediate levels have recognized the following interests as falling within the scope of privacy: medical treatment records and other patient information;[86] an individual's telephone number[87] and address;[88] physical defects;[89] MSN chatting records;[90] and disgraceful photographs.[91] It is apparent that the scope of privacy is expanding to cover a variety of personal information as shown in a number of judicial decisions.

33 To have a better understanding of the subject matters of privacy and personal information, and the liability principles governing individual Internet users and ISPs in violation of privacy, two representative cases are selected and examined as follows.

1   'Human flesh search': Wang Fei Case

34 According to Beijing News, only two out of ten influential 'human flesh search'[92] cases, ranging from 2001 to 2015, have been held to give rise to tortious

---

86   Chongqing Qianjiang District Court decision (2008) Qian Min Chu Zi no 284.
87   Yunnan Province Kunming Municipal Intermediary Court decision, (2004) Kun Min Er Zhong Zi no 785.
88   Shenzhen Bao'an District Court decision (2010) Shen Bao Min Yi Chu Zi no 1034.
89   Ji'nan Lixia District Court decision (1999) Li Min Chu Zi no 276.
90   Shanghai No 1 Intermediary Court decision (2009) Hu Yi Zhong Min Yi Zhong Zi no 1431.
91   Shanghai No 2 Intermediary Court decision (2009) Hu Er Zhong Min Yi Zhong Zi no 451.
92   'Human flesh search' is a Chinese term used for the phenomenon of distributed searching with the assistance of other users of Internet media such as blogs and forums. It is usually used to identify and expose individuals to public humiliation where their identities cannot be established by conventional web search engines. For instance, an Internet user can post a photograph of a person to an online forum, requesting other users who know the person to disclose more information including name and mobile phone number. With the basic personal information, Internet users are able to find out more information such as the person's career and marital status. In a word, the more information that has been disclosed, the easier it is for Internet users to identify a person.

liability.[93] The difficulties in holding liable the infringers of privacy are that it is hard to trace all the infringers who are individuals and to identify who initiated the human flesh search. Moreover, since the posting can be deleted at the end-user's wish, it is difficult to preserve the postings as electronic evidence. It is also challenging to assess damages in an Internet environment where personal information can be disseminated instantaneously to an almost unlimited readership.

35 In 2008, the plaintiff Wang Fei brought a lawsuit in the Beijing Chaoyang District Court which resulted in three consecutive judicial decisions.[94] In this case, the plaintiff's wife Jiang Yan committed suicide because the plaintiff had an extra-marital affair and requested divorce. Jiang posted photos of her husband with the woman involved in the affair on her blog before committing suicide. Later on, her friend posted Wang's disgraceful photos and wrote blogs that disclosed details of the affair to call for a public condemnation of Wang Fei. Many Internet users launched a 'human flesh search' with the traces from the photos and blogs to search for Wang's name, home address, work place, and telephone number, and disclosed this personal information on the Internet. Thereafter Wang and his parents were assaulted at their residences, and Wang was fired by his employer. Wang brought lawsuits against Jiang's friend and three websites involved, and requested damages and compensation for his mental distress.

36 The Court held that an extra-marital affair, however immoral, falls within the scope of privacy. Jiang's friend had infringed upon Wang Fei's privacy by widely disseminating the details of the affair on the Internet together with the personal information of the parties involved.[95] Second, the Court examined a variety of factors, including the method of collection, the scope and the purpose of the disclosure, and the consequences caused by the disclosure to determine whether the disclosure was illegitimate. In this case, the disclosure was meant to condemn the plaintiff Wang Fei's infidelity. It was intentional and the persons who disclosed the information should have been aware of the consequences of the disclosure, which would stir strong public condemnation. Having considered the above-mentioned factors, the Court held that the disclosure

---

93   Special Report 'Only Two out Ten Human Flesh Search Cases Have Been Held Liable,' reported on 7 May, 2015, <http://www.bjnews.com.cn/feature/2015/05/07/362617.html> (accessed 8 October 2015).

94   *Wang Fei v Hainan Tianya Tech Ltd* (2008) Chao Min Chu Zi no 29277; *Wang Fei v Beijing Lingyun Interactive Information Technology Ltd* (2008) Chao Min Chu Zi no 29276, *Wang Fei v Zhang Leyi* (2008) Chao Min Chu Zi no 10930.

95   See *Wang Fei v Zhang Leyi* (2008) Chao Min Chu Zi no 10930.

constituted an infringement of privacy. Clearly, it is a sensible approach to hold that the disclosure of personal information which may not be confidential in some circumstances would nonetheless breach privacy if the disclosure is for an illegitimate purpose and caused harm to the information owner.[96]

37   A related question brought up by this case is whether an unauthorized use of a person's image for non-commercial purposes constitutes a breach of privacy. There is a lacuna in the legislation. The Civil Law only provides that the use of images for commercial purposes is a violation of the right to portrait.[97] However, in the *Wang Fei* case, publishing the disgraceful photographs online was not for any commercial purpose. One of the judgments briefly mentioned that such exposure of the involved parties' images on the Internet violated the parties' privacy.[98] Scholars pointed out that the Tort Liability Law should incorporate a two-pronged provision which clarifies that unauthorized publication of personal images for non-commercial purposes infringes the right to privacy, while the use for commercial purposes without legitimate reason infringes the right to portrait.[99]

38   The case also has implications for the ISP's liability as the safe harbour rules applied. Tianya, a website operator, was exempt from liability since it deleted the content upon Wang Fei's request while the other two websites were held jointly liable for the infringement of the right to privacy and the right to reputation since they took no action after they received the notification.

2   Big Data and Privacy: *Baidu v Zhuye* Case

39   *Beijing Baidu Technology Ltd v Zhu Ye*[100] (*Baidu v Zhuye*) was decided by Nanjing Intermediate Court in May 2015. It overturned the decision made by Nanjing Gulouqu District Court[101] on the nature of HTTP cookies used for data collection and related privacy issues. An HTTP cookie is a piece of data sent from a website and stored in a user's web browser while the user browses that website. Every time the user loads the website, the browser sends the cookie back to the server to notify the website of the user's previous activity. It is used for the web server to collect data from a specific web browser in order to simplify

---

96   *Zhang Jianwen*, The Expansion of Privacy Protection and the Development of the Protection Way in China from 'Faye Wang Case' (2012) 2 Journal of Henan Administrative Institute of Politics and Law 95, 97 f.

97   Art 100.

98   *Wang Fei v Beijing Lingyun Interactive Information Technology Ltd* (2008) Chao Min Chu Zi no 29276.

99   *Jianwen*, 2 Journal of Henan Administrative Institute of Politics and Law 95, 98.

100 (2014) Ning Min Zhong Zi no 5028.

101 (2013) Gu Min Chu Zi no 3031.

the login process. The data sent from the same web browser is identified as one independent Internet user. In this case, Zhu Ye, the plaintiff, used key words such as 'weight loss,' 'breast enhancement' and 'abortion' on Baidu, the largest Chinese search engine service provider, to look for relevant information. Later on, when she accessed other websites, advertisements on the information that has been searched by her on Baidu bounced up from the webpages. Zhu Ye claimed that Baidu had collected her personal information that was revealed by the keywords and disclosed the information to third parties for direct commercial advertisement. She requested an injunction and damages for mental distress.

40 The Nanjing Intermediate Court disagreed with the District Court on three key issues. The first issue was the scope of personal information and privacy. Although overlapping, personal information and privacy are distinct in scope. The Intermediate Court applied the User Data Protection Regulations that define personal information as any identity number, address, telephone number, account number or password which can be used independently or with other information to identify an Internet user, and the time and location where the user surfed the Internet. The Court opined that, although the keywords collected by cookies as a part of 'big data' had a privacy aspect, they were no longer personal information since the data collection was automatic and unspecific to natural persons. Rather, it is the specific web browser that is identified by the data collected by cookies. Therefore, the court concluded that the keywords were not the kind of personal information that can be used to identify a user and thus could not fall under the protection of the User Data Protection Regulations.

41 Second, the Intermediate Court insisted on a strict application of the Tort Liability Law rather than the pro-user approach adopted by the District Court. It considered art 36 of the Tort Liability Law, which imposes liability on both Internet users and ISPs who use the Internet as a tool to harm the interests of another party, and art 12 (1) of the Information Network Regulation, which provides that any user and intermediary that publicizes personal information of a natural person through the Internet and causes harm thereafter is liable for the infringement. The Court held that the automatic collection and analysis of data for commercial advertisement operated by Baidu was an internal process which did not disclose the information to the public. Moreover, there was no evidence of any substantial harm caused to the plaintiff, despite the claimed mental distress. Therefore, the Court opined that the collection and utilization of data did not breach the plaintiff's privacy.

42 Lastly, the Court held that Baidu has performed its duty of care by placing a notice on the webpage for users to opt out of the use of cookies. Therefore, the

fact that Zhu Ye proceeded to use the search engine service implied that she agreed to accept cookies. The Guidelines provided that intermediaries need to obtain implied consent to process general information and express consent to process sensitive information. Since the data collected by Baidu is general information, the express notice provided by Baidu and the implied consent from the user made Baidu's collection and processing of data legitimate under the Guidelines.

IV   Conclusion

43   In 2009, the number of Chinese Internet users soared to become the largest in the world.[102] However, the efficient and almost effortless online transmission of information threatens Internet users' control of their privacy in cyberspace. This is one of the major reasons that compelled Chinese lawmakers to develop the law to protect privacy and personal information. With the fast-paced development of technology, self-regulation for the protection of privacy is worthy of consideration since it provides for more flexibility. In the medium to long term, however, further legislation will be needed.[103]

44   The selected cases illustrate that the scope of privacy is evolving while Chinese society is being reshaped by the Internet, social media, and prosperous e-commerce. It is very challenging, if not impossible, to define the scope of privacy since Internet users almost always provide their personal information to services providers with a click while taking advantages of the convenient services offered. Moreover, ISPs that provide access, file-hosting and search services play an important role in transmitting information that can be used for illegitimate purposes. Therefore, to construct an appropriate indirect liability regime for them is critical for the protection of privacy.

45   The currently scattered legal instruments on privacy protection should be integrated into a more consistent body of law. First, the right to privacy needs to be expressly made a personality right in the text of the Civil Law. Second, since legislators cannot foresee all the fast technological and societal changes, it is better to adopt an inclusive and non-exhaustive approach to the definition of personal information and to clarify what kind of information falls within the

---

102   China Internet Network Information Centre, 'CNNIC publishes 24th Statistical Report on Internet Development in China' (2009), available at <http://chinatraveltrends.com/cnnic-publishes-24th-statistical-report-on-internet-development-in-china> (accessed 8 October 2015).

103   *Hao Wang* (fn 55) 196.

scope of privacy. Third, the Tort Liability Law needs to have a more comprehensive and detailed section on ISPs' liability that covers situations like breach
of personality rights as well as breach of intellectual property rights. Last but
not the least, as the protection of privacy is shifting from concealing personal
information from the sight of the public to the strengthened control of information that guarantees the information will not be misused by intermediaries
or a third party, a balance of interests needs to be maintained between protecting privacy and other social values such as security and freedom of speech.[104]

---

104   *Liu Han*, Privacy Right, Freedom of Speech and the Culture of Chinese Netizens: The
      Struggling Regulation of Human Flesh Search (2011) 4 Peking University Law Journal 870,
      871.

CHAPTER 9

Personality Rights, the Mass Media and the European Convention on Human Rights

Watchdog, Bloodhound or Guard Dog of Power?

Thomas Thiede

1 It has been a long time since *Thomas Carlyle* described the power of the press as 'the fourth estate' in 1841. He elaborated that 'there were three estates in Parliament; but, in the Reporters' Gallery yonder, there sat a fourth estate more important far than they all. It is not a figure of speech, or a witty saying; it is a literal fact.'[1] Indeed, faith in the press as the guardian of truth, the watchdog of the public, the foundation of democracy – in brief, the fourth estate – lies at the heart of the liberal imagination of the western democracies. Liberal theorists have argued that the existence of an unfettered and independent press within each nation is essential for democracy, by contributing to the right of freedom of expression, thought and conscience; strengthening the responsiveness and accountability of governments to all citizens; and providing a pluralist platform and channel of political expression for a multiplicity of groups and interests.[2] Since *Carlyle*, the 'fourth estate' has traditionally been regarded as one of the classic checks and balances in the division of powers,[3] or as *Thomas Jefferson* said, 'Where the press is free and every man able to read, all is safe.'[4]

2 Homage is paid to this dream in virtually all Western States' constitutions, as they contain provisions respecting rights to freedom of speech and the freedom

---

* The manuscript for this text was finalised in late 2014. Only minor changes have been incorporated since that time.

1 Heroes and Hero-Worship (1840).

2 See, for instance, *A Sen*, Development as Freedom (1999), exemplifying this perspective by the famous argument that the free press encourages government responsiveness to public concerns by highlighting cases of famine and natural disasters; he observes '… in the terrible history of famines in the world, no substantial famine has ever occurred in any independent and democratic country with a free press.' Cf *A Sen*, Democracy as a Universal Value (1999) 10 Journal of Democracy 3.

3 *R Kocher*, Bloodhounds or Missionaries: Role Definitions of German and British Journalists (1986) 1 European Journal of Communication 43 ff.

4 *T Jefferson*, Letter to Colonel Charles Yancey (6 January 1816) in: The Writings of Thomas Jefferson, Memorial Edition (1904–4) vol 14, p. 33.

of the media.[5] The rights granted by supranational conventions serve the same intentions. The guarantee of freedom of expression is recognised as a basic human right in the Universal Declaration of Human Rights adopted by the UN in 1948 (UDHR)[6] and – most important to our European perspective – in the European Convention on Human Rights (ECHR). As is well known, rights enshrined in the realm of public international law did not take any meaningful shape until the *Nuremberg* trials after the Second World War, as it was previously assumed that public international law affected states only and did not permit intervention in the internal affairs of states, such that governments could refuse such rights to their citizens as they pleased. However, by 1945 it became clear that this had to change, as Nazi actions and ideology had gone without serious challenge in Germany in the thirties because of *Hitler's* crackdown on dissenting publishers and journalists after the *Reichstag* fire. Due to the Soviet Union abstaining from the vote on the UDHR, the declaration never reached the stage where individuals' rights became actionable. At this point, the political response of the Western European States is historically important: the ECHR was drawn up as a regional equivalent of the UDHC. It borrowed almost word for word from art 19 UDHR to construct art 10 (1) ECHR:

> Everyone has the right to freedom of expression. This right shall include to hold opinions and to receive and impart information and ideas without interference by public authority and regardless of frontiers.

3 Of course, the ECHR does not contain any rules on criminal or tort law, which is at the core of this volume but, due to three peculiarities of the Convention, it seems correct to assume that the findings of the European Court of Human Rights (ECtHR) dealing with the ECHR have the final say in any questions relating to the mass media not national tort and criminal law. Firstly, the ECHR requires the Signatory States of the Council of Europe to provide an effective remedy against human rights violations.[7] Amongst the instruments used by

---

5   The freedom of the press is only mentioned in some constitutions but, where this is not the case, it is usually implied in the freedom of speech.

6   In particular, art 19 UDHR states: 'Everyone has the right to freedom of opinion and expression; this right includes freedom to hold opinions without interference and to seek, receive and impart information and ideas through any media and regardless of frontiers.'

7   See art 13 ECHR: 'Everyone whose rights and freedoms as set forth in this Convention are violated shall have an effective remedy before a national authority notwithstanding that the violation has been committed by persons acting in an official capacity.'

the Signatory States to discharge this duty to provide for an effective remedy
are tort and criminal law. Secondly, any such remedy must be provided regardless[8] of whether the violation was due to governmental, corporate, or an
individual's conduct. Violations, and accordingly remedies, concern not only
the 'vertical' relationship between a public body and individuals, but also the
'horizontal' relationships between individuals.[9] Thirdly, and in stark contrast
to the aforementioned prior state of public international law, the rights enshrined in the ECHR are not limited to inter-state affairs, but are open to court
actions by citizens of Signatory States; applications to the ECtHR against Signatory States can be made by any individual citizen of a Signatory State. As a
result of these three characteristics, affected citizens and media outlets can
bring any noteworthy action in civil or criminal law to the ECtHR, alleging
that the Signatory State does not provide an effective remedy for violations of
freedom of expression; any national law in which the ECHR's jurisdiction is
engaged is ultimately measured and interpreted against the standards of the
ECHR, with which the ECtHR will carry out a very careful scrutiny of interfer-
ences with press coverage and publications.

•••

4   With a view to the beliefs mentioned at the start, it should come as no surprise that the ECtHR has interpreted art 10 (1) ECHR broadly and inclusively.
Evidently, no attempt has been made to restrict those who are entitled to rely
on art 10 ECHR, and 'everyone' does mean 'everyone,' including publishers,[10]
newspapers, and journalists.[11] The ECtHR has frequently emphasized that the
freedom of expression extends to the freedom of the press, as the latter arguably affords the public one of the best means of discovering and forming
an opinion on the ideas and attitudes of their political leaders.[12] The ECtHR

---

8   Of course the Signatory States have a margin of appreciation.

9   See, for instance, ECtHR *Cyprus v Turkey* [GC], 10.5.2001, no 25781/94, § 81.

10   ECtHR *Unabhängige Initiative Informationsvielfalt v Austria*, 26.2.2002, no 28525/95.

11   Cf ECtHR *Sunday Times v the United Kingdom*, 26.4.1979, no 6538/74; *Markt Intern Verlag
     GmbH & Klaus Beermann v Germany*, 20.11.1989, no 10572/83; *Groppera Radio AG and oth-
     ers v Switzerland*, 28.3.1990, no 10890/84.

12   ECtHR *Özgür Gündem v Turkey*, 16.3.2000, no 23144/93, § 58. The ECtHR argues that
     different messages received from a varied press allow the public to choose and form
     its opinions and thus the democratic society is enriched by its pluralism of ideas and
     information; cf *Lingens v Austria*, 8.7.1986, no 9815/82, § 42. Equally the press gives politi-
     cians the opportunity to reflect and comment on the preoccupations of the public thus
     enabling everyone to participate in the free political debate which is at the core of the

highlights this special nexus when describing the role of the mass media as a 'public watchdog.' Concordantly, not only the substance of the ideas and information expressed, but also the form and means of dissemination by which they are conveyed, are protected.[13]

5 The ECtHR has delivered many judgments declaring national laws or court decisions infringe art 10 ECHR and has begun to develop a jurisprudence tailored to the particular needs of the news media. Over the years, it has crystallised its freedom of expression case law into a number of basic principles. Arguably the most important was formulated in 1976 in *Handyside v the United Kingdom* where the ECtHR held that: 'Freedom of expression ... is applicable not only to "information" or "ideas" that are favourably received or regarded as inoffensive, but also to those that offend, shock or disturb.'[14] Given the specific reference to 'opinions,' art 10 ECHR protects the right to criticise, speculate and make value judgements.[15] As a result, polemic, aggressive, exaggerated, provocative and even insulting expressions have been found to fall within the scope of art 10 ECHR and with regard to the press it results in a situation where opinions are not delivered in a sensitive manner, but more often than not in a most insulting manner as 'comment is free.'

6 As the press is seen as the 'public watchdog,' this already significant latitude in communications is extended even further for publications criticising politicians. The free speech infringements most commonly struck down have been in relation to those who wield political power. Here the ECtHR grants a very extensive freedom to comment upon their performance. In the case of *Peter Lingens*, who accused the Austrian Chancellor at the time of 'the basest opportunism' and 'immorality' for seeking a political alliance with a party led by a former Nazi, the ECtHR declared that '[t]he limits of acceptable criticism are accordingly wider as regards a politician than as regards a private individual. Unlike the latter, the former inevitably and knowingly lays himself open to close scrutiny of his every word and deed by both journalists and the public at large, and he must consequently display a greater degree of tolerance.'[16] In essence, politicians, when acting in an official capacity, run the risk that their

---

concept of a democratic society; cf *Prager and Oberschlick v Austria*, 26.4.1995, 15974/90, § 34.

13 Any restriction on the means of dissemination necessarily interferes with the right to receive and impart information *Oberschlick v Austria*, 23.5.1991, no 11662/85, § 57; *Oberschlick v Austria* (No 2) 1 July 1997, no 20834/92, § 34.

14 ECtHR 7.12.1976, no 5493/72, § 48.

15 *Lingens*, 8.7.1986, no 9815/82.

16 *Lingens*, 8.7.1986, no 9815/82, § 42.

reputations may be sullied in the most reprehensible manner in the interests of open discussion on political issues. Additionally, the ECtHR may take into account the prior conduct of a politician: if he or she has been party to harmfully worded attacks on his political opponents, he or she cannot reckon upon delicate treatment in return. This was, for instance, the case in a provocative attack on the late right-wing politician, *Jörg Haider*, where a journalist was protected from private prosecution. The ECtHR emphasised that a 'greater degree of tolerance' applied in respect of a politician, 'especially when he himself makes public statements that are susceptible of criticism.'[17] To sum up, in contrast to some national defamation laws, the ECtHR allows journalists massive latitude in their method of presentation, including exaggeration or even provocation. The scope for comment on wielders of political power is even wider than that for private individuals; the need for open comment on politics is seen as prevailing over the protection of reputation.

7   Of course, the mass media are not only concerned with commenting on politics; their real bread and butter is the reporting of facts. Where journalism is concerned with objectively verifiable statements of fact, their validity is crucial to the recipient. Phrased in terms of tort law: does an untrue statement of fact give rise to liability of the media outlet and the journalist? In its *Goodwin v the United Kingdom* decision, the ECtHR answered this question in the negative when it held: 'the safeguard offered ... to journalists in relation to reporting on articles of general interest is subject to the proviso that they are acting in good faith....' In other words, contrary to the general provisions of tort law, where generally any untrue statement of fact gives rise to liability, if it causes harm, journalists are entitled to fight any claim brought against them if they merely acted in good faith. Arguably with a view to the urgency in reporting news, the journalist has merely to fulfil the duty to endeavour to report as truly as possible; the requirement of diligent information is sufficient. The second core principle in this context, i.e. 'the reporting on issues of general interest,' was set forth in *Bergens Tidende v Norway*.[18] The failures of a local surgeon in inserting breast implants were highlighted in a newspaper article, and his incompetence was pilloried. In reality, the surgeon was not even remotely inept; he had conducted thousands of successful cosmetic operations. Obviously the article had clearly damaged his professional reputation, resulting in pecuniary loss. Nevertheless, the ECtHR submitted that this was not sufficient to override the freedom of the press to impart information on a matter of public concern,

---

17   *Oberschlick*, 23.5.1991, no 11662/85, § 59.
18   ECtHR 2 May 2000, no 26132/95.

as the newspaper had reported on an important controversy relating to public health.[19]

8 With regard to statements of fact, two lessons can be learnt here. First, in the view of the ECtHR, no absolute duty to establish the truth of a report can be imposed on the media. Facts are only to be verified as far as reasonable and appropriate. Second, the ECtHR is inclined to make a broad-brush public interest judgement; this even includes reports of ordeals suffered by women with leaky implants who had suffered damage while under the care of a competent plastic surgeon.

•••

9 Flash forward to the present day – to our age of media consolidation to media oligopolies,[20] the waning circulation of the daily press, etc – and the heroic vision of the mass media and the belief in its value for democracy have lost their sheen. The idea that democracy is strengthened where mass media facilitate greater transparency and accountability in governance by serving in their watchdog role to deter corruption and malfeasance, as well as providing a civic forum for multiple voices in public debate and highlighting problems to inform the policy agenda, seems just a glorified picture of the past.

10 For today's philosophers *Noam Chomsky* and *Edward Herman*, the modern media are but the propaganda arm of big business and big government. In their view, the press is not the 'watchdog of the public,' but the 'guarddog of power.'[21] To them, it is no wonder that so many attribute enormous power to the media not to inform, enlighten and uplift, but to mislead audiences, to close off discussion and buttress authority, to hide the machinations of power, and to control readers and viewers. And, indeed, what should we make of newspapers

---

19   Ibid.

20   Today's Western media is controlled by only a few, whether in the hands of broadcasting oligopolies within each nation, or of major multinational corporations with multimedia empires. See *J Tunstall/M Palmer*, Media Moguls (1991); *A Smith*, The Age of Behemoths: The Globalization of Mass Media Firms (1991); *A Sanchez-Tabernero*, Media Concentration in Europe: Commercial Enterprises and the Public Interest (1993). Contemporary observers caution that the process of media mergers has concentrated excessive control in the hands of a few multinational corporations, which remain unaccountable to the public; see *B Bagdikian*, The Media Monopoly (1993); *L Bogart*, Commercial Culture (1995); *R McChesney*, Rich Media, Poor Democracy: Communication Politics in Dubious Times (1999); *RG Picard*, Press Concentration and Monopoly: New Perspectives on Newspaper Ownership and Operation (1988).

21   See Manufacturing Consent: The Political Economy of the Mass Media (1998).

that are more likely to hold mistaken beliefs about global warming, health care, the war on terror, etc? And what should we make of the fact that media consumers are more eager to satisfy prurient interests and remain informed about some celebrities' dinner schedules than the latest developments in Syria or the intricacies of the Afghan political system. It seems almost as in reply to the ECtHR's public interest criterion when *Oscar Wilde* wrote – in another era, certainly, but his words still resonate – that 'the public have an insatiable curiosity to know everything, except what is worth knowing.'[22]

11 From this perspective, the assumption of the strong position supporting mass media seems to be unfounded. Crucially, freedom of the media is not an end in itself, and the sentiments behind art 10 (1) ECHR are subject to a number of exceptions contained in art 10 (2) ECHR.

> The exercise of this freedom, since it carries with it duties and respon-sibilities, may be subject to such formalities, conditions, restrictions or penalties as are prescribed by law and are necessary in a democratic society, in the interest of national security, territorial integrity or public safety, for the prevention of disorder or crime, for the protection of health or morals, for the protection of the reputation or the rights of others, for preventing the disclosure of information received in confidence, or for maintaining the authority and impartiality of the judiciary.

12 When do any of the exceptions override the freedom of expression and, ac-cordingly, the freedom of the press? Only when the state providing a restricted remedy against the violation of expression can rebut the presumption of art 10 (1) ECHR erected in favour of free expression; in the words of the ECtHR in *Observer and Guardian v the United Kingdom*:[23] 'This freedom is subject to exceptions, however these must be strictly construed and the need for any re-strictions must be established convincingly.' On this basis the 'burden of proof' is reversed. First, the Signatory State defending the restriction of freedom of expression bears the burden of proving its 'necessity in democratic society,' which in turn implies the existence of a 'pressing social need' for the restriction in question. But even when social needs are found 'pressing,' they are not per se overriding, as, secondly, the ECtHR held that '[e]ven when the social need is pressing, the particular infringement, looking at the context and the content of the banned communication, must be "proportionate to the legitimate aims pursued" and the Government bears the burden of passing the proportionality

---

22   The Soul of Man under Socialism (1891).

23   26.11.1991, no 13585/88, § 55; see also *Sunday Times*, 26.4.l979, no 6538/74.

test by adducting sufficient reasons.'[24] This 'proportionality test' is important –
it means that the ECtHR will strike down the restriction in question if its particular application or an aspect of it is nonetheless so disproportionate as to
breach the Convention. This is so if in all the circumstances of the case the
restriction was ineffectual in advancing the value contained in an art 10 (2)
ECHR exception, or was irrelevant to it, or insufficiently justified. The ECtHR
proceeds in this regard on a case-by-case basis. For instance, in *Tolstoy Miloslavsky v the United Kingdom*,[25] the ECtHR held that, although the law of civil
libel might in general terms respond to the social need to protect reputation
from untruths, the lack of proper judicial control over damages at that time
lacked all proportion and constituted a breach of the Convention.

13   Having addressed the high standards for any restriction of the freedom of expression, it seems useful to scrutinise more closely some of the explicitly mentioned values in art 10 (2) ECHR. For the first value, the restriction to protect
one's 'reputation' in relation to the publication of value judgements, I can only
refer to the principle mentioned, namely 'comment is free.' The restriction is
only ever available when the opinion published amounts to an abusive insult
without any meaning for public discourse on the topic – a standard hardly ever
found in any sizeable media outlet.

14   In contrast, with regard to statements of fact, some change appears to be on
the horizon, as some eminent figures in European legal science regard the current state of affairs, where the duty to report only involves verifying information where reasonable and appropriate and its further reduction in cases of
urgency, as highly inappropriate. From the perspective of the subject of these
publications, this principle entails that they bear the risk that false and harmful information is disseminated, which seems almost inevitable if standards
are so low. Such a burden is clearly unjustified, as only the public enjoys the
advantages of being informed and the owner of the mass medium gains the
economic profits. Echoing *Noam Chomsky* and *Edward Herman*, likewise from
the stance of the media recipient the current regime seems rather appalling,
as consumers expect correct information. Even when upholding those initial
sentiments on the role of mass media as guarantors of democracy, one must
surely agree that any such role is not furthered by the dissemination of false
information, but by diligently gathered and presented information supplemented by value judgements on their validity. Last but not least, media outlets
are companies and their product, i.e. the information, is eventually paid for.

---

24   *Handyside*, 7.12.1976, no 5493/72, § 48 f; *Sunday Times*, 26.4.1979, no 6538/74, §§ 62, 67;
     Lingens, 8.7.1986, no 9815/82, § 40.
25   13.7.1995, no 18139/91.

As *Helmut Koziol* has convincingly argued, under the contract between the consumer and the media outlet the latter has to meet the main contractual duty to use its best efforts to determinate the truth – and a duty to point out remaining reasonable doubts.[26] Hence, in order to facilitate liability, three alternatives are discussed, all representing (more or less) conceivable restrictions in the sense of art 10 (2) ECHR. As the public is arguably the beneficiary of the information, State liability towards the victim for the media's non-negligent but objectively false reporting is suggested. Alternatively, the burden of proof could be reversed so that the media owner has to prove that its employees acted with due care. Finally, *Koziol* proposes the media owner's strict liability for false reporting unless even the most diligent investigation would have resulted in the very same report.

15   As explicitly mentioned in art 10 (2) ECHR, the rights or freedoms granted by the ECHR to the other party may restrict the right to freedom of expression. This includes the pivotal personality right to respect for private and family life under art 8 ECHR.[27] Resonating with the aforementioned quote of *Oscar Wilde,* this frequently concerns public figures[28] such as politicians, leading businessmen, artists, sportspeople, entertainment stars and actors, as the public seems keen to gather extensive information on their private lives. The leading case in this regard is *Von Hannover v Germany,*[29] where pictures were published depicting this member of the Monacan monarchy in everyday situations such as playing sports, walking, on holiday and having dinner with friends. The German Federal Constitutional Court (BVerfG, *Bundesverfassungsgericht*) held that *Caroline*, as a public figure of contemporary society, enjoyed the protection of her private life even outside her home, but only if she was in a secluded place out of the public eye 'to which the person concerned retires with the objectively recognisable aim of being alone and where, confident of being alone, behaves in a manner in which he or she would not behave in public.'[30]

---

26   See *H Koziol*, Sachgerechte Haftung der Massenmedien in: H Koziol/J Seethaler/T Thiede, Medienpolitik und Recht (2010) 119 ff.

27   Art 8 ECHR provides: 'Everyone has the right to respect for his private and family life, his home, and his correspondence.'

28   Public figures can be described as persons holding office and/or using public resources and, more broadly speaking, all those who play a role in public life, whether in politics, the economy, the arts, the social sphere, sport or any other domains. See § 7 of Resolution 1165 (1998) of the Parliamentary Assembly of the Council of Europe on the right to privacy.

29   ECtHR 24.6.2004, no 59320/00.

30   BVerfG 15 December 1999, Neue Juristische Wochenschrift (NJW) 2001, 2187; see also BGH (Bundesgerichtshof) 14 May 2002, Versicherungsrecht (VersR), 903 and BGH 19 December 1995, BGHZ (Entscheidungen des BGH in Zivilsachen) 128, 1.

The Constitutional Court attached decisive weight to the freedom of the press, even the entertainment press, and to the public interest in knowing about *Caroline's* private life. In contrast to previous case law, which was largely in favour of the media, the ECtHR disagreed and placed significant emphasis on the protection of privacy. It held that any violation of the right to respect for private and family life is only justified when the published photographs and articles make a contribution to a debate of general public interest.[31] As *Caroline* exercised no official function, the photographs and articles related exclusively to details of her private life and made no such contribution to any public debate.[32] The ECtHR concluded that the German Courts had not struck a fair balance between the freedom of expression and the right to respect for private and family life, and, therefore, that art 8 had been breached. Thus, the decision of the German Federal Constitutional Court was revised and Caroline was ultimately awarded a considerable sum in damages. The ECtHR's approach, to which the Signatory States must adhere, had considerable implications for the tabloid press in Europe, and in an immediate reaction German chief-editors composed an open letter to the German Chancellor heralding the end of western democracy as known if the censorship prescribed by the ECtHR was not stopped. They argued that, as a result of the judgment, the hands of all serious journalists were tied and that they would now be prevented from rapping the knuckles of powerful people.[33] Beside the fact that German democracy still exists and even serious journalists – as *Noam Chomsky* and *Edward Herman* rightly argued – more often than not side with power-wielders, the apprehension that politicians would be included in this arguably strengthened protection of private and family life is unfounded. As mentioned above, politicians must accept greater restrictions on their personality rights than others. Regarding their privacy, it is reasoned that the family situation and social environment of a politician should be regarded not only as interesting for the public but, indeed, of public interest.[34]

---

31   See fn 26 and cf ECtHR *News Verlags GmbH & Co KG v Austria*, 11.1.2000, no 31457/96, § 52
      ff; *Krone Verlag GmbH & Co KG v Austria*, 26.2.2002, no 34315/96, § 33 ff; *Editions Plon v
      France*, 18.5.2004, no 58148/00, § 60.

32   Fn 26, §§ 63–66; cf *Observer and Guardian*, 26.11.1991, no 13585/88, § 59.

33   See the German tabloid BILD, 30 August 2004.

34   If a politician voluntarily courts the media and divulges his private situation for political
      purposes (home story), this would favour the media. Conversely, if the subject of the
      reporting tried to protect his private life from the media as much as possible, any such
      coverage should be respectful and reserved. In other words, the level of voluntary dis-
      closure to the media of private information by a politician should be taken into account.
      A politician who consciously and systematically circulates information about his private
      life to journalists, and thereby exploits the media to raise or maintain his profile, should

16 To sum up, three conclusions must be drawn regarding restrictions on the freedom of expression of the mass media. Firstly, restrictions of an opinion are
hardly available. Secondly, the latitude for the mass media in standards of publication of facts is under pressure. European legal science no longer accepts
lax duties on journalists when disseminating false information. Finally, the
ECtHR makes exceptions to freedom of expression when the right to private
and family life is violated and the resulting publication does not contribute to a
relevant public debate but satisfies only the prurient interests of the consumer.

•••

17 As expected, this report is a provocative stance on the current European situation with the protection of personality rights against mass media. To be clear,
I do not doubt that freedom of expression and of mass media was important
in the development of Western European democracies after the Second World
War. I question the all-important role which freedom of expression apparently
plays in supporting the mass media's strong position, even in cases where others' personality rights are violated. The good intentions eventually leading to
the strong position of the mass media virtually paved the way to today's situation where the mass media present a threat to any person who is named in
a publication. Freedom of the media is not an end in itself but a means to
realise an underlying fundamental goal and, where this idea does not persist,
one should not refrain from challenging the privileges held by the mass media.
As presented, first steps, namely a change regarding a journalist's duties when
presenting fact and the strengthened protection of private life, are leading in
this direction.

18 Without any doubt, Western mass media have amassed great power. For the
future, two principles – both formulated by the French philosopher *Voltaire* –
must be brought in balance. The first is a classical quote on the freedom of
expression: 'We may not like what you say, but liberal society defends to its
death your right to say it.'[35] Nowadays, the second quote, mistakenly attributed
to *Winston Churchill* or even *Stan Lee*, seems to be even more important: 'With
great power comes great responsibility.'[36]

---

not feign surprise if he is unsuccessful in his endeavours to detract media attention from
some particular point.

35   Arguably, the phrase was coined by *EB Hall* (under her pseudonym *SG Tallentyre*) in her
biography of *Voltaire* only to illustrate *Voltaire's* beliefs; cf *SG Tallentyre*, The Friends of
Voltaire (1906).

36   *F-M Arouet (Voltaire)*, Œuvres de Voltaire, vol 48 (1832).

CHAPTER 10

Protection of Patient Personality Rights in China

Ding Chunyan

I   Introduction

1   The term 'personality rights' used in this article refers to civil rights protecting various personality attributes of individuals, namely the 'being' (rather than the 'having') of a human being.[1] It is a unique civil law concept and serves as a 'source right' of a series of legal rights,[2] including the right to physical wellbeing (health, bodily integrity, physical freedom), right to name, image and voice, right to reputation, and right to dignity, liberty and privacy.[3] Personality rights are of fundamental importance for a person to realise his or her inherent value of dignity and to freely develop his or her personality.

2   Chinese law, as a civil law jurisdiction, recognises and protects personality rights. Section 4 of Chapter 5 of the 1986 General Principles of Civil Law (民法通则)[4] made by the National People's Congress stipulates an individual's right to life, right to health, right to name, right to image, right to reputation, right to honour, and right of marital autonomy. Article 2 of the 2001 Interpretations of the Supreme People's Court on the Issues regarding Determining the Tort Liability for Compensation for Mental Suffering (最高人民法院关于确定民事侵权精神损害赔偿责任若干问题的解释) further recognises an individual's right to bodily integrity, right to physical freedom, right to dignity, right

---

1   Whether and to what extent personality rights protection applies to legal entities remains controversial and open for debate: see *G Brüggemeier/AC Ciacchi/P O'Callaghan* (eds), Personality Rights in European Tort Law (2010) 575. Article 110 (2) of the 2017 General Provisions of Civil Law made by the National People's Congress provides that a legal entity and an unincorporated organisation have the right to their name, a right to honour and a right to reputation.

2   *PM Schwartz/K-N Peifer*, Prosser's Privacy and the German Right of Personality: Are Four Privacy Torts Better than One Unitary Concept? (2010) 98 California Law Review 1952.

3   Principle 32 titled 'Protection of the person': see Study Group on a European Civil Code and Research Group on EC Private Law (Acquis Group): Principles, Definitions and Model Rules of European Private Law: Draft Common Frame of Reference (outline edition) (2009) 81.

4   The 1986 General Principles of Civil Law was amended by the Standing Committee of the National People's Congress in 2009.

to privacy[5] and other personality interests.[6] The 2009 Tort Liability Law (侵权责任法) made by the Standing Committee of the National People's Congress provides a wide range of personality rights in art 2, which include the right to life, right to health, right to name, right to reputation, right to honour, right to image, right to privacy, right to marital autonomy and other personality rights and interests. The scope of the personality rights set forth in the 2009 Tort Liability Law is open-ended, thus having a capacity to accommodate unlisted or new personality rights that may develop in the future. More recently, the 2017 General Provisions of Civil Law (民法通则) made by the National People's Congress reiterate in art 109 and art 110 the right to physical freedom, right to dignity, right to life, bodily integrity, health, right to name, right to image, right to reputation, right to honour, right to privacy and right to marital autonomy.

3   Meanwhile, China has been embarking on drafting its Civil Code, which is likely to have a separate Book on Personality Rights.[7] However, there has not been consensus among Chinese legal scholars on a number of issues relating to personality rights, including but not limited to the scope and nature of personality rights, the adoption of the Germanic concept of 'the overarching general right of personality,' the subject of personality rights, the commercial value of personality attributes, the relationship between the law of personality rights and the law of tort, and the legitimate restrictions on personality rights. As Chinese legal scholars have been playing a more and more active and significant role in drafting the Civil Code, a thorough discussion and a better understanding of the above issues relating to personality rights in academia will definitely improve the quality of the Book on Personality Rights of China's new Civil Code.

4   Patients are a special group of natural persons. When doctors perform medical checks, diagnosis or treatment on patients and communicate with them, patient interests in physical wellbeing (life and health, bodily integrity and physical freedom), autonomy, privacy and dignity are at stake. Normatively, patient personality rights should not be compromised merely because they have some physical or mental disease. Patients are entitled to equal personality rights and legal protection with healthy persons.[8] Practically, patients are by and large

---

5   Some jurisdictions, such as the USA, protect autonomy under the right to privacy, but the right to privacy in Chinese law is understood as a separate right from the right to autonomy.

6   However, the 2001 Interpretations of the Supreme People's Court on the Issues regarding Determining the Tortious Liability for Compensation for Mental Suffering have not explained the meaning and the scope of the term 'other personality interests.'

7   *Huang Zhong*, On the Systematic Effects of the Law on Personality Rights as a Separate Book (人格权法独立成编的体系效应之辨识) (2013) 1 Modern Law Science (现代法学) 44.

8   See art 1 (1) of the Convention on the Rights of Persons with Disabilities, which states that 'the purpose of the present Convention is to promote, protect and ensure the full and equal

physically, mentally or emotionally vulnerable and suffer information asymmetry in relation to doctors, especially in a country where the doctor-patient relationship is primarily paternalistic, such as China. Patient personality rights thus deserve close attention and special protection by the law. Moreover, the scientific and technological developments of medicine and biology have created a wide variety of means of exercising patient personality rights, but meanwhile have enabled new and more invasions of them. Therefore, patient personality rights may be used as a legal lens to better understand and frame personality rights.

5 This article aims to contribute to the discourse on the characteristics of personality rights and on personality rights protection in current Chinese law from the perspective of patient personality rights, in particular focusing on two pillars of patient personality rights: patient autonomy and patient privacy. Specifically, the article is divided into five parts. Part two and part three respectively examine the existing legal rules on patient autonomy and patient privacy. Part four discusses four emerging characteristics of patient personality rights in Chinese law. They are the active side of patient personality rights, the posthumous protection of patient personality rights, the commercial value of patient personality attributes, and the legitimate restrictions on patient personality rights. Part five concludes with the implications of the discussion on patient personality rights for codifying personality rights in China.

II   Patient Autonomy

6 Respect for patient autonomy is a cardinal ethical principle in modern medicine.[9] Chinese law has embraced this principle and translated it into three sets of legal rules: (1) informed consent to medical treatment; (2) patient rights over the body; and (3) wrongful conception and birth. The first aims at protecting patient autonomy in making medical decisions, the second aims at protecting patient autonomy over the body, and the last aims at protecting patient reproductive autonomy.

7 It is necessary to mention that some patients may become unable to exercise autonomy when they permanently or temporarily lack mental capacity to make medical decisions due to the illness. There are two solutions in an incapacitated patient case: either the patient has already made advance directive

---

enjoyment of all human rights and fundamental freedoms by all persons with disabilities, and to promote respect for their inherent dignity.'

9   *TL Beauchamp/JF Childress*, Principles of Biomedical Ethics (2001) 114.

for a specified medical treatment before he or she lost mental capacity;[10] or the patient's guardian as legal representative makes proxy medical decisions on his or her behalf.[11] The discussion in this part mainly relates to those patients who have mental capacity and are able to make their own medical decisions.

A   *Informed Consent to Medical Treatment*

1   Legal Rules

8 The law of informed consent to medical treatment has been developed in China since the 1990s. The first enactment providing legal rules on informed consent to medical treatment was the 1994 Regulations on Administration of Medical Institutions (医疗机构管理条例) made by the State Council. Its art 33 provides that the medical institution shall obtain the consent of the patient and the consent and signature of his or her family or the relevant person (关系人)[12] before performing any operation, special examination or special treatment on the patient; where the consent of the patient is unavailable, the consent and signature of his or her family or the relevant person suffice; where neither the consent of the patient nor the consent of his or her family or the relevant person is available, or where other special circumstances occur, the attending doctor shall propose and perform medical treatment after obtaining the approval of the person in charge of the medical institution or an authorised person in charge.

9 Then, art 26 (1) of the 1998 Law on Practising Doctors (执业医师法) made by the Standing Committee of the National People's Congress provides that the doctor shall honestly inform the patient or his or her family of the illness, however the doctor shall avoid any adverse effect of the disclosure on the patient, which means that the doctor may withhold the relevant information on the ground of therapeutic privilege. Article 26 (2) further provides that the doctor, prior to conducting experimental treatment on the patient, shall obtain the approval of the hospital and the consent of the patient or his or her family. Article 37 accordingly imposes administrative and criminal liabilities on those doctors who violate art 26 (2).

---

10   According to art 62 of the 1986 General Principles of Civil Law, a civil juristic act may be conditional, and it will not take effect until the condition materializes. So does art 158 of the 2017 General Provisions of Civil Law. Advanced directive is seen as a conditional civil juristic act in law and a patient's directive will be effective only when he or she becomes incapacitated.

11   See art 10 (1) of the 2010 Basic Standards of Writing Medical Records (病历书写基本规范) made by the Ministry of Health.

12   Because the 1994 Regulations on Administration of Medical Institutions fail to explain the term 'the relevant person,' the meaning of the term is unclear.

10 Articles 55 and 56 of the 2009 Tort Liability Law stipulate the latest legal rules on informed consent to medical treatment. Article 55 (1) sets out the medical staff's duty to disclose medical information and duty to obtain written informed consent to medical treatment, as it provides that during diagnosis and treatment the medical staff shall explain the illness and relevant medical treatment to their patients, and if any operation, special examination or special treatment is needed, the medical staff shall explain the medical risks, alternative medical treatment options and other information to the patient in a timely manner, and obtain the written consent of the patient or, when it is inappropriate to explain the information to the patient, explain the information to close relatives of the patient, and obtain the written consent of the close relatives. Article 55 (2) establishes vicarious tortious liability of the medical institution when its medical staff have breached the above duties and caused harm to the patient. Article 56 provides an exemption of informed consent to medical treatment in the event of an emergency, as it states that where the decision of the patient or his or her close relatives cannot be obtained in an emergency, the corresponding medical treatment may be taken immediately with the approval of the person in charge of the medical institution or an authorised person in charge.

2   Patient Autonomy in Making Medical Decisions

11 It is noteworthy that the 1994 Regulations on Administration of Medical Institutions established a joint-consent mode, which requires the consent of both patient and his or her family or the relevant person before performing an operation, special examination or special treatment on the patient. In other words, the patient does not enjoy exclusive autonomy in making medical decisions; instead he or she has to share the decision-making power with his or her family or the relevant person. Thus the 1994 Regulations on Administration of Medical Institutions only granted the patient limited patient autonomy in making medical decisions. However, it seems that the wording of the 1998 Law on Practising Doctors implies that the joint-consent mode shall be limited to experimental treatments.[13] The 2009 Tort Liability Law ultimately clarifies that it is the patient rather than his or her family or close relative who is entitled to give informed consent to any operation, special examination or special treatment. In other words, the 2009 Tort Liability Law articulated that patients enjoy exclusive autonomy and authority in making their own medical decisions.

---

13   Experimental treatments refers to treatment that does not have sufficient research or clinical evidence to indicate its effect on the treated patient.

12 To facilitate patient autonomy in making medical decisions, current Chinese law imposes on the medical staff a duty to disclose the relevant information (such as the illness, the proposed medical treatment, the medical risks involved, and alternative medical treatment options) to the patient in a timely and appropriate manner. In the event of a failure to disclose the relevant information or a failure to obtain informed consent from the patient, the medical institution will be liable for the patient's damage caused by the failure; meanwhile the breaching medical staff will bear administrative liabilities accordingly.[14]

13 However, patient autonomy in making medical decisions is not absolute and may be restricted in two situations. First, when the patient becomes incapacitated from making medical decisions, it is difficult for the patient to instantaneously exercise autonomy although he or she may have advance directive[15] on whether or not to receive a particular medical treatment before losing mental capacity. In that case, the close relatives of the incapacitated patient will give proxy consent to medical treatment in accordance with the best interests of the patient.[16] Second, when the medical staff, on the ground of therapeutic privilege, withhold the relevant information to avoid serious physical or psychological harm possibly caused to the patient as a result of the disclosure, patient autonomy in making medical decisions is restricted because the patient is unaware of his or her illness and the proposed medical treatment.

B   *Patient Rights over the Body*
1   Legal Rules

14 The current legal rules regarding patient rights over the body may be divided into three categories. The first category is concerned with patient autonomy in determining the separation of a body part or human tissue (such as blood,[17] bone marrow, hemopoietic stem cells, gametes,[18] and organs[19]) from the living body and the use and disposition of the removed body part or human tissue. For example, patients are entitled to determine how long the gamete removed

---

14   For example, art 37 of the 1998 Law on Practising Doctors.

15   See fn 10 above.

16   See fn 11 above; also see art 18 of the 1986 General Principles of Civil Law.

17   See art 2 of the 1997 Blood Donation Law (献血法) made by the Standing Committee of the National People's Congress.

18   See art 3 of the 2001 Measures on the Administration of Human Sperm Banks (人类精子库管理办法) made by the Ministry of Health, and art 14 of the 2001 Measures on the Administration of Human Assisted Reproduction Technology (人类辅助生殖技术管理办法) made by the Ministry of Health.

19   See art 7 of the 2007 Regulations of Human Organ Transplantation (人体器官移植条例) made by the State Council.

from their body will be preserved for the purpose of assisted reproduction, and how to dispose of it in the case of divorce or death. The second category is concerned with patient autonomy in determining the use and disposition of the cadaveric body after death.[20] More specifically, patients have the right to freely decide whether or not to donate the whole or part of their body for organ transplantation.[21] The third category is concerned with patient autonomy in determining how to make use of the human body with the assistance of medical technology. For example, a woman enjoys freedom to decide to be a surrogate mother, bearing a child for others.[22] In addition, patients are entitled to modify or withdraw their decisions over their body at any time as long as it remains practical to do so.[23]

2   Patient Autonomy over the Body

15 Although Chinese law recognises and protects patient autonomy over the body, it does not mean that they enjoy absolute autonomy in this regard. The law sets out various restrictions on the separation of a body part or human tissue, the use of a removed body part or human tissue, and the use of the human body on the ground of social morality. First of all, Chinese law adopts a principle of prohibition of commercialisation in relation to any use of the human body, a removed body part or human tissue. For example, the 2003 Ethical Principles of Assisted Human Reproductive Technology and Human Sperm Banks (人类辅助生殖技术和人类精子库伦理原则) made by the Ministry of Health explicitly established a principle of prohibition of commercialisation,[24] thus banning any commercial dealing with sperm, eggs or embryos, and other

---

20   Ibid.

21   It is noteworthy that the spouse, the adult children or the parents of the deceased are also entitled to decide to donate the whole or part of the body of the deceased unless the latter has made an objection before death: see art 8 (2) of the 2007 Regulations of Human Organ Transplantation.

22   Current Chinese law neither generally prohibits nor expressly permits surrogacy, although the Ministry of Health issues the relevant departmental rules to prohibit medical institutions and medical staff from performing any form of surrogacy procedures, such as art 3 of the 2001 Measures on the Administration of Human Assisted Reproduction Technology.

23   Such as, art 8 (1) of the 2007 Regulations of Human Organ Transplantation.

24   The 2003 Ethical Principles of Assisted Human Reproductive Technology and Human Sperm Banks are made up of these two sets of ethical principles, namely, the set of ethical principles on assisted human reproductive technology and the set of ethical principles on human sperm banks. The principle of prohibition of commercialisation is located in arts 1 (2) and 6 of the first set of ethical principles and art 6 of the second set of ethical principles.

commercial arrangements in the application of assisted human reproductive technology, such as commercial surrogacy. The 2007 Regulations on Human Organ Transplantation (人体器官移植条例) made by the State Council also articulated the prohibition of commercial dealings in human organs no matter whether from the living or the cadaveric body.[25]

16 Second, the law imposes restrictions on patient autonomy in determining how to use a removed body part or human tissue on the ground of public policy. For example, the 2003 Ethical Principles of Assisted Human Reproductive Technology and Human Sperm Banks barred the health care institutions and their staff from performing procedures to facilitate embryo donation for reproduction,[26] thus indirectly restricted patient autonomy in determining the use of their embryos. The rationale for this provision seems to lie in the Ministry of Health's intention to prevent couples from undertaking commercial surrogacy and circumventing the one-child policy through the disguise of embryo donation for reproduction.

17 Third, the law limits patient autonomy over the body for the reason of paternalism, that is, to protect patient interests in physical and psychological health. For example, minors under 18 years old are prohibited from becoming a living organ donor;[27] and living organ donation is strictly limited to a donor and receiver who have a close family relationship,[28] because organ donation will inevitably cause harm to the living donor and only a sufficiently close family relationship may justify a donor's self-determination of harming himself or herself to benefit others.[29]

C   *Wrongful Conception and Birth*
1   Legal Rules

18 Wrongful conception refers to those cases where, due to prenatal medical negligence, an unexpected (healthy or disabled) child is born into a family that sees parenthood as a risk and seeks medical assistance to eliminate the risk. Wrongful birth refers to those cases where, due to prenatal medical negligence, a disabled child is born into a family that wants a child but does not want the responsibilities of caring for a disabled child. There is no specific legal rule regarding wrongful conception and birth actions in Chinese law. However, arts 54 and 57 of the 2009 Tort Liability Law broadly provide tort liability of the

---

25   See art 3 of the 2007 Regulations of Human Organ Transplantation.
26   See art 3 (6) of the first set of ethical principles of the 2003 Ethical Principles of Assisted Human Reproductive Technology and Human Sperm Banks.
27   See art 9 of the 2007 Regulations of Human Organ Transplantation.
28   See art 10 of the 2007 Regulations of Human Organ Transplantation.
29   This restriction may also prevent the disguised trade in human organs.

medical institutions for medical negligence committed by its staff. In wrongful conception and birth actions, the parents may sue the medical institution for damages where the alleged prenatal medical negligence results in the pregnancy and/or the birth of an undesired child.

2   Patient Reproductive Autonomy

19 As medical negligence causes the pregnancy and/or the birth of an undesired child rather than the disability of the child, the legal interest recognised and safeguarded through wrongful conception and birth actions is reproductive autonomy of patients, i.e. their free choice to avoid having a child[30] or a child with a disability.[31] Therefore, as long as patients are able to prove that the alleged prenatal medical negligence deprives them of autonomy to avoid the pregnancy and/or the birth of an undesired child, they are entitled to claim compensation associated with the undesired pregnancy and/or birth. Chinese courts have more and more often adopted the term 'the right to reproductive choice' in their decisions in wrongful conception and birth actions.[32]

20 It is worth noting that Chinese law only provides partial protection of reproductive autonomy. On the one hand, the state's one-child policy substantially restricts the couple's reproductive autonomy to choose to have more than one child in the family.[33] On the other hand, the law neither illegalizes abortion nor provides any limitation on the performance of abortion, as long as the pregnant woman voluntarily chooses to terminate pregnancy.[34] More precisely, the law merely recognises and protects reproductive autonomy to avoid having a child or a child with a disability, which is entirely in line with the State's policy

---

30   See art 51 of the 1992 Women Rights and Interests Protection Law (妇女权益保障法) made by the Standing Committee of the National People's Congress. It was amended in 2005.

31   See art 18 of the 1994 Mother and Infant Health Protection Law (母婴保健法) made by the Standing Committee of the National People's Congress.

32   For example, the author searched for the term 'the right to reproductive choice' in the case database of 'Judicial Opinions of China' (中国裁判文书网), which is the official website of published judicial decisions operated by the Supreme People's Court, and found that there were sixteen wrongful conception and birth cases where the court adopted this term in the judgment.

33   China has allowed all couples to have two children in order to improve the balanced development of population and to deal with an aging population, which is a new 'two-child policy' announced by the Community Party's Central Committee in late October 2015, see 'China to End One-child Policy and Allow Two' BBC News, 29 October 2015, available at <http://www.bbc.com/news/world-asia-34665539>.

34   See the 1957 Reply of the Supreme People's Court on How to Deal with Abortion (最高人民法院关于对堕胎行为应如何处理的批复).

of controlling population growth and eugenics. Therefore, it is understandable for the courts to uphold wrongful conception and birth actions, which exactly aim to protect the couple's reproductive autonomy to avoid having a child or a child with a disability.

III   Patient Privacy

21 The notion of privacy is notoriously difficult to be defined,[35] however two types of privacy interest are commonly accepted: one is the interest in solitude or seclusion (the so-called 'right to be let alone'), and the other is the interest in private information. In the context of patient privacy, these two types of privacy interest will be respectively translated to (1) patient freedom from intrusion upon seclusion, including his or her medical affairs and (2) patient information privacy. As said, the 2009 Tort Liability Law recognises a right to privacy in art 2. Moreover, a series of special laws regulating different types of medical professionals (such as physicians,[36] nurses,[37] rural doctors[38] and expert authenticators dealing with medical negligence cases[39]) also require the corresponding medical professionals to respect and protect patient privacy.

A   *Patient Freedom from Intrusion upon Seclusion*

22 According to art 2 of the 2009 Tort Liability Law, patients are entitled to raise an invasion of privacy claim when someone intentionally intrudes, physically or otherwise, upon their seclusion (such as intruding into the patient's private ward) or into their private medical affairs, which may also be regarded as part of the sphere of the patient. For example, in the case of *Liang v Qingdao People's Hospital* (2003),[40] a group of medical students doing internships at the defendant hospital were observing the plaintiff Liang's abortion surgery without her knowledge and consent. Liang, who received anesthesia during the surgery, was unaware of it, but she felt deeply offended after she knew about

---

35 *AM Conroy*, Protecting Your Personality Rights in Canada: A Matter of Property or Privacy? (2012) 1 Western Journal of Legal Studies 18.

36 See art 22 of 1998 Law on Practising Doctors.

37 See art 18 of the 2008 Regulations on Nurses (护士条例) made by the State Council.

38 See art 24 (3) of the 2003 Regulations on the Administration of the Practice of Rural Doctors (乡村医师从业管理条例) made by the State Council.

39 See art 22 (5) of the 2005 Measures on the Administration of the Registration of Forensic Authenticators (司法鉴定人登记管理办法) made by the Ministry of Justice.

40 See Medical Interns in a Hospital Observed in Abortion Surgery on an Unmarried Woman (未婚女子做人流手术遭医院实习生集体观摩), Fazhi Bobao, 24 September 2004, available at <http://news.sina.com.cn/s/2004-09-24/15554415989.shtml>.

it after the surgery. She sued the hospital for invasion of her right to privacy. The defendant argued that patients, once they chose to use medical services at a hospital, should be presumed to give up their right to privacy and accept whatever way in which the hospital was operated, including medical interns observing the performance of surgery. The Nanqu District Court of Qingdao in Shandong Province rejected the defendant's argument and confirmed the invasion of the plaintiff's right to privacy. The defendant hospital was ordered to pay the plaintiff RMB 10,000 as compensation for mental suffering.

B   *Patient Information Privacy*
1   Medical Confidentiality

23 Chinese law imposes on the holder of patient information an obligation of confidence and tortious liability for breach of confidence.[41] Article 62 of the 2009 Tort Liability Law stipulates that the medical institution and its medical staff shall keep confidential the privacy of the patient, and if any privacy of the patient is divulged or any medical records of the patient are publicised without the consent of the patient, the medical institution shall bear the tortious liability for the harm caused to the patient. In addition, a series of special laws protecting special groups of patients (such as mother and infant patients,[42] venereal disease patients,[43] infectious disease patients,[44] HIV/AIDS patients,[45] drug addicts[46] and patients with mental disabilities[47]) also provide that health information (such as the name, portrait, address, employer, medical records

---

41 Moreover, to safeguard medical confidentiality, art 7 of the 2009 Seventh Amendments to the Criminal Law (刑法第七修正案) made by the Standing Committee of the National People's Congress imposes criminal liability on three types of parties: (1) any staff of the medical institution who, in violation of the statutory provisions, sells or illegally provides to others the personal information of patients obtained during their performance of duties or provision of service; (2) any person who illegally obtains the personal information of patients by stealing or any other means; and (3) any legal entity who commits either of the two crimes described above.

42 See art 36 (3) of the 2001 Measures on the Implementation of the Mother and Infant Health Care Law (母婴保健法实施办法) made by the State Council.

43 See art 36 (3) of the 2012 Administrative Measures on the Prevention and Treatment of Venereal Diseases (性病防治管理办法) made by the Ministry of Health.

44 See art 12 of the 2004 Law of Prevention and Treatment of Infectious Diseases (传染病防治法) made by the Standing Committee of the National People's Congress.

45 See art 39 of the 2006 Regulations on Prevention and Treatment of HIV/AIDS (艾滋病防治条例) made by the State Council.

46 See art 7 (2) of the 2011 Regulations on Drug Rehabilitation (戒毒条例) made by the State Council.

47 See art 4 (3) of the 2012 Mental Health Law (精神卫生法) made by the Standing Committee of the National People's Congress.

and other identifiable personal information) of these special groups of patients shall be kept confidential.

24 Chinese courts uphold breach of medical confidentiality claims even when the reason for the divulgement of patient health information is unclear as a matter of fact. For example, in the case of *Cun Lili v Beijing Anorectal Disease Hospital* (2014),[48] the plaintiff Cun had been in the defendant hospital to receive medical treatment for a hemorrhoid and anal fissure for around one month in 2006, and in 2012 she found that part of her medical records at the defendant hospital was contained in a digital disk sold online. Cun sued the defendant for breach of medical confidentiality. Although the No 2 Intermediate Court of Beijing could not ascertain the reason for the leakage of the health information, it still held that the defendant had breached its duty of confidence and infringed the plaintiff's right to privacy. The defendant was ordered to pay the plaintiff RMB 12,000 as compensation for mental suffering.

25 However, medical confidentiality may be subject to a wide range of restrictions in Chinese law. First, patient health information should be reported by information holders to or used by the public security authority, the procuratorate or the court for the purpose of criminal investigation.[49] Second, patient health information regarding infectious disease cases or suspicion cases should be reported to the government.[50] Third, patient health information may be used for the purpose of monitoring health care quality, medical research and teaching.[51] Fourth, patient health information may be accessed and used by 'the involved parties' (当事人) whose personal and property rights and interests directly relate to the health information of the patient concerned, provided that the patient's rights, in particular the right to privacy, be protected.[52]

---

48   The case docket number is (2014)二中民终字08046号.

49   See art 108 of the 2012 Criminal Procedure Law (刑事诉讼法) made by the National People's Congress and art 14 of the 2002 Rules on the Administration of Medical Records of Medical Institutions (医疗机构病历管理规定) jointly made by the Ministry of Health and the State Administration of Traditional Chinese Medicine.

50   See art 30 of the 2004 Law on Prevention and Treatment of Infectious Diseases (传染病防治法) made by the Standing Committee of the National People's Congress, and art 39 of the 2003 Regulations on the Urgent Handling of Public Health Emergencies (突发公共卫生事件应急条例) made by the State Council.

51   See art 6 of the 2002 Rules on the Administration of Medical Records of Medical Institutions.

52   See art 23 of the 2008 Provisional Rules on the Administration of Health Records (卫生档案管理暂行规定) jointly made by the Ministry of Health and the State Archives Bureau.

2   Patient Right of Access to and Control of Health Information

26 Apart from medical confidentiality, the patient's right of access to and control of his or her own health information is another indispensable aspect of
patient information privacy. On the one hand, art 10 of the 2002 Regulations
on the Handling of Medical Malpractice (医疗事故处理条例) made by the
State Council enables patients to photocopy and duplicate their own medical
records, so does art 61 (2) of the 2009 Tort Liability Law. On the other hand,
Chinese law fails to stipulate for the patient's right to control the disclosure,
sharing and uses of his or her own health information. Without the legal en-
titlement, it is impossible for patients to actively exercise privacy rights over
their own health information, such as by authorising a third party to use the
health information for a profit or non-profit purpose.

IV   Emerging Characteristics of Patient Personality Rights

27 The dogmatic characteristics of personality rights are extra-patrimonial and
highly personal, therefore unhereditable, inalienable, beginning with the birth
and terminating with the death of a human being.[53] Personality rights have
been traditionally considered a province of tort law,[54] which emphasised the
'defensive' structure of personality rights.[55] However, the characteristics of
personality rights are far from being settled in various jurisdictions.[56] China is
not an exception and much controversy focuses on the relationship between
the law of personality rights and the law of tort, the posthumous protection
of personality rights, the commercial value of personality attributes, and the
legitimate restrictions on personality rights. Patient personality rights (in particular the two pillars of personality rights relating to patient autonomy and
patient privacy), which have greatly developed since the last century, serve as
a lens to understand the above controversies regarding the characteristics of
personality rights.

---

53   *J Neethling*, Personality Rights: A Comparative Overview (2005) 38 Comparative and International Law Journal of South Africa 223.

54   *G Resta*, The New Frontiers of Personality Rights and the Problem of Commodification:
European and Comparative Perspectives (2011) 26 Tulane European & Civil Law Forum
33 f.

55   *Resta* (2011) 26 Tulane European & Civil Law Forum 36 f.

56   *Neethling* (2005) 38 Comparative and International Law Journal of South Africa 224 f.

A   *Active Side of Patient Personality Rights*

28 Personality rights possess both active and passive sides.[57] The active side grants
    the subject 'sovereignty' or 'power' over the object of the personality right,
    while the passive side imposes on others the 'duty' to respect the same object,
    prohibiting them from committing any infringement.[58] Patient autonomy in
    making medical decisions presents a good example in this regard. Specifically,
    patients enjoy the right to bodily integrity and are entitled to legal protection
    from any wrongful intervention into their body. This is the passive side of pa-
    tient autonomy. Moreover, it is inevitable and also necessary for doctors to
    perform various intervening medical treatments on patients for therapeutic
    purposes. Therefore, in the context of medical care, the passive side of patient
    autonomy carries less weight due to the realistic need for medical interven-
    tion, and more emphasis is given to its active side: the patients have the 'power'
    to determine whether, how and to what extent doctors can interfere with their
    bodily integrity for therapeutic purposes and ultimately to determine how to
    deal with their own body, health and life.

29 To facilitate patients in exercising the active side of patient autonomy, Chinese
    law adopts a special term 'informed consent to medical treatment,' which plays
    two roles in law. In terms of the passive side of patient autonomy, the patient's
    informed consent acts as complete defence for the doctor, who is thus free
    from tortious liability for the intervention into the patient's bodily integrity.
    The more important role of the patient's informed consent relates to the active
    side of patient autonomy. Informed consent promotes self-determination of
    the patient and acts as his or her expressed prior authorisation to the doctor,
    who thus follows the patient's medical decision by conducting a medical inter-
    vention of the authorised type, in the authorised manner and for the autho-
    rised purpose. Therefore, the law not only needs to prevent patients from the
    infringement of bodily integrity, but also needs to facilitate them to actively
    make an autonomous medical decision, for example, by imposing on doctors a
    duty to make timely and appropriate disclosure of the relevant information.[59]

---

57   Some Chinese legal scholars argued that personality rights do not have an active side be-
     cause the subject is often restricted by law in freely deciding how to use his or her person-
     ality attributes (for example, the law disallows the subject to sell his or her own organs):
     see *Li Yongjun*, On the Legal Protection of Personality Rights from the Perspective of the
     Nature of Personality Rights (从权利属性看人格权的法律保护) (2012) 1 Studies
     on Law and Business (法商研究) 16. However, this point of view suffers from a logical
     problem, namely that legal restrictions on the active side of personality rights cannot
     negate the existence of that side of personality rights.
58   *A Popovici*, Personality Rights: A Civil Law Concept (2004) 50 Loyola Law Review 354.
59   See no 6 ff of this article.

30 By the same token, it is of great significance for the law to extend its function in facilitating patients in exercising the active side of patient autonomy over their body, that is, in self-determining whether to remove and how to use a body part or human tissue, how to use the cadaveric body after death, and how to make use of the human body with the assisted medical technology. The law cannot oversee the active side of patient reproductive autonomy and patient information privacy either. However, current Chinese law has not provided the necessary legal mechanisms to enhance the active side of these patient personality rights. As analysed above, Chinese law of patient information privacy focuses on the passive side of patient privacy (i.e. medical confidentiality) and provides very few rules to promote its active side (i.e. the patient's right of access to and control of health information).[60]

B   *Posthumous Protection of Patient Personality Rights*

31 As a natural person's capacity for rights starts at birth and ends at death, he or she can only enjoy and exercise various civil rights, including personality rights, during the lifetime.[61] However, this legal rule does not necessarily contradict the view that the legal protection of personality right may extend to the period before the birth and to the period after the death of a human being. The typical example of the former is the tortious liability for prenatal injury and that of the latter is the posthumous protection of authorship in copyright.[62] Both patient autonomy over the body and patient information privacy involve the issue of posthumous protection.

32 As mentioned above, a patient, through actively exercising the right to autonomy over the body, may freely decide how to preserve, use and dispose of a removed body part or human tissue after death, or whether and how to donate his or her cadaveric body after death.[63] The validity of the patient's self-determination on these issues will not be prejudiced because of the death; Chinese law protects patient autonomy regarding the posthumous use and disposition of his or her removed body part, human tissue or cadaveric body even though the patient as the decision maker has already passed away at the moment of the use and disposition. For example, the law generally will not allow the wife to use her deceased husband's frozen sperm or the frozen embryo created with her deceased husband's sperm to conceive a baby if the husband

---

60   See no 23 ff of this article.

61   See art 9 of the 1986 General Principles of Civil Law.

62   Such as art 20 of the 1990 Copyright Law (著作权法) made by the Standing Committee of the National People's Congress, amended in 2010.

63   See no 6 ff of this article.

had clearly rejected any posthumous use of his sperm or the embryo created
with his sperm.

33 Similarly, although a patient can no longer actively exercise the right of access to and control over his or her health information after death, his or her
previous decision on how to use personal health information and the passive
side of patient information privacy (i.e. posthumous medical confidentiality)
still deserve posthumous protection.[64] There are arguably two justifications for
providing posthumous protection of patient information privacy. One is that it
better serves the interest and expectation of living patients in terms of privacy
protection. If the legal protection of patient information privacy were to van-
ish once patients died, patients would likely become more reluctant to disclose
sensitive health information to doctors and medical institutions, even at the
cost of avoiding medical care, because they might worry about the possible
disclosure and abuse of their private health information after death. The second justification is that posthumous protection of patient information privacy
better serves the interest of the patients' close relatives, who may have mental
suffering due to the unlawful posthumous disclosure and use of the patient
health information.

34 It is noteworthy that posthumous protection of patient personality rights
in Chinese law is not the continuation of personality rights without a subject.[65] It is embedded in the context of the injured feeling of the patient's
close relatives,[66] which is similar to the approach accepted in France and
Switzerland.[67] For example, art 3 of the 2001 Interpretations of the Supreme
People's Court on the Issues regarding Determining the Tort Liability for Compensation for Mental Suffering grants the close relatives of the deceased a
claim for compensation for mental suffering, which is caused by the posthumous infringement of the name, image, honour, reputation, privacy and the
cadaveric body of the deceased.

C   *Commercial Value of Patient Personality Attributes*

35 Personal attributes may be corporeal or incorporeal: the former include the
human body, and removed body parts or human tissue, while the latter include

---

64   For example, art 4.1 of the Declaration on Promotion of Patients' Rights in Europe (1994).

65   But this view is upheld in Germany and Austria: see fn 53 above, at 243.

66   For more detailed discussion: see *Ge Yunsong*, Civil Law Protection of Personality
      Interests of the Deceased Possessed during the Lifetime (死者生前人格利益的民
      法保护) (2002) 4 Studies on Comparative Law (比较法研究) 2 f.

67   *Neethling* (2005) 38 Comparative and International Law Journal of South Africa 243.

name, image, voice and private personal information. Personality attributes are traditionally considered external to the market realm, which is nevertheless no longer true nowadays. Personality attributes, especially incorporeal ones, have gradually acquired commercial value and are increasingly treated as immaterial commodities that can be sold, bought and licensed in the market.[68] This new phenomenon gives rise to a number of legal issues: (1) whether the law shall recognise and protect the commercial value of personality attributes; (2) whether the commercial value of personality attributes shall constitute a separate and independent right from personality rights of the subject; and (3) if yes, whether this right shall be patrimonial, alienable and hereditable.

36   By and large, Chinese law does not recognise the commercial value of corporeal patient personality attributes due to the principle of prohibition of commercialisation in relation to the human body, removed body parts and human tissue (such as human organs, gametes and embryos),[69] although they may meet the actual needs of the market.[70] However, Chinese law protects the commercial value of incorporeal patient personality attributes, recognising that patients are entitled to freely decide who, under what conditions and for what purposes may exploit their private health information, which is conceived as the active side of patient privacy.[71] Meanwhile, the law provides patients with compensation for mental suffering caused by unauthorised exploitation of private health information, which is conceived as the passive side of patient privacy.

37   Moreover, according to art 20 of the 2009 Tort Liability Law, where any harm caused by the infringement of personality rights gives rise to pecuniary damage to the victim, the tortfeasor shall pay compensation in the amount of the loss sustained by the victim as the result of the tort; and if the loss sustained by the victim cannot be determined and the tortfeasor obtained some benefit from the tort, the tortfeasor shall pay compensation in the amount of the benefit obtained. By applying this rule, the patient whose private health or

---

68   See *Resta* (2011) 26 Tulane European & Civil Law Forum 42.

69   Art 3 (right to the integrity of the person) of the European Charter of Fundamental Rights states a similar principle, i.e. the prohibition on making the human body and its parts as such a source of financial gain, while art 8 (protection of personal data) does not provide a similar limitation.

70   For example, there are underground markets of commercial surrogacy and trade in human organs, gametes, and embryos in China.

71   It is worth noting that the enforceability of a contract relating to the commercial exploitation of personality attributes may be subject to the protection of human dignity of the subject.

biological information has been exploited without authorisation by a pharmaceutical company is entitled to claim the latter's unlawfully earned profits as a result of the unauthorised use.

38 However, Chinese law does not recognise that patients have a separate and independent right (distinct from their personality rights) over the commercial value of their incorporeal personality rights, let alone provide for any legal rules relating to the transferability, alienability and hereditability of that right.

D   Legitimate Restrictions on Patient Personality Rights

39 Patient personality rights are subject to a wide range of legitimate restrictions, which may be classified into three major types: paternalism, social morality, and public interest. For example, paternalism is the underlying rationale for curtailing patient autonomy in making medical decisions, where the doctor withholds the relevant information regarding the illness and/or the proposed medical treatment from a patient in order to avoid serious physical or psychological harm possibly caused to the patient as a result of the disclosure.[72] In this case, patient autonomy gives way to paternalistic protection of the patient. Paternalism also justifies restrictions on patient autonomy in making living organ donation.[73]

40 Patient personality rights are also restricted by social morality. Although there are the actual market needs for the commercial exploitation of corporeal personality attributes, Chinese law articulates the principle of prohibition of commercialisation in relation to the human body, removed body parts and human tissue, because such commercial exploitation violates the predominant morality in society. Moreover, public interest widely restricts patient personality rights. One example is the state's one-child policy, which curtails both patient autonomy in embryo donation for reproduction,[74] and patient reproductive autonomy in having more than one child in the family.[75] As another example, medical confidentiality protection is subjected to various restrictions for the public interest in public security, justice and public health.

41 The greater the restriction on patient personality rights, the less protection that the law provides for the development of patient personality. Unfortunately, Chinese law suffers from excessive restrictions and the unclear scope of such restrictions on patient personality rights. For example, patient health

---

72   See no 7 ff of this article.

73   See no 13 ff of this article.

74   Ibid.

75   See fn 33 above.

information may be accessed and used by 'the involved parties' whose personal and property rights and interests 'directly relate to' the health information of the patient concerned.[76] However, the law adopts the vague terms 'the involved parties' and 'directly relate to' without further explanation, which easily leads to the abuse of the restrictions on patient privacy in practice.

v Conclusion

42 Chinese law has been establishing a basic legal framework to protect patient autonomy and patient privacy, however there is much room for improvement so as to fully and effectively promote patient personality. First of all, the law needs to pay more attention to the active side of patient personality rights by providing well-designed and detailed rules to facilitate patients in exercising autonomy in making medical decisions, autonomy over own body and autonomy in making reproductive decisions and in exercising their right of access to and control over their own health information. Second, the law needs to work out a set of legal rules to address the issue of posthumous protection of patient personality rights and the issue of commercial exploitation of patient personality attributes, because the relevant rules in current law are highly undeveloped. Third, the law needs to narrow down and clarify the scope of the legitimate restrictions on patient personality rights, limiting them to what is necessary and proportionate.

43 Meanwhile, the above discussion on patient personality rights may shed light upon China's ongoing codification of personality rights. The importance of the active side of personality rights in effect implies a desirable relationship between the law of personality rights and the law of tort. No doubt, the law of tort has been playing an important and indispensable role in terms of the passive side of personality rights, sanctioning the infringement of personality rights through an injunction or an award of damages. However, the traditional 'defensive' structure of personality rights focusing on the passive side is no longer sufficient to fully and effectively protect individuals' personality rights and to develop their personality. Beside the law of tort, legal rules aiming at promoting the active side of personality rights should be established through the general law (e.g. the Civil Code) and the special law (e.g. the Personal Data Protection Law), which should equally become an indispensable part of the law of personality rights in China. Moreover, Chinese lawmakers need to

---

76   See fn 52 above.

thoroughly consider the issues of posthumous protection of personality rights and the commercial value of incorporeal personality rights before addressing them in the Civil Code. They should also be extremely cautious when allowing restrictions on personality rights, as excessive restrictions create a risk of undermining the inherent value of human dignity and the greatest chance of personality development.

CHAPTER 11

On the Independence of Personalities and Restrictions on the Status of Spouses

Fan Liying

I   Introduction

1 As natural persons, spouses are entitled to enjoy independent personalities as well as relevant rights such as the right of name, right of personal liberty, reproductive right and right of privacy. After marriage, the right of personality as a result becomes subjected to the status of spouse: the right of name turns into the right of marital surname in accordance with the marriage, the right to sexual freedom develops into the right to cohabit bound by the status of spouse as the result of the specialization of sexual relationship. The enforcement and realization of the reproductive right has to accept restrictions on account of other legal provisions; the right of privacy becomes the object of the right to know for the benefit of the marriage. 'Man is born free; and everywhere he is in chains.' While enjoying independent rights of personality, spouses have to be bound by their mutual status for the benefit and interests of each other and their family.

2 'Personal relation' refers to a social relation that has the property of being personal and is inseparable; its subject aims at special moral interests rather than economic ones.[1] The relationship between spouses falls into the scope of rights of status but it is different from other personal relations for it has to depend on the existence of spousal status and thus exists only between husbands and wives. The personalities of spouses are independent yet subject to their status.

II   Right of Name and Right of Marital Surname

A   *Legal Character of the Right of Name and the Right of Marital Surname*

3 The right of name refers to the right of a natural person to determine, use and change his own name in accordance with the legal provisions. General opinion

---

1   *Guo Mingrui/Fang Shaokun*, The Civil Law (2000) 4.

holds that the right of name is a kind of right of personality and a very important one too. Although name and surname are just signs for certain people,
their existence is a crucial indication of an independent personality.

4   The right of marital surname refers to the surname that comes through marriage. Spouses can choose their own surname.[2] As natural persons, spouses
have independent personalities as well as the right of name, however, after the
marriage, their surnames will change in line with their spousal status. Thereby,
most countries and regions view the right of marital surname as an effect of
marriage.[3] And the right of marital surname reflects the character of the right
of status.

B   *The Option of Marital Surname*

5   Legislation in most foreign countries and regions allows husband and wife to
choose by agreement the marital surname. For example, art 750 of the Japanese
Civil Code states: 'Husband and wife assume the surname of the husband or
wife in accordance with the agreement made at the time of the marriage.' and
art 1000 in the Civil Code of Taiwan states: 'The husband and the wife should
keep his or her own surname. Unless one party shall prefix to his or her surname
that of the spouse in writing at the household administration authority …'[4]
The General Principles of Civil Law of the People's Republic of China set out in
art 99 that 'citizens shall enjoy the right of personal name and shall be entitled
to determine, use or change their personal names in accordance with relevant
provisions. Interference with, usurpation of and false representation of personal names shall be prohibited.' Therefore the conclusion can be drawn that
the spouses enjoy the right to choose their surname.

6   Since it is the general practice for other countries to allow the husband and wife
to choose by agreement to put the other spouse's surname into his or her own
surname, China should adopt the same interpretation. But can spouses choose
by agreement a third surname as their marital surname? Most countries and
regions take a negative attitude towards this, but China has no definite provisions on it while there are two different opinions amongst Chinese scholars. In
my opinion, the right of marital surname, as a kind of right of status, is a sym-
bol of spousal status and the choice must therefore be between the husband's
and the wife's surnames. No provisions can be found in legislation anywhere
that the spouses may choose a third surname as their marital surname.

---

2   *Yu Yanman*, The Original Theory of Family Law (2007) 219.
3   *Yu* (fn 2) 219.
4   *Wang Zejian*, Introduction to Civil Law (2003) 620.

C   *Reversion to Original Surname*

7   When it comes to whether or not spouses can revert to their own original surname after having taken a marital surname, relevant statements can be found in art 1000 of the Civil Code of Taiwan, China that '... the party who prefixed to his or her surname that of the spouse may revert to his or her own surname. But only one change may be made during the continuance of the marriage relationship.'[5] On the topic of reversion to the original surname for the widowed or divorced spouses, there exist mainly two kinds of legislation. One allows each spouse to choose, after divorce or in widowhood, the surname, including keeping the marital surname and reverting to the original surname. As is stated in § 1355 of the German Civil Code: 'The widowed or divorced spouse retains the family name. He may, by declaration to the registrar, reassume his birth name or the name that he had until the determination of the family name, or attach his birth name or the name he had at the time of the determination of the family name before or after the family name.' The other approach provides that a widowed wife has to keep the marital surname in widowhood until her remarriage. Take art 143 of Italian Civil Code as an example: this prescribes that the wife shall add the husband's surname and, even if the husband dies, the widow has to keep this surname until she remarries. There are no such provisions in China, but the prevailing view is that each spouse is entitled to decide whether to keep the marital surname or return to his or her original surname during or after the marriage.

III   **The Right of Sexual Freedom and the Right of Cohabitation for Spouses**

A   *Legal Characters of the Right of Sexual Freedom and the Right of Cohabitation for Spouses*

8   The right of sexual freedom means that spouses have a fully discretionary right over their sex life. It belongs to the rights of personality. No one, including the husband, can have sex with the wife against her will.

9   The right of cohabitation refers to the right of each spouse to ask the other to cohabit and live together. And correspondingly, each spouse assumes the duty of cohabitation and living together. Most countries and regions have made legislative provision for the duty of cohabitation in the context of the rights of spouses. For example, art 215 of the French Civil Code states that 'Spouses

---

5   *Wang* (fn 4) 620.

mutually oblige themselves to a community of living.' Article 752 of the Japanese Civil Code also prescribes that 'husband and wife shall cohabit, and shall cooperate and aid each other.' The Marriage Law of the People's Republic of China also regards separate living and the nonexistence of mutual affection as reasons for granting divorce, which indirectly gives effect to the right and duty of cohabitation for spouses.

B   Exercise of the Right of Cohabitation and Inviolability of the Right of Sexual Freedom

10 Spouses have both the right and the duty of cohabitation, however this right needs their joint wills and the husband cannot force the wife to have sex. Faced with sexual violence or threats from the husband, the wife has the right to refuse. This is exactly like the right to refuse any extramarital rape, as it is the guarantee of independent personality and personal freedom for women and shows that the former embraces the latter. Thereby some countries such as the United Kingdom and Germany have legislatively or judicially recognised that rape can be committed by the victim's husband (marital rape).[6] In China there are no criminal regulations that exclude husbands from being liable for rape, but judicial practice provides some recognition of marital rape: during marriage, a husband's sexual violation is not judged as rape, but during a period of estrangement or divorce proceedings, such conduct will be rape.[7] Personally I agree with the judicial practice. In the relationship of marriage, marital rape involves the infringement of a personal interest which turns the sexual violation into family violence. This infringement violates the wife's sexual freedom and the wife is entitled to claim divorce and damages from the husband.[8]

---

6 In the United Kingdom, marital rape was recognised for the first time by the Supreme Court in *R v R* [1992] 1 Appeal Cases (AC) 599. German law gave up using the phrase 'extramarital sexual intercourse' by stating in § 177 of the German Criminal Law (amended in 1998) that:
    'Whosoever coerces another person
    1. by force;
    2. by threat of imminent danger to life or limb; or
    3. by exploiting a situation in which the victim is unprotected and at the mercy of the offender, to suffer sexual acts by the offender or a third person on their own person or to engage actively in sexual activity with the offender or a third person, shall be liable to imprisonment of not less than one year.'
7 First Criminal Tribunal of the Supreme People's Court of the People's Republic of China. Reference for Criminal Adjudication.1999 (3), 2000 (2).
8 *Guo Weihua*, Study on the Right of Sexual Freedom – with discussion of the legal protection on victims of sexual infringement (2006) 309–316.

C   *Legal Consequences of Nonperformance of Cohabitation*

11 When either spouse refuses to cohabit without reasonable cause, the other party may bring a claim to enforce the right of cohabitation. But the adjudication of cohabitation cannot be an act under coercion. Therefore when the party who refuses to cohabit without reasonable cause does not respond to the judgment, the corresponding legal consequences would be well worth studying.

12 (a) The other party may initiate divorce proceedings specifying the circumstances that justify divorce. According to art 32 of the Marriage Law of the People's Republic of China, the court shall grant a divorce if the spouse applied to court for divorce and one of the following circumstances applies: if either spouse cohabits with another person; if both spouses have lived separately due to lack of mutual affection for two years; or if other circumstances such as a declaration of disappearance have led to the spouses living apart without reasonable cause. Other countries adopt similar provisions. For example, art 140 of Swiss Civil Code articulates that when either spouse refuses to cohabit without important reasons, the other party may bring proceedings for divorce at any time during the marriage provided that they have lived separately for at least two years.

13 (b) The other party may claim for compensation on the ground of damage. As is set forth in art 46 of the Chinese Marriage Law, in circumstances of bigamy, cohabitation with another, or maltreating or deserting any family member, the innocent party shall be entitled to claim damages for divorce. All these circumstances entail the nonperformance of cohabitation. The innocent party shall not claim damages without filing for divorce.

14 (c) The other party may refuse to undertake the duty to support where the circumstances justify its abatement. Most countries and region do not stipulate this in explicit terms and the opinion of jurists vary. In Japan, some believe that this support between spouses reveals the nature of the relationship involved in marital life and that this duty cannot be exempted by refusing to cohabit, while others strongly disagree.[9] Some scholars from Taiwan, China, hold positive attitudes towards it, believing that it would be against the principle of good faith for spouses to require to undertake the duty to support in the absence of cohabitation. And judicial practice endorses this view.[10] These two different

---

9   *Shi Shangkuan*, The Theory of Family Law (1980) 265 f.

10   *Yang Yuling*, General Effect of Marriage. Treatise on Family and Succession of Civil Law (1985) 40.

opinions exist also in China.[11] Personally speaking, I think since both the duty to support and the duty of cohabitation are legal duties based on the status of spouses, the nonperformance of cohabitation can be used as a defence to the duty of support.

IV   Personal Reproductive Right and the Reproductive Right of Spouses

A   *Definitions of the Personal Reproductive Right and the Reproductive Right of Spouses*

15 The possessor of a reproductive right is entitled to decide whether to give birth or not as well as the time and manner of birth. The right embraces both the right to bear a child and the right not to do so.

16 It is generally believed that the reproductive right belongs to rights of personality in civil law. But when it comes to whether it is a right of personality or a right of status, jurists have not yet reached agreement.[12] In my opinion, the theory of personality rights accords with the nature of the reproductive right. However, according to the one-child policy in China, the exercise of this right is connected with status, because it can only be exercised on account of spousal status and with permission. Thus the reproductive right refers to the enjoyment of the right while the reproductive right of spouses refers to the enforcement and realization of the right.

17 Although the enforcement of the right needs the joint efforts of the spouses, the reproductive right is enjoyed separately by husband and wife. Article 51 of the Law on the Protection of Rights and Interests of Women in China states that: 'Women have the right to child-bearing in accordance with relevant regulations of the state as well the freedom not to bear any child.' This provides legislative authority for the right of women to refuse to bear a child. Thereby, whether the wife chooses to take birth control or to have an abortion, she shall not infringe the husband's reproductive right. That is to say, the husband cannot conduct tort litigation on the ground that the wife refuses to get pregnant.

---

11   *Yu* (fn 2) 230; *Shao Shixing*, Analyses on the duty of cohabit and of royalty of spouses, Law Reviews (2001) 1.

12   *Yu* (fn 2) 79–81.

B   *When the Wife Makes Bold to Terminate the Pregnancy, the Husband*
     May File for Divorce

18 Due to the physiological differences between men and women, the wife has
    the last word on the reproductive right. Just because the natural order can-
    not be changed does not necessarily mean that the husband's reproductive
    right should be ignored. The law may not force the wife to give birth to chil-
    dren, but it can provide remedies for infringement of the reproductive right.[13]
    The Third Interpretations of the Supreme People's Court about Several Issues
    Concerning the Application of the Marriage Law of the People's Republic of
    China prescribes in art 9 that 'The court shall not support the pleading made
    by the husband for damages on the ground of unauthorized termination of
    pregnancy by his wife and infringement on his reproductive rights; where both
    husband and wife dispute over childbearing, resulting in the actual rupture of
    emotional affection, if a party pleads a divorce, the people's court shall deal
    with it in accordance with the provisions in art 32 (3) of the Marriage Law of
    the People's Republic of China after mediation fails.'

C   *When the Wife Has a Child Extramaritally with a Third Person,*
     the Husband May Claim Damages

19 When the wife has an illegitimate child with another man during the marriage,
    she is considered by judicial practice to have infringed the husband's property
    right rather than his reproductive right.[14] According to art 2 of the Tort Liability
    Law in China, those who infringe civil rights and interests shall be subject to
    tort liability under this law and 'civil rights and interests' as used here includes
    the right of life, the right of health, the right of reputation, the right of honour,
    the right of self image, the right of privacy, marital autonomy, guardianship,
    ownership and other personal and property rights and interests. According to
    prevailing opinion, the reproductive right falls within the scope of protection
    of the right of personality. When the reproductive right of a natural person
    is infringed, the infringer shall bear civil liability. The birth of an illegitimate
    child to the wife would cause double damage to not only property rights but
    also the reproductive right and gives rise to liability accordingly.

---

13 *Jiang Yue/Hu Zhijian*, Selected Cases of Law of Marriage and Law of Sucession (2004) 38.
14 The Supreme People's Court of the People's Republic of China holds in its reply of 2 April
    1992 that if, during the marriage, either spouse has a child with a third person and hid the
    truth, causing the other party bring up the child by reason of misapprehension, the de-
    ceived party may claim the costs of upbringing and the sum requested should be granted
    according to the circumstances.

v   The Right of Spousal Privacy and the Spousal Right to Know

A   *Legal Character of the Right of Spousal Privacy and the Spousal Right to Know*

20   The right of privacy refers to an independent right of personality that enables a natural person to keep his or her private life secret, and enjoy private freedom as well as protecting the private space against illegal disturbance.[15] The right of spousal privacy, ie the right of privacy between the spouses, is a kind of personality right entitling each spouse to prevent the illegal access or disclosure of private information by the other spouse, to keep his or her private life free from disturbance by the other spouse, and to make private decisions without the other spouse's interference. The right of privacy of spouses, like the general right of privacy, is one of the basic rights of personality that guarantee private life by protecting it from intrusion. Nevertheless, due to the particularity of the relationship between husband and wife, the scope of spouses' privacy is narrower than that of general citizens.

21   The right to know refers to the right of every person to have access to whatever he or she wishes to know. And the spousal right to know means the right of spouses to have mutual acknowledgement of some of their private information on the ground of their conjugal relation. It belongs to the rights associated with spousal status.

B   *The Dividing Line between the Right of Spousal Privacy and the Spousal Right to Know*

22   Spousal privacy is embodied mainly in private information, private life, personal vocation and interpersonal relationships and all of these come into the domain of the right of privacy. Each spouse is entitled to have some access to the other's privacy as stated above.

23   (a) Spouses mutually enjoy the right to know private information such as that relating to physical condition, living habits, income, and previous marriages and offspring, if any. And knowing this private information may not be an infringement of the other's rights so long as they are not disclosed without the other's authority. Previous love affairs do not fall into the scope of the right to know, since they do not relate to spousal privacy.

24   (b) Conversely, spousal privacy does not extend to personal life, physical condition, personal belongings or private space. Journals, letters and other correspondence fall within the scope of personal privacy unless they should be made public for the benefit of the marriage and the family.

---

15   *K Larenz*, Methodology of Law, translated by Chen Aie, Taiwan, Wu-nan Press (1996) 313.

25 (c) When it comes to the choice of vocation or domicile, joint consultation and decision-making are needed by spouses as regards the family's interests. § 1356 of the German Civil Code states that 'in the choice and exercise of a gainful employment, spouses must take the necessary account of the concerns of the other spouse and the family.'

26 (d) Each spouse enjoys the right to know if there is any bigamy, cohabitation with a third person or adultery by the other spouse. If either spouse makes a follow up and takes photographs for evidence when he or she has adequate reason to believe that the other spouse has engaged in the above-mentioned forms of behaviour, the courts shall admit such evidence.

27 Generally speaking, any private information that concerns the interests of spouses and their family is no longer private and falls within the scope of the spousal right to know.

C   *Judicial Harmonization of the Right of Spousal Privacy and the Spousal Right to Know*

28 There are no specified provisions on the dividing line for the right of spousal privacy and the spousal right to know and therefore judicial decisions are needed. *Karl Larenz* is said to have observed that there is such broad scope for judicial decisions here because the elements of the opposing rights lack clear dividing lines. Whether rights or principles, provided that the dividing lines are obscure, there will inevitably be conflicts because how the opposing rights are to be balanced cannot be precisely detailed. Once there is conflict, one right has to surrender to the other or both of them have to give way to some extent for the sake of the reconstruction of peace in law.[16]

29 The right of privacy is judged by the International Covenant on Civil and Political Rights as a derogative right. Here, derogation refers to restrictions on and suspension of the right, meaning that the right of privacy has to be restricted or suspended in some circumstances, for example, in the public interest or in the face of a superior interest.[17] Since both the right of privacy and the right to know constitute important social interests, reconciling them becomes a question of the balancing of interests.

30 (a) The order of protection of the two rights. Between the right of privacy and the right to know, which one has priority? The answer needs to follow the principle of public order and good morals. If the personal privacy of either party

---

16   *Guo Mingrui/Fang Shaokun*, The Civil Law (3rd edn 2010) 150.

17   *Wang Yuanyuan*, A Study of Connotations and Restrictions on the Right of Privacy. Constitutionalism of China. <http://www.calaw.cn/mclude/shownews.asp?newsid=496>.

does no harm to the other, then the right of privacy prevails, while in case of the breach of mutual loyalty or social morality, the right to know has precedence.

31 (b) Restrictions on the right to know. Each spouse can obtain private information about the other by enforcing the right to know, but this should be done only for the purpose of litigation in which the private information is disclosed as evidence in court. In spite of the derogation for the benefit of spouses, the right of privacy should not be infringed. No one should find out or disclose the husband or wife's private information, not even the other spouse.

Index